What readers are saying about *Rails for PHP Developers*

This is a thorough and approachable introduction to Ruby and Rails for PHP programmers from fellow developers who are well-versed in both Ruby and PHP.

▶ **Paul M. Jones**
Lead Developer on the Solar Framework for PHP

As a PHP developer, I found the book focused well on the transition from coding PHP to coding Ruby (and Rails) and that it gave great examples of translating common PHP idioms to Ruby.

▶ **Matthew Weier O'Phinney**
PHP Developer and Zend Framework Core Contributor

The quality of the writing is superb, the challenges and examples are engaging, and the PHP to Ruby information is a valuable resou~~rce~~.
The exercises are nice, are short, and follow the topic well, giv~~ing~~ readers some creative time between each chapter.

▶ **Mislav Marohnić**
Prototype JavaScript Framework Core Developer

This is an enjoyable book packed with great information and usable examples. I like the organization of the book and the gentle, informal voice with which the authors cover many complex topics. It's easy to read, yet it has plenty of substance and depth to give the reader a great introduction to Rails.

▶ **Bill Karwin**
MySQL Guild and Former Zend Framework Project Leader

Rails for PHP Developers

Rails for PHP Developers

Derek DeVries

Mike Naberezny

The Pragmatic Bookshelf
Raleigh, North Carolina   Dallas, Texas

Our Pragmatic courses, workshops, and other products can help you and your team create better software and have more fun. For more information, as well as the latest Pragmatic titles, please visit us at

http://www.pragprog.com

ISBN-10: 1-934356-04-2

ISBN-13: 978-1-934356-04-3

Printed on acid-free paper with 50% recycled, 15% post-consumer content.

First printing, January 2008

Version: 2008-1-15

Contents

Acknowledgments

Derek would like to thank Melissa, daVinci, and his new baby girl, Sevilla, who was born during the writing of this preface.

Mike would like to thank Kathy for her support and his parents for buying his first computer, the Commodore 64.

We'd like to thank our reviewers: Bill Karwin, Mislav Marohnic, Tim Fletcher, Paul M. Jones, Matthew Weier O'Phinney, Dallas DeVries, Laura Thomson, and Chuck Hagenbuch. Their expertise, time, and effort have been invaluable to us.

We'd like to thank the Pragmatic Programmers for giving us a great opportunity to spread the word of Rails and our editor, Susannah, for keeping us on track.

Thanks to everyone building open source software that we use and love, from Rails to PHP. They truly make our working lives so much easier to enjoy.

Preface

There is no doubt that by now you've heard all of the hype about Ruby on Rails. It has been generating a lot of buzz with the promise of making web applications fast and simple to create, and you may be wondering what the big deal is. We know that PHP has been doing this for years and has proven quite capable by its use in large companies such as Yahoo. You may be wondering whether it's worth the time investment to learn Rails and Ruby, when you already have PHP under your belt.

What Rails Offers

Rails embraces a general development philosophy that sets a high priority on creating maintainable code. By following some simple guidelines, you should be able to keep a uniform pace of development and be free to change your code with little fear of breaking existing functionality. Rails achieves this by cherry-picking proven web development patterns and best practices. These are two of the most important principles Rails follows:

- Convention over configuration

- Don't repeat yourself (DRY)

Rails defines the directory structure of your application for you and sets a series of conventions for naming files, classes, and database tables. It takes advantage of these conventions to tie together your application without a lot of configuration. You may initially be resistant to the idea of Rails telling you how to structure your application, but your first Rails application will quickly demonstrate the efficiency that these conventions offer you. By choosing smart defaults, Rails allows you to focus on the functionality of your application instead of on the skeleton.

Rails developers tend to be almost religious about the DRY principle. Functionality is written cleanly once, and only once. Rails provides an environment that makes it easy to consolidate shared code between different components of your application.

Rails gives first-class importance to testing. Writing code is always done in parallel with tests to ensure the code works as intended and will continue to work when things around it change. In PHP, the uptake of testing culture has been slow, and the methodologies for testing entire applications are not clear. Ruby's dynamic and flexible object model, along with its standard library, makes unit testing easy. The Rails stack builds on this to provide clear, built-in support for testing all parts of a web application from the first line of code.

Who Should Read This Book

This book is meant for PHP developers who are interested in adding Rails to their toolsets. There are a lot of books on Rails now, but PHP developers have a unique way of thinking about problems that are built around the PHP mind-set. This book aims to guide your learning in Rails based on your existing knowledge of programming in PHP. An understanding of object-oriented programming in PHP will help but is not entirely necessary. This should be something you start to pick up naturally while programming in Ruby.

Through this book, you will likely learn valuable lessons from Rails that will inform future PHP development. Rails assembles a collection of patterns and practices that are not new in themselves. Many of the patterns in Rails can be implemented in other languages and may help inspire some new approaches in your PHP code. However, the greatest feature of Rails by far is Ruby! Throughout the book, we will explore the power and productivity of Rails together. As you read, also be open to Ruby itself, and be sure to absorb how Ruby forms the foundation of Rails.

Resources

All code samples are available as an archive online.[1] This book is interactive, so make sure to download and view the sample code as you work. Reading Ruby code is one of the best ways to learn the language.

---

1. http://www.pragprog.com/titles/ndphpr/source_code

We have built a companion website for this book that is also available online.[2] We will keep this website up-to-date with further code examples, resources, and answers to frequently asked questions. Be sure to subscribe to the feed to keep up-to-date with future articles.

PHP and Rails: A Personal View

Since the introduction of PHP 5, we've witnessed an evolution in PHP's capabilities. Perhaps even more than changes in PHP itself, we've seen a transformation in the way programmers use it. Object-oriented programming has become more commonplace. As a result, professional software engineering practices such as unit testing have become more practical and accessible to PHP developers.

We were early adopters of PHP 5. When Rails came along, we were already sold on writing object-oriented, well-separated applications with tests in PHP. Initially, we were a bit skeptical and didn't have much incentive to try Rails. We're glad we did. We're now excited about Rails and enjoy building applications with it. We think you will as well, but you'll need to read the book and draw your own conclusions. We've designed this book to be the guide that we wished we had when we were in your shoes.

There are some software methodologies that we believe are applicable to nearly all projects, such as the importance of object orientation and unit testing. These opinions show in our writing. However, many other factors determine how an application should be built and what tools should be used. We believe that PHP, Ruby, and Rails are all just tools you can choose from to build great applications.

It also might interest you to know that in our consulting practice, Maintainable Software,[3] we still develop roughly half of our new applications in PHP 5 (with the other half being mostly Rails). This should tell you that we think PHP is a formidable platform, and it's not about "switching" from one to the other. Learning Rails is just about having a new tool to apply to your problems when it's a good fit.

---

2. http://railsforphp.com
3. http://maintainable.com

About the Code Examples

There are many different ways of building PHP applications. Many PHP projects are developed from scratch, and an increasing number are developed using one of the many frameworks available. In our examples, we chose a framework-agnostic approach to programming PHP so that you can understand examples without previous knowledge of any specific PHP framework.

To save space in the book, we usually leave off the leading <?php tag when the example contains only PHP code. This means that if you want to run these examples on your own, you'll need to add this, or else PHP will simply echo the code back to you.

We capitalize references to Ruby—the programming language—and Rails—the framework. When you see ruby or rails in all lowercase, we are instead referencing commands used to invoke the Ruby command-line interpreter or the Rails framework generator, respectively.

PHP and Ruby code snippets use an icon in the sidebar to easily differentiate between examples written in the two languages.

PHP
preface/hello.php
```php
function sayHello() {
  print "Hello World!";
}
```

Ruby
preface/hello.rb
```ruby
def say_hello
  print "Hello World!"
end
```

About the Environment Used

Examples and screenshots in this book were created with Mac OS X and Safari, but the examples should run in all modern development environments. Rails operates under the assumption that you have some basic knowledge of command-line operations. It is well worth learning the command-line basics of your preferred environment if you haven't already done so.

Command-line examples are shown running in a bash shell, so you may find that you need to make some small adjustments based on your environment.

Command-line prompts in this book display the base name of the current working directory. The following example shows a command run from the newsletter directory:

```
newsletter> ruby script/console
```

Version Requirements

Throughout the book, we compare code examples between PHP and Ruby. The PHP examples will work on PHP 5.1 or newer. For those of you who are still working primarily with PHP 4, you may occasionally see PHP features mentioned that you haven't used yet, such as exceptions. You'll want to consult the PHP manual on these as you go.

The Ruby and Rails examples will all run on recent Ruby versions but are especially geared toward Ruby 1.8.5 and newer. Before we give any examples in Ruby, we talk about the installation and give you some pointers on where to get the software you'll need.

The Rails code is intended to work on Rails 2.0 or newer. We take full advantage of new features and conventions in this version of Rails, so most of the code will not work correctly on previous versions.

How to Read This Book

The goal of this book is to get you up to speed with both the Ruby language and the Rails framework. To do this, we've divided the book into three parts:

- Part I, "From PHP to Rails"

- Part II, "Building a Rails Application"

- Part III, "PHP to Ruby at a Glance"

The first part—"From PHP to Rails"—introduces the Model/View/Controller pattern with the conversion of a simple PHP application to Rails. This part then presents an introduction of Ruby to lay the foundation for building a larger Rails application.

The second part—"Building a Rails Application"—guides you through an in-depth application tutorial, from project conception all the way to deployment. This part will cover the meat of building web applications "the Rails way."

The third and final part—"PHP to Ruby at a Glance"—provides an in-depth reference that maps PHP syntax and idioms to comparable Ruby and Rails code. We provide one-to-one corresponding Ruby and PHP code wherever possible to make the translation easy.

Both Ruby and Rails are invaluable development tools with their own respective strengths and weaknesses. By the end of this book, you'll have a good understanding of both these tools and will be able to add not only one but two new tricks to your development toolbox. Although we'll use PHP to drive our learning of Rails, Rails can help us learn about PHP as well. As developers, we're always on a quest to find faster and more efficient ways to do our job. We hope that Rails inspires you to do just that.

Part I

From PHP to Rails

## Chapter 1

Getting Started with Rails

In this chapter we'll begin our Rails journey by focusing on the basic concepts that drive the Rails framework. We'll then get up and running quickly by installing Rails and building a small test application.

The Rails framework is built using the Ruby programming language, and a better understanding of Ruby is essential to mastering Rails. Don't worry if you're not familiar with Ruby, though. Many developers end up learning Ruby as they are learning Rails. The next few chapters will get you up to speed with the Ruby language and how the Ruby programming philosophy differs from PHP.

1.1 Rails as an Extension of Ruby

David Heinemeier Hansson extracted Rails from an application he wrote for his company, 37signals. He released it as open source in 2004, and there is now a group of developers on the core team actively applying features and patches to Rails. David's original framework actually began in PHP, but he later found Ruby to be a much better fit for what he needed to do.

You'll find the expressiveness of Ruby embraced fully in Rails to create language conventions that are specific to Rails. The Rails core team is concerned about creating a syntax that is friendly to humans. In languages such as C and PHP, we sometimes get lost in curly brackets and semicolons that make us feel like programs are written for machines. In good Ruby programs like Rails, programs always feel like they are written for humans.

Rails takes advantage of numerous powerful Ruby features that allow classes and methods to be created and modified at runtime. By using the dynamic nature of Ruby, we can write incredibly flexible programs. This dynamic nature can also help keep our application code as clean and DRY as possible.

The Rails framework is composed of several different Ruby libraries. As an introduction to Rails, let's start by taking a look at the different components that make up the framework.

1.2 The Components of Rails

Rails is a full stack framework, which means it contains all the tools needed to get a basic application up and running. The Rails stack is split into various components that we'll often refer to by name. These are some of the components that we'll talk about most.

ActiveRecord

> This is the heart of most Rails applications and is an *object relational mapper* (ORM) that maps database tables to objects in our application. We'll use this exclusively when interacting with the database.

ActionPack

> This part of Rails handles the request/response cycle and includes the template and rendering part of our application.

ActiveSupport

> This part of Rails provides shared code that is used to build many of the other Rails components. It also contains additional functionality ranging from multibyte character support to date and time logic.

ActionMailer

> This part will help us build and send email messages from within our application.

Rake

> This is a tool used to execute different tasks in our application. These tasks include running tests, building documentation, and doing much more. This is not a component of the Rails package per se but is a Ruby tool that is tightly integrated into the Rails workflow.

Some components such as ActiveRecord and Rake are not exclusive to Rails and are pretty useful as independent libraries outside the framework. We'll go over each of these components in more depth later as we interactively learn Rails. Although we'll learn most of Rails by writing code, making the transition from PHP to Ruby and Rails is more than learning a new language syntax. Before we start coding, let's go over some of the Rails conventions that will inform the decisions we make as we write our applications.

1.3 Opinionated Software

The Ruby and Rails culture is quite different from that in PHP, and this is reflected in both the code and the community. Rails is considered opinionated code, and it's important to understand where and why Rails expects you to follow certain coding principles and conventions.

Rails code has been heavily influenced by the coding style prevalent in Ruby, and the Rails community places a high importance on code beauty and readability. Although Ruby often allows more than one way to do something, only one approach is usually considered correct by community standards. Rubyists always give priority to clear and consistent code over complex or cryptic code.

Rails is built with a distinct vision of how web applications should be written. The Rails team regularly takes the role of a benevolent dictator by imposing opinions they think are in your best interest when writing software. Don't get too worried if you initially are taken back by some of these choices. Sometimes it takes a while to get used to a different way of working. We suggest you follow the conventional workflow for at least your first couple Rails applications. As the adage goes, "It's good to learn the rules before you decide to break them."

Embracing the 80/20 Rule

The Rails framework aims to remain simple by following the 80/20 rule. Rails aspires to solve 80 percent of the most common issues encountered when building a web application. This means that Rails limits or rejects features and patches that will not benefit the majority of developers using it. There is an important drive in the Rails community to keep the framework as lightweight as possible and to avoid unnecessary feature bloat.

This does not mean that Rails cannot handle your application's needs. It just means that the solution might not be in the core Rails framework and is not much different from PHP in this respect. Rails makes it quite easy to override behavior or add custom functionality to your application using a Rails plug-in. If you're running into a issue with the framework, there is a good chance that someone may have already written a Rails plug-in or Ruby library that solves your problem.

Following Conventions

Rails takes coding standards further by imposing rules and conventions that are fairly easy to follow. Some of these decisions such as class and database naming conventions are typically left to the developer when creating a new application in PHP. You'll quickly notice that not having to make these judgments yourself actually speeds up development time and creates a more consistent code base between different teams members and projects.

Your first instinct may be to do things the way you've always been doing them in PHP. Although old habits die hard, you'll be rewarded for following the path of least resistance in Rails.

Increasing Productivity Through Beauty

It may seem like a strange statement, but one of the core ideas behind Rails is that of maintaining a beautiful code API. One of the prime motivating factors behind productive employees is that they enjoy the code they are working with. You'll notice that the Rails framework goes to great lengths to provide an API that is predictable and beautiful to work with.

A good example of this concept is in validation declarations. Ruby's flexible syntax enables us to call methods without parentheses. This results in creating a naturally readable validation syntax that is obvious to even those with no Ruby programming experience.

```
class Movie < ActiveRecord::Base
  validates_presence_of :title, :on => :create
end
```

This example validates that a title is present when a movie is created. The code is quite expressive and is easy to read and maintain.

1.4 The MVC Pattern and Rails

One of the most important opinions that Rails asserts is how to organize your application code. Rails uses the classic design concept of
Model/View/Controller (MVC) to do this. MVC is a pattern used to manage applications that apply some type of user interface. The concept
actually dates back to the 1970s but in recent years has become quite
popular in creating web applications. It is used in varying forms within
most modern web frameworks. A fairly large number of MVC-based
frameworks exist for PHP as well, and prior knowledge of any of these
will also help you grasp how MVC works in Rails.

MVC splits your code into three distinct roles of responsibility and aims
to clearly separate your domain logic from your user interface logic.
If you use a PHP template engine such as Smarty, Flexy, or Savant,
you already understand how important this is in creating maintainable code. The MVC pattern goes a little further than most PHP template solutions by adding a layer between the database and templates.
The controller layer is the plumbing that connects the business and
database logic to the template logic.

Model

The model is the foundation of your application and consists of the
nonvisual aspects of "things" in your application. The model contains
all your interaction with the database as well as any behavior that
enhances or changes data in the database. This includes simple formatting and validation of the data as well as some data integrity.

Being nonvisual usually makes testing this type of data simple and
reliable. The main goals of the model layer is to represent your data in
a way that can be used among various interfaces without duplicating
code. When you think "model," you should think business logic.

View

The view is the visual representation of your application, as well as simple logic specific to rendering the user interface. In web applications,
this is usually (X)HTML markup or JavaScript code. In today's Web 2.0
world, you may also need to render XML in response to web service
requests. When you think "view," think of your application's front-end
logic and templates.

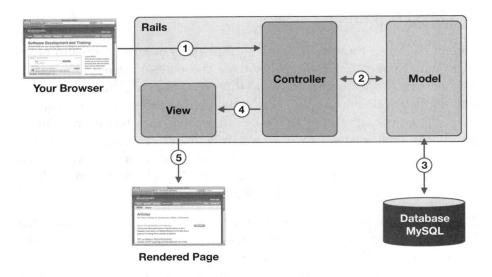

Figure 1.1: MODEL/VIEW/CONTROLLER

Controller

The controller directs the traffic by handling requests sent to your application and determining the right code to execute. It plays an important role in keeping your data loosely coupled by acting as an intermediate layer between the model and the view.

The controller also maintains the state of your application using cookies and session data. When you think "controller," think of the event handler that ties together the model and view layers.

The diagram in Figure 1.1 illustrates the three components of MVC and shows a typical request/response cycle associated with Rails.

1. The browser sends a request to your application in the form of a URL and GET/POST parameters.
2. The controller figures out what part of your code should deal with this particular request. It then asks the model layer for any data needed to perform that action.
3. The model queries the database to change or retrieve data and hands the results back to the controller.
4. The controller passes the data to the view for use in the page template.

5. The controller renders the view in a response sent back to the browser.

Now that we have an idea of how the MVC pattern is used to organize code in our application, we'll put it to use by building a Rails application using these principles. Before we build an application, however, we need to get Rails installed.

1.5 Installing Ruby and Rails

Installation is different on various platforms, and there are some great packages that simplify the Rails install process. You can find the most up-to-date install process on the Rails download page.[1]

Although often thought of as a single unit, Ruby and Rails are two separate packages. Rails is a framework written in the Ruby language, not unlike frameworks such as Cake and the Zend Framework in PHP. To get Rails working, your first step will be to get Ruby installed on your machine. We recommend installing Ruby version 1.8.6 or newer. You can find detailed information on installing Ruby across a variety of platforms in the download area of the Ruby website.[2]

Once you have Ruby installed, we have to take a quick look at package management in Ruby. The most common method of distribution for Ruby packages and libraries is through *RubyGems*. RubyGems is a package manager similar to PEAR for PHP, and Rails is most easily installed on your computer through a gem. We recommend installing RubyGems 1.0.1 or newer, which you can download from the Ruby-Forge website.[3]

Once you've downloaded the latest version of RubyGems, unpack the contents, and run the following (as root when appropriate).

```
src> cd rubygems-*
rubygems-1.0.1> ruby setup.rb

install -c -m 0644 ...
...done.
No library stubs found.
```

---

1. http://rubyonrails.org/down
2. http://www.ruby-lang.org/en/downloads/
3. http://rubyforge.org/frs/?group_id=126

This will install all the necessary files to get us going with RubyGems, along with the gem command. The gem command is what we'll use to install Rails.

This book was written using Rails 2.0.2, and you'll need at least this version to run the code example in this book. If you already have a previous version of Rails installed, you need to first remove any existing Rails gem to make sure you're using the version that the book is written to work with. All gem install/uninstall commands need to be run as the root user on *nix-based systems.

```
work> gem uninstall rails
Successfully uninstalled rails version 1.2.3
Remove executables and scripts for
'rails' in addition to the gem? [Yn]   Y
Removing rails
```

Let's now install Rails.

```
work> gem install rails
Successfully installed rails-2.0.2
```

Congratulations, you should now have Ruby and Rails up and running on your system. To make sure that we're working with the correct version of Rails, we can run the rails command with the -v option.

```
work> rails -v
Rails 2.0.2
```

Although Rails works with a variety of databases, the examples in this book assume you are using MySQL. You may even have MySQL on your system already since it is often the database of choice for PHP developers.

Rails is an opinionated web framework, and one of the opinions is that you will use Subversion.[4] Doing so will reward you with nice features of Rails that integrate well with Subversion. Although not necessary to follow this book, knowledge of Subversion will come in handy while deploying your application, installing third-party plug-ins, and submitting patches to Rails itself if you decide to contribute to Rails.

1.6 Creating a Rails App

The best way to learn Rails is to actually make something, so we are going to do just that. We will dive right into creating a small Rails

---

4.   http://subversion.tigris.org/

What Is Subversion?

Subversion is a version control system that allows you to track and manage changes in your application's source code. We realize that there are many different kinds of PHP developers. Some developers work with tools such as Dreamweaver and FTP. Others work with tools such as Vim and Subversion. Regardless of exactly where you fall in the spectrum, we highly recommend looking into using a source control system. Subversion is the preferred software by most Rails developers because it is free, easy to use, and more powerful than similar free tools such as CVS.

application to help clarify the MVC pattern a little more and to get you accustomed to how code is organized in Rails.

For our first Rails application, we need to create a simple form to collect email addresses for a company newsletter. Before saving any emails, we validate that the address is unique and formatted correctly. We then notify users of any errors that happen during the operation.

Each Rails application is stored within its own directory. To create a new application, move to the location where you store your work. From here we issue the rails command along with our application name to create a new application. As of Rails 2.0.2, Rails uses SQLite3 as the default database. We'll use the -d option to specify MySQL instead.

```
derek> cd work
work> rails -d mysql newsletter
create
create   app/controllers
create   app/helpers
create   app/models
create   app/views/layouts
create   config/environments
...
create   log/test.log
```

This creates the newsletter/ directory along with a collection of other files and directories that are to become the skeleton of our new Rails application. If we take a further look at the directory structure, we'll see something like that shown in Figure 1.2, on the next page.

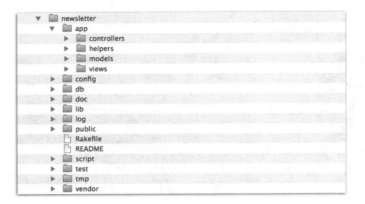

Figure 1.2: APPLICATION DIRECTORY STRUCTURE

We will store most of our Rails application's code in the app/ directory within our project. If we take a look inside, we will see where the
MVC pattern fits in. We have three directories to separate each aspect
of MVC. We also have an additional helpers/ directory that we'll cover
in more detail in Chapter 5, *Working with Controllers and Views*, on
page 109.

There are quite a few files and directories overall here, but we need to
focus on only a few to get started. All configuration for our new application is done within the config/ directory. We'll start by configuring our
database.

Configuring the Database

MySQL is the perfect place to store all the emails we're collecting for
this application. The first step is to create and configure the database
to work with our application. The database configuration for our application is stored in config/database.yml and is written as a YAML file.[5]

YAML is a simple file format that is gaining popularity lately because of
its human-friendly syntax. You'll see Rails uses YAML as an alternative
to Ruby to define configuration in a few areas.

---

5. YAML stands for YAML Ain't Markup Language and rhymes with "camel." Learn more
at http://www.yaml.org.

Let's open this file to take a better look. You'll probably first notice that there are three different database configurations in the file. Rails uses the idea of execution environments and has three different environments to execute code: development, test, and production. A different database is used in each of these environments. We'll discuss environments in more depth in Section 6.2, *Using Rails Environments*, on page 154. For now, we're just starting the development phase of our application, so we need to configure only the development environment.

`getting_started_with_rails/newsletter_1/config/database.yml`

```
development:
  adapter: mysql
  encoding: utf8
  database: newsletter_development
  username: root
  password:
  socket: /tmp/mysql.sock
```

Rails already assumes we are using the mysql database adapter on localhost. It has also given us a suggestion to follow in regards to the name of the database. This section is where you'll enter your MySQL username and password so that your application can connect. The default configuration uses a username of root with a blank password.

Once you have saved your MySQL username and password to this file, you can create the newsletter_development database in the means you are most comfortable with. We like using the mysqladmin command.

```
newsletter> mysqladmin -u root -p create newsletter_development
```

After we have the database connection set up, we need to create a table to store our newsletter subscribers. This application is quite simple, and we need only a single table to store the email addresses. We'll name this table using the plural form of what it is storing—subscribers. We'll keep the table simple with only two columns: id and email.

```
CREATE TABLE subscribers (
  id int(11) NOT NULL auto_increment,
  email varchar(255) default NULL,
  PRIMARY KEY (id)
) ENGINE=InnoDB DEFAULT CHARSET=latin1;
```

Once we've created this table, we're ready to fire up a server to get our new application working in the browser.

Starting Up the Server

Rails comes bundled with a server called WEBrick that works great for development work; it will save us any additional installs at this point. The script to start this is located in the script/ directory and has to be run from the root directory of your application. Pop open a new console window to do this.

```
work> cd newsletter
newsletter> ruby script/server
=> Booting WEBrick...
=> Rails application started on http://0.0.0.0:3000
=> Ctrl-C to shutdown server; call with --help for options
[2007-12-01 17:37:10] INFO WEBrick 1.3.1
[2007-12-01 17:37:10] INFO ruby 1.8.6 (2007-03-13) [i686-darwin8.9.1]
[2007-12-01 17:37:10] INFO WEBrick::HTTPServer#start: pid=13 port=3000
```

This message means the server has started on our machine. That's right—there's no Apache web server to install and no VirtualHost directives to configure as you would for your PHP environment. All you have to do is start script/server whenever you want a little web server to test your Rails work. WEBrick is great for getting started quickly with development but is not recommended for production use. We'll discuss a more production-ready solution in Chapter 10, *Deploying the Application*, on page 235.

WEBrick will continue to log to the console as requests are made to your application. You will need to keep the console running for the application to remain accessible from the browser, and you can shut down the server at any time by hitting Ctrl+C.

As a rule of thumb, we don't need to restart our server to see changes take effect in our application. There are a few exceptions to this rule. You'll need to restart the server when changing anything within the config/ directory. If we were to change the database configuration now, we would need to restart WEBrick so that Rails loads with the correct settings. We also might need to restart the server if you see the error message "Routing Error: No route matches..." Restarting the server can be done by hitting Ctrl+C on the console running the server and then restarting it.

```
^C[2006-12-17 16:45:02] INFO  going to shutdown ...
[2006-12-17 16:45:02] INFO  WEBrick::HTTPServer#start done.

newsletter> ruby script/server
=> Booting WEBrick...
```

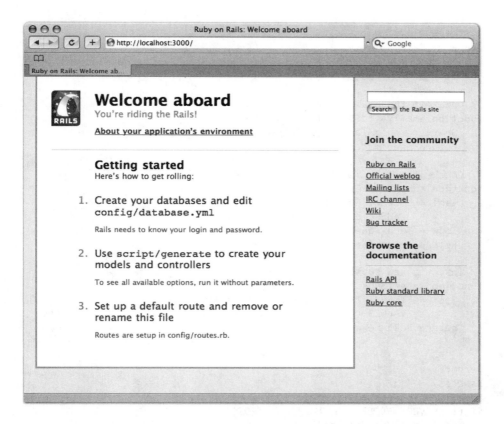

Figure 1.3: RAILS GREETING

Now that the server is going, you can access your new Rails application by visiting http://localhost:3000 in your browser. Rails will greet you with the welcome screen shown in Figure 1.3.

This is proof that things are up and running, and Rails will provide you with some friendly links to various online resources.

The Newsletter App in PHP

Let's first take a look at how our entire newsletter application would look as a PHP script. We will then go over how this script could be split up to use the MVC pattern in a Rails application.

PHP   getting_started_with_rails/newsletter.php

```php
<?php
$dbh = new PDO('mysql:host=localhost;dbname=newsletter_development',
               'root', '');

// Check if the email format is valid
function emailValid($email) {
    $pattern = '/^[a-z0-9_.-]+@[a-z0-9-]+\.[a-z.]+$/i';
    return preg_match($pattern, $email);
}
// Check if a user is already subscribed
function subscriberExists($dbh, $email) {
    $sql = "SELECT COUNT(*) AS cnt FROM subscribers
            WHERE email=".$dbh->quote($email);
    $row = $dbh->query($sql)->fetch();
    return !empty($row['cnt']);
}
// Insert a new subscriber into the list
function insertSubscriber($dbh, $email) {
    $sql = "INSERT INTO subscribers (email)
            VALUES (".$dbh->quote($email).")";
    return $dbh->exec($sql);
}


$error   = '';
$success = '';
$email   = isset($_POST['email']) ? $_POST['email'] : '';
if ($_SERVER['REQUEST_METHOD'] == 'POST') {
    if (!emailValid($email)) {
        $error = "Email is an invalid format. Please try again.";
    } elseif (subscriberExists($dbh, $email)) {
        $error = "Email already exists on our list.";
    } elseif (insertSubscriber($dbh, $email)) {
        $success = "Thank you, You have been subscribed.";
    }
}
?>

<!DOCTYPE html PUBLIC "-//W3C//DTD XHTML 1.0 Transitional//EN"
"http://www.w3.org/TR/xhtml1/DTD/xhtml1-transitional.dtd">
<html>
  <head><title>Subscribe to our Mailing List</title></head>
  <body>
    <h2>Subscribe to our Mailing List</h2>
    <div style="color: red">
      <?php echo htmlentities($error, ENT_QUOTES) ?>
    </div>
    <div style="color: green">
      <?php echo htmlentities($success, ENT_QUOTES) ?>
    </div>
```

```
   <form method="post" action="/newsletter.php">
     <input type="text" name="email" size="25" />
     <input type="submit" />
   </form>
  </body>
</html>
```

This is a lot of code, but don't worry because we'll break down each part for you. This PHP script combines all the logic and markup in a single file. This is not necessarily a best practice or modern programming technique in PHP, but it should be straightforward enough for any PHP developer to understand. This procedural style of programming is actually pretty convenient for a simple script such as this, but you would probably find yourself repeating code as this application grows.

There are three distinct sections of this code that can be separated into different files to facilitate reuse. With a little more knowledge on the MVC pattern, let's see whether we can figure out how we might split this up to fit the pattern.

Extracting the Model Code

The PHP functions defined in this code all have to do with subscribers. We validate the subscriber's email format, see whether the subscriber already exists, and finally create the subscriber record.

`PHP`

getting_started_with_rails/newsletter.php

```php
// Check if the email format is valid
function emailValid($email) {
    $pattern = '/^[a-z0-9_.-]+@[a-z0-9-]+\.[a-z.]+$/i';
    return preg_match($pattern, $email);
}
// Check if a user is already subscribed
function subscriberExists($dbh, $email) {
    $sql = "SELECT COUNT(*) AS cnt FROM subscribers
             WHERE email=".$dbh->quote($email);
    $row = $dbh->query($sql)->fetch();
    return !empty($row['cnt']);
}
// Insert a new subscriber into the list
function insertSubscriber($dbh, $email) {
    $sql = "INSERT INTO subscribers (email)
             VALUES (".$dbh->quote($email).")";
    return $dbh->exec($sql);
}
```

Extracting and combining all the code that deals with subscriber information seems to make a lot of sense. This type of code will become part of our model layer, because it deals with the data of a "thing" (subscriber) in your application. Let's take a look at how we would create our subscriber model in Rails.

Instead of manually creating new files to extract this code, we'll be using code generation to build the structure for us. The script/generate command will build the stubs of code we need to put together our application. We use it here to create a Subscriber model. Navigate to the root level of your application, and run the following.

```
newsletter> ruby script/generate model Subscriber
exists   app/models/
exists   test/unit/
exists   test/fixtures/
create   app/models/subscriber.rb
create   test/unit/subscriber_test.rb
create   test/fixtures/subscribers.yml
create   db/migrate
create   db/migrate/001_create_subscribers.rb
```

The script takes two arguments here: model is the type of object we want to create, and Subscriber is the name of the model we are creating. The script outputs a list of files created, which includes everything we need to get going with the subscriber model. At this point we need to focus only on the single file where we define the object that represents a subscriber in our application. Let's open app/models/subscriber.rb to take a look at the Subscriber class.

Ruby getting_started_with_rails/newsletter_1/app/models/subscriber.rb

```
class Subscriber < ActiveRecord::Base
end
```

Taking a look at this file shows there isn't much there. Ruby uses a single inheritance model just like PHP. Although object inheritance in PHP uses the extends keyword, inheritance in Ruby is defined using the less-than symbol (<). In this case, the functionality of our Newsletter class is slightly deceiving, because this model inherits all the functionality built into the ActiveRecord::Base class.

Your Subscriber model controls everything that goes in and out of the subscribers table we created. The ActiveRecord::Base class that Subscriber inherits from is a high-level database abstraction layer. This layer is known as an *object relational mapper* because it maps each model directly to a database table using a specific naming convention. By naming our table as the lowercase plural form of our model class, the database table and corresponding model class are automatically linked.

Taking a look back at our PHP code, there are three things we need to accomplish with this model code.

- Validate that the email format is correct.
- Validate that the subscriber email doesn't already exist.
- Insert the subscriber.

Let's start with the validation of the data for this model. Each column in our database maps directly to an attribute on our model class. We can validate data being inserted into the database by adding simple declarations on our ActiveRecord model. In this case, we'll use two built-in validation rules to make sure that the email column is both formatted correctly and unique. We'll add the validates_format_of and validates_uniqueness_of methods, respectively, to accomplish this.

`Ruby` getting_started_with_rails/newsletter_2/app/models/subscriber.rb

```ruby
class Subscriber < ActiveRecord::Base
  validates_uniqueness_of :email,
                          :message => "already exists on our list"
  validates_format_of :email,
                      :with => /^[a-z0-9_.-]+@[a-z0-9-]+\.[a-z.]+$/i
end
```

Each of these rules is passed the name of the column we are validating as the first parameter. We've added a :message parameter to validates_uniqueness_of to override the default error message given when the validation fails.

We use the :with option to validates_format_of to specify the regular expression the email has to match in order to validate. This particular regular expression checks for the most basic of email validation by looking for an at sign (@) and dot (.) in the address. Rails uses Perl-style regular expressions, which means we can reuse the same pattern used in the PHP preg_match function.

Once these validation rules have been set, Rails will intercept any insertion or updates we make to the subscribers table to make sure the data is valid. If the data fails any of the validation rules, Rails gives a list of errors so that you know what went wrong.

Believe it or not, we don't even need to create a function to insert the record. This functionality is already inherited from ActiveRecord, which we'll see later when we save the record. Between generating the model

---

A Symbol of Our Friendship

You have probably noticed by now that Ruby has a data type not present in PHP. A symbol is created by using a string of characters preceded by a colon such as the following.

```
:my_symbol
```

Symbols provide a lightweight replacement for strings when we're naming things in Ruby, and we discuss them in further detail in Section 11.2, *Symbols*, on page 266.

---

code and adding these validation rules, this finishes up the code needed to implement the requirements of our PHP functions.

Extracting the Controller and View Code

The next bit of PHP code in our example is responsible for flow control. It directs what to do when the HTML form is submitted.

`PHP` getting_started_with_rails/newsletter.php

```php
$error   = '';
$success = '';
$email   = isset($_POST['email']) ? $_POST['email'] : '';
if ($_SERVER['REQUEST_METHOD'] == 'POST') {
    if (!emailValid($email)) {
        $error = "Email is an invalid format. Please try again.";
    } elseif (subscriberExists($dbh, $email)) {
        $error = "Email already exists on our list.";
    } elseif (insertSubscriber($dbh, $email)) {
        $success = "Thank you, You have been subscribed.";
    }
}
```

This code invokes the functions needed to handle the submitted data. It then assigns variables for our template based on what happens. This type of code is part of the controller layer because it handles the request and passes information from the subscriber data to the template.

Creating the Controller

We can generate a controller in Rails by using the same generator script we used to create our model. We need to name this the Subscribers controller because of its role in handling actions that deal with subscribers in our application.

Figure 1.4: ACTION MISSING THE TEMPLATE

```
newsletter> ruby script/generate controller Subscribers
exists  app/controllers/
exists  app/helpers/
create  app/views/subscribers
exists  test/functional/
create  app/controllers/subscribers_controller.rb
create  test/functional/subscribers_controller_test.rb
create  app/helpers/subscribers_helper.rb
```

Different "pages" within our application are defined by new methods within our controller. These methods are commonly referred to as *actions* because of the role they play. They handle the flow of application logic and are often named using verbs. We'll use an method named create to handle the action of creating new subscribers.

We create methods in Ruby using the keyword def, followed by the name of the method and the parameters in parentheses. The parentheses and parameters are optional in Ruby and in this case have been left out for brevity. The body then follows, and the method is closed using the end keyword. We've also added a single-line comment using the hash (#) character.

`Ruby` `getting_started_with_rails/newsletter_2/app/controllers/subscribers_controller.rb`

```ruby
class SubscribersController < ApplicationController

  # create a new subscriber
  def create
  end

end
```

Each action in a Rails controller maps to a default URL based on the name of the controller and action. To run the create action in our Subscribers controller, redirect your browser to http://localhost:3000/subscribers/create. Unfortunately at this point, we don't have an associated template for this action. Without this template, we are shown the error in Figure 1.4, on the previous page.

Rails wants to render a template, but the template file is missing! Of course, this is because we have not created a template for the page yet. Rails helps out here by showing us exactly where it is looking for the missing template. All template/view code belongs in the app/views directory. This location is further split up by controller. Since we're writing the create action within the SubscribersController, we will need to create the corresponding template in app/views/subscribers/create.html.erb.

Creating the View

Let's give this application a face by extracting the template code. This should be fairly simple because it is mostly HTML with just a small amount of PHP presentation logic sprinkled in.

`PHP` `getting_started_with_rails/newsletter.php`

```php
<!DOCTYPE html PUBLIC "-//W3C//DTD XHTML 1.0 Transitional//EN"
"http://www.w3.org/TR/xhtml1/DTD/xhtml1-transitional.dtd">
<html>
  <head><title>Subscribe to our Mailing List</title></head>
  <body>
    <h2>Subscribe to our Mailing List</h2>
    <div style="color: red">
      <?php echo htmlentities($error, ENT_QUOTES) ?>
    </div>
    <div style="color: green">
      <?php echo htmlentities($success, ENT_QUOTES) ?>
    </div>

    <form method="post" action="/newsletter.php">
      <input type="text" name="email" size="25" />
      <input type="submit" />
    </form>
  </body>
</html>
```

Separating this markup into a different file gives the UI designer a clean template to work with that is absent of business logic. It also lets you easily swap in a different style of template if you wanted to render an XML or JavaScript representation of the data.

The most common type of view in Rails is written in Embedded Ruby and is most often referred to as ERB. The extension on these views is written as .html.erb, which describes the MIME type of the response along with the rendering engine used to create it. In this case, we need to return HTML for our response.

ERB is a template system that allows Ruby to be embedded and evaluated within a text file. It works similarly to how native PHP is commonly used within HTML markup. We can invoke the Ruby interpreter using the <% tag and exit using %>. Outputting an expression within the tags uses the same convention as PHP short tags by adding an equal sign in the opening tag. <%=.

Let us now translate this code to ERB by creating app/views/subscribers/create.html.erb. The code looks quite similar to that in the original PHP script. There are a few important translations that we've made when converting this to ERB. The Ruby variables we use are prefixed with an at sign (@) instead of the dollar sign ($) we're familiar with in PHP.

`Ruby` getting_started_with_rails/newsletter_2/app/views/subscribers/create.html.erb

```
<!DOCTYPE html PUBLIC "-//W3C//DTD XHTML 1.0 Transitional//EN"
"http://www.w3.org/TR/xhtml1/DTD/xhtml1-transitional.dtd">
<html>
  <head><title>Subscribe to our Mailing List</title></head>
  <body>
    <h2>Subscribe to our Mailing List</h2>
    <div style="color: red"><%= h(@error) %></div>
    <div style="color: green"><%= h(@success) %></div>

    <% form_tag :action => "create" do %>
      <input type="text" name="email" size="25" />
      <input type="submit" />
    <% end %>
  </body>
</html>
```

We've also introduced the idea of *helper methods*. A helper method is simply a function that we use within our view to help render our markup. We've used the h helper method in our Ruby code to get the equivalent functionality of htmlentities in PHP.

We've also used a helper method named form_for to create the form in our view. We've passed a single argument to this method that specifies what action the form will post to. In this case, the form will post back to the same create action we created in our subscribers controller. The do/end style of syntax used with this method is an example of a

Is It Dangerous to Put Logic in Templates?

Of course not, provided it is presentation logic. Presentation logic is code such as simple loops of data, determining the class of a particular HTML element, or choosing whether an element should be displayed at all. Avoiding all logic in the template would require writing much more code than necessary to get around the restrictions. There is a slippery slope when allowing PHP or Ruby to be integrated into markup, but with the right discipline, these solutions can be quite elegant and easy to understand.

What Is the .rhtml Extension Used For?

Before Rails 2.0, ERB views that rendered HTML had an .rhtml extension. This was phased out in favor of a more extensible solution that met the need to render different templates for the same action (such as create.xml.erb). The .rhtml extension was around for quite a while, and there is a good chance that you'll still see it around in older Rails applications.

Ruby block. This allows us to use a single method to build both the opening and closing tags of this form. We'll learn more about blocks in Section 2.9, *Understanding Blocks*, on page 51.

Rails has an immediate feedback cycle just like PHP. We can view the changes we've made by simply hitting Refresh in the browser. Rails now proudly displays the newsletter submission form shown in Figure 1.5, on the next page. All that is left is actually hooking the parts together in the controller.

Processing the Form

If we refer to the original script, the remaining logic we need to extract from our PHP has to do the following.

1. Get the email variable posted from the form.
2. Validate the email.
3. Insert the subscriber's email.
4. Assign a message to notify the user of what happened.

Figure 1.5: CREATE SUBSCRIBER FORM

When the subscriber form is submitted, it will send a POST request to the same create action we're using to display this form. This is actually quite similar to what we're doing with the PHP version of the newsletter application.

Ruby

`getting_started_with_rails/newsletter_3/app/controllers/subscribers_controller.rb`

```
Line 1   class SubscribersController < ApplicationController

           # create a new subscriber
           def create
      5       if request.post?
                @subscriber = Subscriber.new(:email => params[:email])
                if @subscriber.save
                  @success = "Thank you, You have been subscribed."
                else
     10            @error = @subscriber.errors.full_messages[0]
                end
              end
           end

     15  end
```

In PHP, we checked the request method via $_SERVER['REQUEST_METHOD']. The Rails version does a similar check using the request.post? method call on line 5. Our validation has been handed off to the model itself and will be automatically be checked when we save the data. At this point we can go ahead and create the record.

When the email is posted to Rails action, we'll be able to access it using the params data structure. This data structure holds any information that would be in the $_GET or $_POST superglobals in PHP. It is accessed in the same way as an associative array in PHP.

> ### Instance and Local Variables
>
> The "Ruby way," and generally accepted rule, is to name local variables using all lowercase letters with underscores.
>
> ```
> my_variable = "hey there!"
> _123 = "another variable..."
> ```
>
> Instead of using $this-> to access instance variables within an object, Ruby uses a @ prefix on variables.
>
> ```
> @message = "six less characters to type than $this->!"
> ```
>
> We can find more details on the difference between variables in PHP and Ruby in Section 11.3, *Variables*, on page 279.

To create a new record in the database, we instantiate a new Subscriber object using its new method. This would be similar to calling new Subscriber() to construct an object in PHP.

```
@subscriber = Subscriber.new(:email => params[:email])
```

The arguments passed in are a set of key/value pairs that correspond directly to the name of columns in that table. This will assign the email column with the value we gathered from the form. Finally, invoking the save method will insert this record into the subscribers table.

The save will return true if the save was successful, at which point we'll set the success message. If one of our validation rules is violated, the save will return false. In this case we can retrieve an array of validation errors by calling errors.full_messages on the @subscribers object. In this example we need to display only the first error message found.

Instance variables assigned in this action will become available in our view template. This means that both @error and @success will be accessible in the view.

Finishing up the logic for this controller completes our conversion. Refresh the newsletter app in your browser to test the final result. Try saving a new email or entering invalid data.

> ### What Is a Question Mark Doing on a Method Name?
>
> Adding a question mark at the end of a method name is valid syntax and fits a certain convention in Ruby. We typically add a question mark to the end of a method if it returns a boolean value. It's as if we're asking the object a question with a yes or no answer: "Are you a post request?"

1.7 Chapter Review

Congratulations! We have finished our first Rails application. Although this was a simple application, we have already learned quite a few important concepts in Rails:

- We learned some of the many conventions and opinions that Rails makes about building web applications.
- We learned that code generation makes it easy to create our files in an organized way.
- We learned how the MVC pattern works as well as how to identify and separate the different aspects of our code. The benefits of using MVC will really pay off as we work our way into a larger application.
- We learned how Rails has much built-in functionality to take care of things we may have created custom functions for in PHP.

1.8 Exercises

Here's some extra exercises that you can try on your own:

- We looked at only a few of the many files created by the generators we used. Take a look through the rest of the files created when we built our newsletter Rails application.
- Try adding columns to the subscribers database table and the form used to submit our subscriber data. How would you save these additional values when they are submitted to the create action?
- We used some simple conditional logic using if/else in our controller code. Try conditionally displaying the error and success <div> tags in the view depending on the value of the @error and @success variables.

## Chapter 2

Beginning Ruby Code

The previous chapter gave you a small taste of Rails, but now it's time to step back a bit to look at some basics—the elements of Ruby code you'll need to know to become a successful Rails developer. This chapter will get you, a PHP developer, quickly started down the road to understanding Ruby as a language and a little bit about the power it gives Rails. Along the way, we'll refer to your PHP experience to accelerate your understanding of each topic.

Ruby is a fully object-oriented language. If you are familiar with object-oriented programming in PHP, you have a good start. Ruby has some powerful object-oriented features that will be an exciting addition to what you may know in PHP. Don't worry if you are not familiar with object-oriented code! Starting now with Ruby is a great time to learn. Objects in Ruby are not scary or complicated.

2.1 Seeing Ruby as a General-Purpose Language

There are some things that PHP may have deeply embedded in your brain that work completely differently in Ruby. The first thing you might have to unlearn is the web browser.

PHP is one of only a handful of languages that was developed specifically for writing web applications. It is so specific to the Web that it's sometimes difficult to separate the PHP language from all the goodies it has bundled to support web development, such as the functions htmlentities() and nl2br(). Most of us write our first PHP scripts as "Hello World" pages—from the first experiment, we're in the web browser.

Back in the mid-1990s, Rasmus Lerdorf released the first version of PHP to the public. In this early form, it was a limited set of tools designed simply to make his tasks of developing dynamic web pages easier. It has since grown to be much more, but its focus remains the same—developing web applications. You can write all kinds of applications in PHP now, but for a large number of developers, programming PHP means working with the web browser.

Close to the same time as PHP emerged, Yukihiro "Matz" Matsumoto released Ruby to the public. Although many people outside of Japan think that Ruby is relatively new, PHP and Ruby are in fact close to the same age. Whereas PHP was created out of Rasmus's need for a better way to make dynamic web pages, Matz created Ruby out of his sheer dissatisfaction of doing any kind of programming with the languages available at the time.

PHP and Ruby are very different in this regard. Although they can both be applied to many of the same problems now, their histories are radically different. PHP grew organically over time, evolving as the Web evolved, and the language we now know as PHP was developed by many different contributors who bolted on different features to make PHP more suitable for solving their web problems. Ruby, especially in the early years, remained the vision of largely one man who was architecting his ideal language.

Matz created Ruby as a general-purpose language. He drew inspiration from many different languages that were available at the time, including Perl, Lisp, Smalltalk, and Python. For Matz, Ruby has always been about building his ideal language rather than solving a set of specific problems. Although Ruby has many contributors like PHP, Matz has always remained Ruby's architect and project leader. If you've ever been frustrated with all the little inconsistencies that make PHP so colorful, you may come to appreciate the design of Ruby that has resulted from it largely being the focus of one man striving for perfection over years of effort.

Since Ruby is a general-purpose language, many different kinds of developers have taken it and applied it to their particular problems. This was the case when David Heinemeier Hansson wanted to use Ruby for developing web applications. His extensions to Ruby became Ruby on Rails.

Many other kinds of developers have also extended Ruby in different ways for solving their own problems. Most of these problems don't have anything to do with the Web, so Ruby alone isn't particularly optimized for the Web out of the box like PHP.

2.2 Interacting with Ruby

A breadth of other kinds of libraries and tools are available for Ruby that allow it to do all kinds of things unrelated to Web. For us web developers, one of the best things to come out of this is Interactive Ruby (IRB).[1]

Once you have Ruby installed on your computer, you'll notice that the command ruby does the same thing as php—it silently waits for a script to be streamed in on stdin. That's not particularly friendly or useful for us at this point, so exit with Ctrl+C if you tried it.

Another command is installed with Ruby that starts IRB. It's called— you guessed it—irb. Fire up IRB with the irb command, and let's start interacting with Ruby.

```
irb>
```

The first thing you'll see in IRB is the prompt. You can try pressing Enter a few times, and you'll be always be brought back to the prompt, just like your shell. Let's try our first Ruby command.

```
irb> print('Hello world!')
Hello world!=> nil
irb>
```

Ruby's print works like its counterpart in PHP. The biggest difference is that Ruby statements don't always end in a semicolon as they do in PHP. We can use the semicolon to put together multiple statements on a line, but otherwise we won't need it in Ruby.

Also, notice that Ruby's print does not automatically append a newline to the string to be printed. That's why we see that =>nil next to the string we printed. PHP's print() works the same way.

Ruby also has another method, puts ("put string"), that does append the newline. Let's try that one.

---

1. In some PHP versions, you can use php -a on the command line to get an interactive PHP interpreter.

```
irb> puts 'Hello world!'
Hello world!
=> nil
irb>
```

Now the "Hello world!" string was printed on its own line. We also introduced another change: the puts statement has no parentheses.

All function calls in PHP need parentheses, but there are a few exceptions—notably, echo, print, include, and a few others. You're allowed to leave off the parentheses in PHP for these few cases only because they are not actually functions. They're language constructs. You probably do this already but don't think about the distinction between constructs and functions.

Ruby is a bit simpler inasmuch as everything you "call" will be a method (a method is a function attached to an object). There's no differentiation between methods and constructs that matter for syntax like in PHP. Method calls never require parentheses in Ruby, and there are no special cases. Just like the semicolon, you can leave them off unless you need them for a specific purpose such as grouping.

You've just learned two important aspects of the Ruby language. First, Ruby is consistent, and exceptions to the rules are rare. Instead of remembering the few places where parentheses can be left off, you can just leave them off all the time. Second, there's generally more than one way of doing something. Use the parentheses or leave them off—the decision is up to you.

Let's continue with our IRB session.

```
irb> puts 'Hello world!'
Hello world!
=> nil
irb>
```

Since puts just prints out the string and doesn't return anything, we get back nil just as we would get back NULL in PHP. Each time we type an expression into IRB, the result will be printed.

Let's try another expression that returns something more useful.

```
irb> 2 + 2
=> 4
irb>
```

IRB is every Ruby programmer's favorite calculator. Try some other expressions to get comfortable with IRB.

When you finish using IRB, you can exit by typing exit. You can also exit by typing quit. Finally, you can just press Ctrl+D. Like most aspects of Ruby, there's more than one way to do it. You can find your preference, and Ruby lets you do what you like, even when it comes to saying goodbye. It's your Ruby.

As we move forward, we'll continue to use IRB quite a bit. Interacting with the Ruby interpreter in this way is a great way to learn and test code. Later, we'll even see how Rails extends IRB for interacting with our entire web application. For now, let's keep progressing by learning about variable assignment in Ruby.

2.3 Objectifying Everything

Many languages such as PHP and Java support object-oriented programming but aren't pure object-oriented languages. One of the reasons that they are not "pure" is that they have primitive types. These languages have the notion of things that are not objects.

In PHP, we work most frequently with these types. Examples of primitive types include integers, floats, strings, and booleans. We can store data in them and pass them around, but they aren't objects and don't do anything useful on their own.

Ruby is radically different from these languages because it has no primitive types at all. Ruby is a purely object-oriented language like Smalltalk. In Ruby, everything is a full-blown object.

As a result of being objects, everything in Ruby accepts method calls, even nil.[2] In PHP, a string isn't smart enough to do anything on its own. If we wanted to get the length of a string, we'd call the strlen() function and pass the string to it. Since a string is a full-blown object in Ruby, we can ask it directly to report its length.

```
irb> greeting = "Hello World!"
=> "Hello World!"
irb> greeting.length
=> 12
```

In PHP, variables always start with a dollar sign ($). This makes it easy for the PHP compiler to identify variables as it reads our code. Ruby doesn't have this requirement.

---

2. In Ruby, nil is the equivalent of PHP's NULL.

Local variables don't need any prefix at all. The variable shown previously is simply called greeting instead of the familiar $greeting in PHP.

Matz has often been quoted as saying although many languages are optimized for compilers, Ruby is optimized for humans. You probably don't enjoy typing dollar signs all day, so Matz has shifted the burden to his compiler. The same goes for the dot. In Ruby, the dot is used to dereference objects, where PHP uses an arrow like in $object->method().

Earlier, we assigned the string object containing "Hello World" to the variable called greeting. We then called the method length, and IRB reported the result. Interestingly, we don't need the intermediate variable at all.

```
irb> "Hello World!".length
=> 12
```

That probably looks bizarre right now. Since everything in Ruby is an object, methods can be chained to everything. That's why the .length can be chained directly after the quotes.

With our "Hello World!" string still contained in the variable greeting, let's try another method.

```
irb> greeting.upcase
=> "HELLO WORLD!"
```

In PHP, we'd use strtoupper() and pass the string $greeting into it. Ruby doesn't have a large collection of global functions like strlen() and strtoupper() that operate externally on variables.

A key to understanding the differences between PHP and Ruby is grasping the concepts that everything is an object and objects internalize the methods to perform operations on them.

2.4 Accepting Ruby's Object World

As a PHP developer, you might read the ideas presented previously and think that having everything be an object is code bloat or perhaps a little too far-fetched. We'd like to assure you that this isn't the case, and Ruby's world of objects can solve a very practical PHP problem in a simple way.

One of the most common problems of learning PHP is memorizing the order of the arguments for its frequently used functions. We'll call this the "needle or haystack" problem.

Even seasoned PHP veterans often have trouble remembering whether the needle or haystack argument comes first, since they aren't always used consistently throughout PHP.

To illustrate the problem, let's consider two common array functions in PHP and look at their usage.

PHP beginning_ruby_code/php/needle_haystack.php

```php
in_array($needle, $haystack);

array_push($haystack, $needle);
```

In PHP, nearly all the array functions take an array to operate on as the first parameter. This is true of array_push(), as shown in the example. However, in_array() is an exception to the rule and takes the array as the second parameter instead. This is an inconsistency that PHP developers just need to remember and can easily be a source of confusion.

Our memorization problem occurs because of the nature of procedural programming. Since the PHP functions aren't methods attached to any particular object, we must pass everything the function needs to work on as parameters. The more parameters a function requires, the harder it is for us to remember them and the order. Having some inconsistencies just compounds the problem.

Ruby solves this problem with object orientation. Let's look at the Ruby equivalents for PHP's in_array() and array_push(). Try this in IRB.

```
irb> fruit = ['apple', 'orange']
=> ["apple", "orange"]
irb> fruit.include? 'banana'
=> false
irb> fruit.push 'banana'
=> ["apple", "orange", "banana"]
irb> fruit.include? 'banana'
=> true
```

In Ruby, an array is an object, and the common operations you need to do on an array are methods of that object. Once we have our array object, we just call include? or push. Each one needs only one parameter since the methods are attached to the object on which they will operate. Since there's only one parameter now, there's no source of confusion or inconsistency! Looking at Figure 2.1, on the next page, we can see that different objects can even implement methods of the same name. Both String and Array implement their own reverse method.

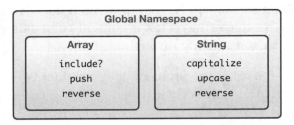

Figure 2.1: METHOD ORGANIZATION

This example is an important one because it demonstrates a fundamental difference between Ruby and PHP. In PHP, the types we use all the time, such as strings and arrays, have no methods. We largely need to use procedural functions on these, which can occasionally be confusing.

In Ruby, everything is an object, and the objects internalize their methods. Not only does this help with remembering parameters, it also serves to organize the Ruby universe. Instead of having many procedural functions in a global space like PHP, Ruby packages all its methods neatly into the objects that need them.

We hope you can see by this example that Ruby's object-oriented nature can actually make things simpler and thus make our lives easier.

2.5 Assigning to Variables

In the previous sections, we've already made some assignments. We've assigned strings and arrays to variables. It seems simple enough, but there are some things to learn. Let's look at how assignments in Ruby really work and how they differ from PHP.

There are two types of assignment in PHP. The equals operator (=) is used for assign by value, or "making a copy." The equals-ampersand operator (=&) is used for assign by reference, or "making a link."

In Ruby, there is only one assignment operator: equals (=). It behaves quite a bit differently than its PHP counterpart, so let's have a look at it in IRB.

```
irb> a = 'foo'
=> "foo"
irb> b = a
=> "foo"
```

You can see from the helpful IRB output that the variables a and b each contain "foo". You can try also just typing the variable names to view their values.

```
irb> a
=> "foo"
irb> b
=> "foo"
```

On the surface, it looks like the assignments worked like in PHP. However, Ruby behaves very differently, and it's important for us to understand how.

A string in Ruby is an object, and that object has methods. Calling the a.reverse! method will cause the String object to reverse itself. Go ahead and try it.

```
irb> a.reverse!
=> "oof"
irb> a
=> "oof"
```

As you can see, a has reversed itself. Now inspect the variable b.

```
irb> b
=> "oof"
```

It is also shown as reversed! Was that unexpected?

In Ruby, the assignment operator always assigns by reference. It does not create copies, as we expect from PHP. Instead, it creates links. Let's look again at how we assigned them.

```
irb> a = 'foo'
=> "foo"
irb> b = a
=> "foo"
```

Here, the literal "foo" is an object by itself. It's an instance of the String class. You can even call methods on it directly like "foo".size (try it!). We assigned a reference from this String object to the variable a. We then assigned that reference to the variable b.

It's important when writing Ruby code to remember that everything is an object and assignments are always by reference. Let's try another one just to make it sink in. This time we'll start with a PHP example.

PHP   beginning_ruby_code/php/assign_array.php

```php
$a = array();
$b = $a;

$a['foo'] = 'bar';

var_export($a);  // => array()
var_export($b);  // => array('foo' => 'bar')
```

In the previous PHP code, we assigned $a by value to an empty array. We then assigned $b by value to $a, which created a copy of the empty array in $a. Thus, we have two separate, empty arrays in $a and $b.

We know that after the previous PHP code has run, $a will contain an associative array with one element, but $b will still be an empty array.

Let's try that in IRB.

```
irb> a = {}
=> {}
irb> b = a
=> {}
irb> a['foo'] = 'bar'
```

The {} is shorthand for Hash.new. Ruby's Hash is similar to PHP's associative array. On the first line, we created a new Hash and assigned a reference to the variable a. We then assigned that reference to the variable b.

Inspecting both of the variables...

```
irb> a
=> {"foo"=>"bar"}
irb> b
=> {"foo"=>"bar"}
```

...we can see that even though we didn't explicitly modify b, it was shows the same value as a. This is exactly the opposite of what happened in the PHP example.

This is because both a and b contain a reference to the same Hash object.

Take a few minutes to play with other strings and hashes on IRB and observe the results before continuing. Remember that when you make assignments in Ruby, you are really creating references.

> **Functions and Methods**
>
> If you haven't done much object-oriented programming, you may wonder what the difference is between a function and a method. A *method* is simply a function that is bound to an object. Every *function* in Ruby is indeed bound to an object, so we'll always refer to them as methods.

2.6 Writing Methods and Passing Parameters

The world inside the Ruby interpreter is about object interactions. Everything is an object. Objects send methods, or messages, to other objects. We are now approaching the point where we can write Ruby programs beyond simplistic examples. This means we will be spending most of our time writing methods for our objects.

We've written Ruby methods in earlier examples, but we've glossed over the details. Ruby has some interesting rules that we must learn to write effective methods and has some magic to discover. Understanding these will go a long way to helping you understand what's really happening when you start digging into Rails programming.

Defining a Method

The basics of defining a method are the same in both Ruby and PHP. We've seen them both before, but let's look at them again quickly before exploring deeper. Here is an example of a method with one parameter in PHP.

`PHP` beginning_ruby_code/php/method_basic.php

```php
class Parrot {
    public function say($word) {
        // say it here
    }
}
```

Here's that same code written the Ruby way.

`Ruby` beginning_ruby_code/ruby/method_basic.rb

```ruby
class Parrot
  def say(word)
    # say it here
  end
end
```

In Ruby, the parentheses around the parameters for say are optional. The popular Rails programming style is to always include them unless the method has no parameters.

Let's add a second parameter to the method and make it optional.

PHP   `beginning_ruby_code/php/method_basic_2.php`

```php
class Parrot {
    public function say($word, $mocking = true) {
        // say it here
    }
}
```

If we want control over whether Parrot says the word in a particularly mocking or funny way, we use the optional $mocking parameter. Of course, any good parrot will make fun by default (at least on TV), so that's how we've set this up. Here's the same code in Ruby.

Ruby   `beginning_ruby_code/ruby/method_basic_2.rb`

```ruby
class Parrot
  def say(word, mocking = true)
    # say it here
  end
end
```

As you can see from the earlier Parrot examples, your PHP knowledge translates directly into Ruby. Basic method declaration and optional parameters work the same way. The biggest difference for the most common cases is just the syntax.

Now that we have reviewed the basics of writing methods in both Ruby and PHP, let's look at some more advanced cases.

Passing Named Parameters

If you've been programming PHP for a short time, you should already know some best practices for writing methods that apply to Ruby as well. For example, your methods should be relatively short—anything more than twenty lines or so indicates the method is doing too much.

Your methods should also avoid having too many parameters. If your method takes more than three parameters, that could also be a sign that your method is doing too much. A method with too many parameters can be confusing. However, sometimes even a small number of parameters can confuse as well.

The parameters in the Parrot examples are positional parameters; that is, their order is all that differentiates them when the method is called. There are times when order alone can make parameters ambiguous. Positional parameters can't help us in these situations. Let's consider a Cube in PHP.

`PHP` `beginning_ruby_code/php/method_params_unnamed.php`

```php
class Cube {
  public function __construct($height = 10, $width = 10, $depth = 10)
  {
    // check and then store parameters
  }
}
```

Somewhere later in the code base, perhaps in another file, we then instantiate a new Cube.

`PHP` `beginning_ruby_code/php/method_params_unnamed_usage.php`

```php
$c = new Cube(10, 20, 50);
```

Without seeing the signature of the constructor method, it's easy to forget the order. Does height go first? Does the width go second, or is it the depth? This lack of clarity is a problem. As both PHP and Ruby programmers, we should strive for programs that are easy to read and understand.

When implemented, the Cube class would probably have methods like setHeight() and setWidth(). One way to remove the ambiguity in this particular example is to take the parameters off the constructor method entirely and just always call these methods explicitly after creating the object. However, that's painful. We can do better.

An alternative is to use named parameters. PHP actually doesn't support named parameters, but you can fake them effectively. You can do this by passing them as an associative array.

If the Cube constructor method instead took a single parameter, an associative array of options, instantiating it would be as follows.

`PHP` `beginning_ruby_code/php/method_params_array.php`

```php
$c = new Cube(array('height' => 10, 'width' => 20, 'depth' => 50));
```

In the earlier example, we made setting the options of Cube clearer by simulating named parameters with an associative array. We've managed to make the code more readable while avoiding the hassle of three separate calls to methods like setHeight(). A fair number of PHP programs use this technique.

Now that we've looked at how named parameters can help some situations and can be faked in PHP, let's look at the equivalent in Ruby.

You might be disappointed to learn that Ruby doesn't have support for named parameters at the language level either, although it is planned. This helps your learning curve because we currently fake it in Ruby just like in PHP—with a twist.

Like an associative array is passed in PHP, a hash is passed in Ruby.

`Ruby` `beginning_ruby_code/ruby/method_params_naive_hash.rb`

```
c = Cube.new({'height' => 10, 'width' => 20, 'depth' => 50})
```

Ruby's hash is more convenient than PHP's associative array in this case because it just uses the {} braces. Losing the baggage of the array word makes the method a little more readable.

There's another improvement to be made. Although you can use strings for the keys just like PHP, idiomatic Ruby uses symbols. Let's make this change.

`Ruby` `beginning_ruby_code/ruby/method_params_symbolized_hash.rb`

```
c = Cube.new({:height => 10, :width => 20, :depth => 50})
```

The hash now looks a little cleaner and is easier to type as a bonus.

Ruby has one more important trick up its sleeve. Although the previous uses are legal, they are actually the marks of a beginning Ruby programmer. The best way is this.

`Ruby` `beginning_ruby_code/ruby/method_params_idiomatic_hash.rb`

```
c = Cube.new(:height => 10, :width => 20, :depth => 50)
```

When faking named parameters with a hash became a popular pattern, Ruby added a shortcut that allows you to leave off even the {} braces!

The rule is simple: when the last parameter in a method call is a hash, you can leave off the {}, and Ruby will know that you want to make a hash. With this knowledge, you are better prepared to understand Rails because this technique is used everywhere. In fact, if Cube were an ActiveRecord model, you would instantiate it exactly as shown in the previous example.

In the newsletter application, we introduced views and helper methods. Most of the built-in Rails view helpers also use this technique. Here's an example from the views of the application we'll build in Part II.

Ruby | beginning_ruby_code/ruby/method_params_helper.rb

```ruby
<%= submit_tag "Create", :class => "submit" %>
```

You should now recognize that submit_tag is a method, and it takes two parameters. The first is a string, and the second is a hash.

You now understand that simulated named parameters work the same in PHP and Ruby. The primary difference is that Ruby has evolved its syntax to encourage the pattern and make it more convenient. You're on your way to understanding the Ruby mechanics that make Rails so popular. Next, we'll take a look at some of the unique idioms Rails uses to control the program flow of our applications.

2.7 Controlling Program Flow

Ruby is designed to allow you to write programs that are closer to natural language. As such, it offers more flexibility in control structures and more vocabulary than PHP.

Let's pretend we are developing an application that has an administration interface. Only users who are the administrator can access certain functions of the application, and we want to have a simple check of whether a User model has the administrator privileges. If not, we'll simply return.

In PHP, this might look like the following.

PHP | beginning_ruby_code/php/control_if_not.php

```php
public function edit() {
    if (! $this->user->isAdmin() ) {
      return;
    }
}
```

That's pretty straightforward PHP code and would be a common way to do it. Let's translate that code directly into Ruby.

Ruby | beginning_ruby_code/ruby/control_if_not.rb

```ruby
def edit
  if ! @user.admin?
    return
  end

  # ...
end
```

In the PHP language, if-not combinations are common. However, this is not popular in Ruby. It works, but it's not the best way to write this code in Ruby.

One simple addition that Ruby has is the unless keyword. Let's rewrite that action to use unless.

Ruby | beginning_ruby_code/ruby/control_unless_before.rb

```
def edit
  unless @user.admin?
    return
  end

  # ...
end
```

Removing the not operator has made the code easier to read. This code is more readable than the if-not combination. As a result, most good Ruby programs tend to favor it.

However, Ruby allows yet another improvement to be made.

Ruby | beginning_ruby_code/ruby/control_unless_after.rb

```
def edit
  return unless @user.admin?

  # ...
end
```

The Ruby grammar permits *statement modifiers*, which allow the condition to come after the statement, as shown earlier. You can also use if as a statement modifier.

This is an interesting feature that does not have an equivalent in PHP. It might look a little strange at first, but try saying it out loud. It's much closer to natural language to say "return unless user is admin" than "if not user is admin return."

When writing your Ruby programs, you should strive for clarity and readability above all else. You can write control structures in Ruby that look quite similar to PHP, but that's not the best way to write Ruby. When writing control structures, you want to try to use the expressiveness Ruby offers to make your code read as close to natural language as possible.

With these thoughts in mind, most control structures are quite similar in Ruby and PHP. For many side-by-side comparisons of PHP and Ruby control structures, check out Section 11.7, *Control Structures*, on page 300. We won't repeat those examples here, but take a look at them before moving on. The most interesting control structure that Ruby offers is the block. We'll explore blocks in Section 2.9, *Understanding Blocks*, on page 51. Before we get there, let's look at handling errors in both PHP and Ruby.

2.8 Handling Errors

In this section, we'll take a look at PHP's dual error model and the different approach that Ruby takes when handling errors.

PHP Error Messages

Prior to PHP version 5, PHP had only one built-in mechanism for handling errors: the PHP error messages. These are the kinds of errors that PHP itself will output most of the time.

Here's an example of one such error that occurs when an undefined function has been called.

PHP
`beginning_ruby_code/php/error_fatal.php`

```php
<?php
undefinedFunction();
echo '...and execution stopped';
?>
// => PHP Fatal error: Call to undefined function undefinedFunction() in
//    /filename.php on line 3
```

In the case of this error, the function called does not exist, so PHP clearly has no way to continue. The call to echo() is never reached, and there is no way for the program to recover from this error.

PHP errors vary in severity. Some errors, such as the E_FATAL error shown earlier, terminate the execution of the program immediately. However, this is not the case for all PHP errors. Consider the following example.

PHP
`beginning_ruby_code/php/error_warning.php`

```php
<?php
function foo($bar) {}

echo foo();
echo '...but execution has continued!';
?>
// => PHP Warning: Missing argument 1 for foo(), called in /filename.php
//    on line 4 and defined in /filename.php on line 2
//    ...but execution has continued!
```

In this code, a function is called without all its required arguments. Clearly this is a mistake, and in almost all cases, the function will not behave as it was intended by the author. However, interestingly, execution continues!

This example is more interesting than the first because unless the user has explicitly set an error handler with set_error_handler(), a program can continue along with unintended consequences.

Handling PHP Error Messages

In the previous examples, the errors generated were because of bad code and were avoidable. However, many PHP functions generate error messages that are simply unavoidable. In these cases, our programs must be smart enough to anticipate the errors and silence them.

For example, when trying to connect to a database, it's not possible to know ahead of time whether a mysql_connect will fail because of server conditions that are beyond the program's control.

In the next example, the database connection fails.

PHP

beginning_ruby_code/php/mysql_connect_naive.php

```php
<?php
$db = mysql_connect('foo', 'user', 'password');
echo '...but execution continues!';
?>
// => PHP Warning: mysql_connect(): Can't connect to MySQL server on
//      'localhost' (4) in /code/php_pain_ruby_revelation/- on line 2
//      ...but execution continues!
```

This is very bad PHP code but is also a common mistake. The previous code is "naive," or without any error checking. The mysql_connect() call is expected to always succeed, and it does—usually.

When it doesn't, the PHP error message is generated. Clearly, the program does not have the connection that it is expecting to use, but execution continues anyway. Since the error was never handled, very bad things can happen downstream in the code.

Here's the same code but with the appropriate error handling.

PHP

beginning_ruby_code/php/mysql_connect_error_checking.php

```php
$db = @mysql_connect('localhost', 'user', 'password');
if (! $db) {
    // hopefully more sophisticated error handling
    die('database connection failed');
}
```

This is a common idiom in PHP programming. First, we prepend the silence operator (@) to mysql_connect() to make sure if the connection fails that the PHP error message isn't leaked. Second, we check whether the result of mysql_connect() is not a resource. If not, we do something to deal with the error. Finally, the connection was successful if we make it all the way through.

This is all inconvenient compared to the first example where we had just a single call to mysql_connect(). Unfortunately, it's necessary for writing sound PHP programs using the mysql extension (and many others). It is an exceptional condition, but we still must deal with it and similar ones every step of the way. This becomes very tedious, and scripting languages are supposed to provide convenience.

PHP Exceptions

Ordinarily, we expect our programs to run through without encountering major errors, such as the database that went down in the earlier examples. When these kinds of errors occur, they are not normal—they are exceptional.

PHP 5 introduced a powerful construct called *exceptions*. Most other languages have some variation of exceptions, including C++, Java, Python, and Ruby. Exceptions provide a convenient way of wrapping blocks of code and handling any exceptional conditions at the bottom.

To demonstrate exceptions, let's take a look at some code that is similar to the previous code but uses the pdo extension instead. PDO is the standard data access library that was also introduced with PHP 5. Although it is capable of raising the normal PHP error messages like the mysql extension, it defaults to throwing exceptions instead. Let's look at a small piece of code using PDO to see PHP exceptions in action.

PHP · beginning_ruby_code/php/pdo_exception.php

```php
try {
    $db = new PDO('mysql:host=localhost;dbname=test', 'user', 'pass');

    $rows = $db->query('SELECT * from people');

    foreach ($rows as $row) {
        print_r($row);
    }
} catch (PDOException $e) {
    die("Error!: " . $e->getMessage());
    // ... or something more sophisticated
}
```

Notice that when connecting to the database with $db = new PDO, this code performs no error checking. It's similar to the first (and more convenient) mysql_connect() example that didn't bother to check errors.

In fact, the previous code has many places that major errors could occur but are not explicitly checked: once in the connection, once in retrieving the result set, and once for retrieving each row from the set. These are all sources of errors that would otherwise have to be checked individually with if blocks.

All of the errors are exceptional. They are expected to succeed, but we still need to plan a rescue mission for when they don't. This is exactly what the try/catch block provides.

When any code inside the try fails and throws an exception, PHP will immediately jump to the corresponding catch to handle the failure. This removes the burden of having to check for major errors every step of the way.

Even better, the try/catch blocks can be nested to an arbitrary depth. Functions can be called deep into your program, and if an exception occurs anywhere, it will bubble up to the first catch that can rescue it.

Finally, PHP exceptions are objects. Unlike the old PHP error messages that just contain a string message and an integer code, exceptions package up detailed information about the source of error in the backtrace. PHP's base Exception class can also be subclassed, such as PDOException, as shown earlier. This makes it simple to check the source of an exception.

Exceptions allow you to structure your code more clearly than the old error messages and make handling major errors much more convenient.

Ruby Error Messages

Ruby's error messages are similar to those in PHP. A Ruby error message may not necessarily stop the execution of the script.

Ruby beginning_ruby_code/ruby/warning.rb

```ruby
MY_CONSTANT = 1
MY_CONSTANT = 2
puts "...but execution continues!"

# => -:2: warning: already initialized constant MY_CONSTANT
#    ...but execution continues!
```

In the previous example, a constant is defined twice. Ruby warns that the constant has already been initialized but continues along anyway to print the message.

However, fatal errors will halt execution.

Ruby

`beginning_ruby_code/ruby/fatal.rb`

```ruby
foo(}
puts "...and execution stopped"

# => -:1: parse error, unexpected '}', expecting ')'
```

Here, a method foo is called, but the curly brace was mistakenly used instead of the closing parenthesis. In this case, Ruby cannot parse the file and halts execution before printing the message.

Error messages can and do occur in Ruby. However, the important differentiation between Ruby and PHP here is that the Ruby errors are easily found up front and can be corrected easily. They are not usually traps to be found later in execution.

There are no situations in Ruby where error messages happen as a result of common operations like opening files or database connections. These are always exceptions, just like the convenient PHP exceptions we saw in the previous section. Once your Ruby program is free from more obvious defects like the ones shown earlier, you have to worry only about handling errors through the exceptions!

Ruby's Rescue Mission

Although you'll find PHP code using both styles of error handling, Ruby uses exceptions as the standard way of handling all errors. PHP exceptions occur when throw is called and are trapped in try/catch blocks.

PHP

`beginning_ruby_code/php/raise_exception.php`

```php
<?php
function demoIt() {
    try {
        throw new Exception('Error!');
    } catch (Exception $e) {
        die($e->getMessage());
    }
}
demoIt();
?>

// => Error!
```

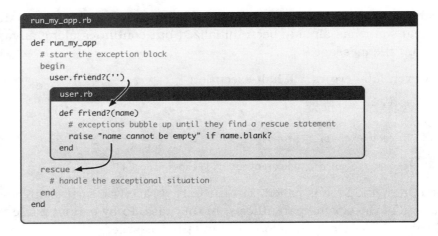

Figure 2.2: RESCUING EXCEPTIONS

Ruby exceptions are similar. An exception is raised by calling raise. We place the code for the rescue mission in the rescue section of a begin/end block. As shown in Figure 2.2, raising an exception can be arbitrarily deep and will always bubble up to the nearest rescue statement.

Ruby beginning_ruby_code/ruby/raise_exception.rb

```ruby
def demo_it!
  begin
    raise 'Error!'
  rescue => e
    abort e.message
  end
end
demo_it!

# => Error!
```

Notice that in rescue => e, we didn't specify a type of exception to rescue. This will cause all exceptions to be rescued. A specific type of exception can be rescued by naming it after rescue, such as rescue ActiveRecord::RecordNotFoundError. It's also optional to leave off the destination variable => e if one isn't required.

As you can see from the previous examples, exceptions in PHP and Ruby are similar. PHP 5 developers should feel right at home with Ruby in this regard. PHP 4 developers will find exceptions to be a breath of fresh air compared to the more "manual" error checking.

Ruby's exceptions provide some additional features absent in PHP exceptions. We'll talk more about Ruby exceptions in Section 12.4, *Exceptions*, on page 349. For now, the key idea is that Ruby's exceptions are as convenient as those in PHP 5, but without inconsistencies in the error model to remember.

Unlike exceptions, our next topic doesn't have as easy of a reference point in PHP. Blocks are a defining part of Ruby but are one of the more difficult concepts to grasp for PHP developers since they have no direct translation in PHP.

2.9 Understanding Blocks

There are many aspects of the Ruby language that make it different from other languages. From a PHP developer's perspective, there are really two defining characteristics of Ruby that stand out above others. The first characteristic is that Ruby is a fully object-oriented language.

The second characteristic is a language feature known in computer science as *closures*. If you have done any JavaScript programming, you may already be familiar with closures but might not know them by name. The Ruby language has deep support for closures, and they are used extensively throughout the language. In Ruby, they're simply called *blocks*, so that's how we'll refer to them from now on.

PHP is not the only language that lacks a direct equivalent of blocks. Many other languages, such as Java, also do not have them. Because of this, many developers seem to think that blocks are an obscure language feature for advanced users. Although blocks may be a new concept to you, they are extremely useful. Understanding them is vital to becoming proficient with Ruby and its libraries.

Using Your First Block

Although there is no direct translation of blocks in PHP, we can make some analogies to PHP that will help build up an understanding toward blocks. Let's start with a simple loop that prints a familiar jingle.

PHP   beginning_ruby_code/php/blocks_99_bottles.php

```php
function print_bottles($num) {
  print "$num bottles of beer on the wall\n";
}

for ($bottles = 99; $bottles > 0; $bottles--) {
  print_bottles($bottles);
}
```

When the code is executed, PHP evaluates the condition in the for loop. As long as the condition is true, PHP calls our print_bottles() function on each iteration.

The for and function keywords are built-in constructs of the PHP language. They are built into the language, in the same way that semicolons and curly braces are built in.

Only a select number of control constructs that are built in to PHP allow code to be attached to them with curly braces. It's not possible to add new control constructs to PHP without writing a PHP extension (in the C language).

With the PHP example still in mind, let's look at the idiomatic Ruby version.

Ruby   beginning_ruby_code/ruby/blocks_99_bottles.rb

```ruby
99.downto(1) { |num| puts "#{num} bottles of beer on the wall" }
```

It uses some unfamiliar syntax, but it's also quite declarative. It is almost like we would speak or write: ninety-nine down to one, sing the lyrics. This is an important aspect of the Ruby architecture. Ruby is designed to encourage programs that read like a natural language.

We already know what the Ruby version will do, so now we need to understand how it does that and why it looks the way it does.

By this time, you should recognize that 99 is an object that has a method called downto. The extra code attached to downto, the odd-looking bit with the curly braces and goalposts that does the printing, is called the block.

The downto method in the Ruby example serves the same purpose as our PHP example that counted down with the for construct. The downto method iterates over the numbers, temporarily passing control to the attached block on each iteration.

The Anatomy of a Block

Compare downto's block to our PHP function print_bottles().

Ruby `beginning_ruby_code/ruby/blocks_99_bottles.rb`

```ruby
99.downto(1) { |num| puts "#{num} bottles of beer on the wall" }
```

PHP `beginning_ruby_code/php/blocks_99_print_alone.php`

```php
function print_bottles($num) {
  print "$num bottles of beer on the wall\n";
}
```

There are many similarities between the Ruby block and the PHP function. This is because the Ruby block is actually just a function in another form. A block is a function without a name, or an *anonymous function*.

A block can receive parameters, in this case just the bottle count, and these go between the goalposts. When there are no parameters, the goalposts can be left off. The rest of the block is executable code, just like any other Ruby method.

As we discussed earlier, PHP has only a select number of built-in language constructs like for that can have code blocks attached to them. Ruby is different from PHP in this regard.

Ruby methods have a secret. Every method in Ruby, whether it be a built-in one or one you create, has the capability of being passed a block. If 99's downto method was in pure Ruby, it might look like this.

Ruby `beginning_ruby_code/ruby/blocks_downto_with_call.rb`

```ruby
class Integer
  def downto(value, &block)
    n = self
    while n >= value
      block.call n
      n -= 1
    end
    return self
  end
end
```

Notice the &block parameter at the end of the downto definition. When a block of code is passed to a Ruby method, it can be captured into a variable.

That's right, the actual code in the block (our lyrics printer) is converted into an object, an instance of the Ruby class Proc, and stored inside a variable. The ampersand (&block) tells Ruby to store this object in the the variable called block.

The keyword self in this example refers to the object itself, which in this case is the integer 99. Consider our earlier sample implementation of downto, and now look at our jingle again.

`Ruby` `beginning_ruby_code/ruby/blocks_99_bottles.rb`

```ruby
99.downto(1) { |num| puts "#{num} bottles of beer on the wall" }
```

When the downto method is called, it is given two parameters: value contains the number of bottles for the countdown, and block contains the block to call on each iteration that prints the lyrics.

The inside of the downto method should be straightforward. In fact, it looks a lot like our PHP example. It counts down from the Integer object's value (in our case, 99) to value by using a while loop.

On each iteration of that while loop, it yields control to the code in the block by calling the block.call method. Any parameters given to block.call are passed to the goalposts in the block.

Yielding to the Block

In the previous section, we looked at how the Integer class might implement the downto method. We developed this sample implementation using block.call to yield control to the block for each iteration of the countdown.

`Ruby` `beginning_ruby_code/ruby/blocks_downto_with_call.rb`

```ruby
class Integer
  def downto(value, &block)
    n = self
    while n >= value
      block.call n
      n -= 1
    end
    return self
  end
end
```

The previous implementation is good for starting to understand blocks, but it is not always necessary (or desirable) to capture the block into a variable as shown earlier. Now that the concept has been established, we can look at the preferred way of yielding to blocks.

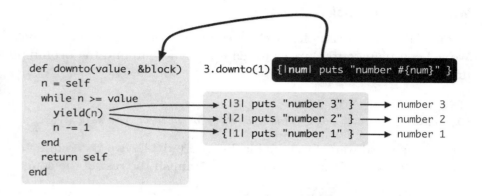

Figure 2.3: YIELDING TO A BLOCK

Here is an alternate implementation of downto.

Ruby beginning_ruby_code/ruby/blocks_downto_with_yield.rb

```ruby
class Integer
  def downto(value)
    n = self
    while n >= value
      yield n
      n -= 1
    end
    return self
  end
end
```

As you can see in this alternative example, the block is not captured into a variable. The block is there but invisible. As we said earlier, every Ruby method has a secret.

The special yield method is called that yields control to the block like block.call did. If we take a look at Figure 2.3, we can get an idea of how yield works.

When you start writing your own methods that use blocks, always use yield in this way unless you need to capture a Proc into a variable for more advanced uses.

Writing Longer Blocks

In all of the prior examples, we've been using only one form of block. We've been using curly braces to tell Ruby where to find the beginning and end of the block.

Ruby | beginning_ruby_code/ruby/blocks_99_bottles.rb

```ruby
99.downto(1) { |num| puts "#{num} bottles of beer on the wall" }
```

There's a second way of writing blocks where the keywords do and end are used in place of the curly braces. Let's finish the rest of the song.

Ruby | beginning_ruby_code/ruby/blocks_99_bottles_do_end.rb

```ruby
99.downto(1) do |num|
  puts "#{num} bottles of beer on the wall, " +
      "#{num} bottles of beer!"

  puts "Take one down, pass it around!" unless num == 1
end
```

This form is nicer when writing blocks that span multiple lines.

Ruby doesn't restrict how you use the curly braces or the do/end form. You can have blocks with curly braces spanning multiple lines or blocks with do/end on a single line.

Like many things in PHP, just because you can do it does not make it a good idea. In the vast majority of Ruby programs and situations, the community uses curly braces for blocks on the same line and the do/end form for multiple lines. We suggest you follow that lead also.

Blocks are a complex but important feature to learn in Ruby. Don't worry if you think you don't have a full grasp of blocks quite yet. They should begin to make more sense as we start using them within the context of our Rails application in Chapter 4, *Modeling the Domain*, on page 85. We also discuss some additional uses and features of blocks in Section 12.1, *Blocks*, on page 311.

2.10 Chapter Review

We are starting to see some of the philosophies that set Ruby apart from PHP, and many of these ideas heavily influence how we write code in Rails. We'll expand upon this in the next chapter by learning more of the specific features and language syntax that make Ruby unique.

Let's review what else we learned in this chapter:

- We learned how useful the Interactive Ruby interpreter is when playing around with Ruby syntax. This gives us immediate feedback without the need for a browser.

- We learned how Ruby emulates named parameters using hashes and how important this is to understanding common Rails method calls.

- We got our first taste of Ruby blocks. Blocks are one of biggest aspects of Ruby that differentiate it from PHP, and we learned about how useful they can be.

- We saw how Ruby uses exceptions to consistently handle errors and how this is so different from PHP's error handling.

2.11 Exercises

Here's some extra exercises that you can try on your own:

- In IRB, try calling the methods method on a Ruby string. This performs reflection on the object to list to which messages the object responds. Play around with calling various methods to see what else you can do with a string.

- Try raising some exceptions in Ruby. See what happens when you raise an error in IRB. Try enclosing your raise statement in a rescue block to catch the exception.

- We showed a possible implementation of Integer#downto that yields a value to a Ruby block. Try to build an implementation of Integer#upto using the same idea.

Chapter 3

Embracing the Ruby Philosophy

In the previous chapter, we started using IRB and wrote our first lines of Ruby code. Now, it's time to look at more advanced Ruby material so we can begin to understand the Ruby philosophy and what makes Ruby special. Once you're comfortable with the material in this chapter, we'll head back to Rails, and we will put your Ruby skills to work tackling a more serious web application in Part II of this book.

3.1 Thinking in Objects

One of the most important steps in understanding Ruby is to learn how to think in terms of objects. In this section, we'll begin to reshape our thinking by looking at some examples.

Data Is Dumb

Every PHP developer's first program consists of mostly the same thing. It's usually an HTML file with PHP bits embedded. The file consists of calls to PHP functions that do interesting things, such as echo() or htmlentities().

Even as our PHP programming abilities grow and we begin using classes and start to think in a more object-oriented way, we are always using the same built-in PHP functions in the same old way.

PHP   ruby_philosophy/php/in_and_out.php

```php
$upcasedName = strtoupper($theName);

$commaSeparated = implode(',', $anArray);

$saferToOutput = htmlentities($myData);
```

Whether we think about it or not, this kind of usage trains us that data is dumb. We put data into variables, variables go into functions, and new variables come out. This is the essence of procedural programming. Since all PHP programs rely on the functions built into PHP, it's sometimes difficult to escape this thinking even as our own programs become more advanced.

Toward Smart Objects

Variable types such as strings, numbers, and arrays are just data. They're dumb and can't do anything on their own. We must call functions to operate on them. If we need to reverse the string, round the number, or sort the array, we call a function to do the work. We pass the variable into the function and get a variable back out.

Along the same thinking, functions themselves aren't very smart either. A function is simply a little machine that manipulates data. It doesn't know much about the data it's manipulating. For example, strrev() cares that the first parameter is a string, but it doesn't care whether the string is your dog's name.

Object orientation gives us a different way of thinking about our data. We can create objects that have both data and functions to work on that data, which we call *methods*. Instead of having dumb variables and dumb functions, we can encapsulate everything into smart objects.

PHP   ruby_philosophy/php/object_person.php

```php
class Person {
    private $name;

    public function __construct($name) {
        $this->name = $name;
    }

    public function setName($name) {
        $this->name = ucfirst($name);
    }

    public function getName() {
        return $this->name;
    }
}

$mike = new Person('Michael');
$mike->setName('mike');

print $mike->getName();
// => Mike
```

In the earlier example, we created a Person object. This Person object has methods to set and get the person's name.

This style of programming has many advantages, but the primary one is encapsulation. It brings together variables and functions into something smarter—an object. The object's methods (its functions) are now much smarter and more specialized than anything not in an object could be. The getName() method knows not only that the name is a string but that it is a name of a specific person.

In the previous example, our Person is pretty smart. Our program can assign a new name with the setName() method and can call the getName() method to get back the name of each person created.

Let's look at the same code in Ruby.

`Ruby` `ruby_philosophy/ruby/object_person.rb`

```ruby
class Person
  def initialize(name)
    @name = name
  end

  def name=(name)
    @name = name.capitalize
  end

  def name
    @name
  end
end

mike = Person.new('Michael')
mike.name = 'mike'
puts mike.name
# => Mike
```

Objects allow us to model our problem domain in code. This is why our ActiveRecord classes are called *models*. To make our programs more understandable, we try to model our objects as close as possible to the real-life things that they represent. In this case, our Person class is the code representation of a real person. Let's take a look at some of the differences in how we define classes in PHP and Ruby.

Although the syntax is obviously different, the Ruby version of a Person looks similar to the PHP version. You've probably noticed a subtle difference in how we assign and access the data for the object. Instead of the setName() and getName() methods, we have name= and name, respectively. Setting the name value for a person is an assignment operation, and Ruby embraces this idea by using a special syntax. Although the name= syntax seems a little unusual at first, it makes perfect sense when assigning data to an attribute of our object.

There is another important difference in the name method of our Ruby class. You may wonder how we ever get the value of @name since we aren't using a return statement. Ruby implicitly returns the last statement evaluated in any method. Although we could also write this as return @name, the accepted Ruby convention is to omit the return keyword when it isn't needed.

3.2 Understanding Attributes

Ruby and PHP take different approaches when it comes to sharing data between methods of a class definition. PHP uses data members to share data, where each data member is typically declared at the top of a class definition. These data members can be declared with a different visibility keyword depending on their purpose.

Ruby does not use data members but instead shares data using instance variables. These variables do not need to be declared anywhere within our class and are completely encapsulated within the object. There is no equivalent of PHP's public data member, and adding public accessor methods is the only way to access and modify instance variables.

In PHP, we can declare data members as either public, private, or protected.

`PHP` ruby_philosophy/php/member_visibility.php

```php
class Book {
    protected $title;
    public $price;

    public function __construct($title, $price) {
        $this->title  = $title;
        $this->price  = $price;
    }

    public function getTitle() {
        return $this->title;
    }
}

$book = new Book("Frankenstein", 9.95);
print $book->getTitle()."\n";
// => Frankenstein
```

```php
$book->price = 10.95;
print $book->price."\n";
// => 10.95
```

The previous PHP code declares two data members. The $title attribute is protected, and we added a getter method named getTitle() to retrieve it from outside of the class. We declared the $price attribute as public. This makes it easy to access data for this attribute but difficult to change the implementation of price. If we wanted to calculate tax before returning the price, we would need an additional method such as getPrice(). Now let's take a look at the Ruby translation of this class.

Ruby   ruby_philosophy/ruby/member_visibility.rb

```ruby
class Book
  def initialize(title, price)
    @title, @price = title, price
  end

  def title
    @title
  end

  def price
    @price
  end

  def price=(price)
    @price = price
  end
end

book = Book.new("Frankenstein", 9.95)
puts book.title
# => Frankenstein

book.price = 10.95
puts book.price
# => 10.95
```

The @title in the Ruby code works similarly to our PHP and has a getter method. In Ruby, we've named this method directly after the instance variable it returns. We also have a @price instance variable, but since we have no public data declarations in Ruby, we need to add both getter and setter methods. The setter method is also named directly after the instance variable, but this time is appended with an equals sign (=) in the name. Because of Ruby's flexible syntax, we can now use these methods to access and assign the @price as if were a public attribute. However, we still have the flexibility to change the implementation of how we return the price data.

Defining getter and setter methods tends to become quite repetitive. We can dynamically add these methods using a few special Ruby class methods. Attribute methods allow us to declaratively assign which of our instance variables we want to become available as attributes.

Ruby   ruby_philosophy/ruby/attr_methods.rb

```ruby
class Book
  attr_reader    :title
  attr_accessor :price

  def initialize(title, price)
    @title, @price = title, price
  end
end
```

The attr_reader :title method declaration replaces our title getter method, and the attr_accessor :price replaces both the getter and setter methods for @price. There is also the attr_writer method for adding a setter method without the corresponding getter.

3.3 Method Visibility

Like PHP, Ruby methods can be declared public, private, or protected. This makes sense, since methods are ultimately how we access any object data in Ruby. Just as in PHP, all methods in Ruby are assumed public unless declared otherwise. In Ruby we can declare the visibility of multiple methods at a time. Making a single protected declaration will establish every method below as a protected method until we declare a different access. This cuts down on repetition and nudges us to group together methods with similar visibility. Typically we group public methods at the top of a class definition to exclude the need for any public visibility declaration.

PHP   ruby_philosophy/php/method_visibility.php

```php
class MyClass {
    public function myPublicMethod() {}

    protected function myProtectedMethod() {}

    protected function anotherProtectedMethod() {}

    private function myPrivateMethod() {}

    public function mySecondPublicMethod() {}
}
```

Ruby ruby_philosophy/ruby/method_visibility.rb

```ruby
class MyClass
  # default is public
    def my_public_method
    end

  protected
    def my_protected_method
    end

    def another_protected_method
    end

  private
    def my_private_method
    end

  public
    def my_second_public_method
    end
end
```

The difference between protected and private methods in Ruby is subtle and has nothing to do with inheritance as it does in PHP. A protected method in Ruby can be called from any object instance of the same class.

Ruby ruby_philosophy/ruby/method_protected.rb

```ruby
class Employee < User
  def initialize(name)
    @name = name
  end

  # we can call the given user's protected "name"
  # because it is also a User class
  def compare(user)
    self.name == user.name
  end

  protected
    def name
      @name
    end
end

joe  = Employee.new('joe')
jane = Employee.new('jane')

puts joe.compare(jane)
# => false
```

```
puts jane.name
# => protected method `name' called for #<User:0x1eac08 @name="Jane">
```

Since Jane's name method is declared as protected, we cannot call it publicly. We can, however, call this same method in the implementation of Joe's compare method since Joe is also an instance of User.

A private method in Ruby can be executed only within the context of the same object or derivative object.

`Ruby` `ruby_philosophy/ruby/method_private.rb`

```
class User
  private
    def format(value)
      value.capitalize
    end
end

class Employee < User
  def initialize(name)
    # format can only be called by this instance
    @name = format(name)
  end
end

jane = Employee.new('jane')
puts jane.format
# => private method `format' called for
#    #<Employee:0x1edf48 @name="Jane"> (NoMethodError)
```

Notice that unlike PHP, the private format method is inherited into the User subclass.

With a little better understanding of object attributes and visibility under our belts, let's take a look at how Ruby uses object types.

3.4 Understanding Typing

PHP and Ruby are similar in that they are both dynamically typed languages. This means that variables are assigned types as they are used in context. You don't need to declare the types of variables before they are used, and variables may change types as they are used.

```
irb> foo = 'bar'
=> "bar"
irb> foo = 42
=> 42
```

In the previous example, the variable foo is assigned a string object containing bar. It is then reassigned to the numeric (Fixnum) object 42. In both cases, the type of foo was never declared. Ruby simply stores something new inside it each time. PHP works the same way, and we probably don't even think of this as a feature.

Although both PHP and Ruby are dynamically typed, this is where the similarity in their typing ends. PHP is a very loosely typed language. If you try to add an integer to a string, it works fine. Let's try that in Ruby.

```
irb> a = 2
=> 2
irb> b = '2'
=> "2"
irb> a + b
=> "2"
TypeError: String can't be coerced into Fixnum
        from (irb):7:in `+'
        from (irb):7
```

If this were in PHP, adding $a + $b would work just fine. PHP will take whatever types it gets and try to make the best of it. This usually works fine and occasionally produces a result we aren't expecting. As we see from the earlier example, Ruby doesn't even try. It just gives us an error message.

Lucky for us, Ruby has a solution for this type mismatch. Most objects implement a collection of methods that will convert the object to different data types. In this case, we can get the result we want by using the to_i method to convert our String into a Fixnum.

```
irb> a = 2
=> 2
irb> b = '2'
=> "2"
irb> a + b.to_i
=> 4
```

Duck Typing

You'll often hear the term *duck typing* when programming in Ruby. This concept comes from the phrase "If it walks like a duck and quacks like a duck, then it's probably a duck." In Ruby this means that when we are using objects, we are concerned about what they can do, and not the actual type of the object. Instead of checking whether an object is in fact a duck, we just make sure that it either quacks or walks.

Since PHP is a dynamic language, we are usually not concerned about the specific type of data being passed around. We concatenate integers to strings and add strings to integers without a second thought. PHP 5 changed this a little by implementing object-oriented features that are more conscious of data types. New constructs such as interfaces and type hinting are aimed directly at enforcing that the objects we pass around are of a specific class.

Advocates of statically typed languages argue that not enforcing types is dangerous to the stability of a program. PHP 5 is interesting as a language because to some extent it embraces both sides of the argument. It is a loosely typed language for its primitive types but can be a strictly type language for objects, depending on how the program is written.

Let's look at how PHP can provide type safety for objects and how this is different from Ruby's typing philosophy. A type hint in PHP requires that an object inherits or implements a specified type.

`PHP`   ruby_philosophy/php/duck_typing.php

```php
class Duck {
    public function waddle() {
        print "duck waddling...\n";
    }
}

class Goose {
    public function waddle() {
        print "goose waddling...\n";
    }
}

// only accept Duck
function go(Duck $duck) {
    $duck->waddle();
}

go(new Duck);
// => duck waddling...

go(new Goose);
// => Argument 1 passed to go() must be an instance of Duck
```

In this case, we state that the go method accepts only Duck objects. Our goose object also implements the waddle method but cannot go since our function accepts only ducks. If we take a look at the Ruby version, we'll see that Ruby doesn't care about the type and will make anything waddle as long as it has a waddle method.

Ruby `ruby_philosophy/ruby/duck_typing.rb`

```ruby
class Duck
  def waddle
    puts "duck waddling..."
  end
end

class Goose
  def waddle
    puts "goose waddling..."
  end
end

def go(duck)
  duck.waddle
end
go Duck.new
# => duck waddling...
go Goose.new
# => goose waddling...
```

Since both ducks and geese are part of the Anatidae family of birds, we could update our PHP example by making the Duck and Goose classes inherit from this same parent class. Then instead of enforcing a Duck type, we could enforce that the object was an Anatidae.

This once again begins to reach limitations if we wanted to pass a waddling Walrus object to go(). Creating a Waddling object interface might be our next step, but we may instead determine at this point that the easiest solution is to copy the Ruby example and eliminate the type hint. The code still works, and chances are that in practice we wouldn't be passing the wrong object to this function anyway.

PHP `ruby_philosophy/php/duck_typing_no_hint.php`

```php
// only accept Duck
function go($duck) {
    $duck->waddle();
}

go(new Duck);
// => duck waddling...

go(new Goose);
// => goose waddling...
```

Type hints have not been universally adopted by PHP developers, and this updated version is how many people use PHP already. Not taking advantage of the type hinting mechanism can promote polymorphism.

At the same time, the restrictions imposed by type hinting can have benefits, especially with larger libraries and teams.

Generally, we don't enforce types in many areas of our own PHP programs. Rather than lose some flexibility and depend on PHP to crash when types collide, we write automated unit tests to ensure that our programs behave in the expected ways. Ruby takes this same approach when dealing with all objects.

Methods as Messages

When invoking a method on a Ruby object, we'll often refer to this as "passing a message to the object." When the object receives the message, it invokes the corresponding method with the given arguments. In the previous example, a Duck object responds to the waddle message. When we send this message, the duck responds with a string. The difference in terminology is subtle but important.

We know that with duck typing, the behavior of an object is more important than the type. Ruby follows up with this idea by letting us easily interrogate the behavior of an object.

Ruby | ruby_philosophy/ruby/respond_to.rb

```ruby
class Duck
  def waddle
    puts "duck waddling..."
  end
end

duck = Duck.new
puts duck.respond_to?(:waddle)
# => true

puts duck.respond_to?(:climb)
# => false
```

This syntax demonstrates why it is useful to view a method call as a message. The respond_to? method is available on every object in Ruby and is our way of asking the object "Do you respond to this message?" We can do a similar inspection in PHP using the is_callable function.

PHP | ruby_philosophy/php/respond_to.php

```php
class Duck {
    public function waddle() {
        print "duck waddling...\n";
    }
}
```

```
$duck = new Duck;
$waddle = is_callable(array($duck, 'waddle'));
var_export($waddle);
// => true

is_callable(array($duck, 'climb'));
$climb = is_callable(array($duck, 'climb'));
var_export($climb);
// => false
```

The biggest usage difference is that new methods can be added to classes and objects at runtime in Ruby. It's important to have the ability to examine behavior, and Ruby makes it easy to do so.

Along with the concept of sending messages is a way of invoking behavior using an explicit send method to send our message.

Ruby   ruby_philosophy/ruby/send.rb

```
mike = Person.new('Mike')

mike.send(:name)
```

Using the syntax mike.send(:name) does the same thing as doing mike. name but allows us to invoke a method name that we may not know until runtime. This is similar to using the call_user_func function in PHP.

PHP   ruby_philosophy/php/send.php

```
$mike = new Person('Mike');

call_user_func(array($mike, 'getName'));
```

The concepts of interrogating the behavior of an object and invoking a variable method name at runtime are not unique. We can already do these things in PHP. The need to understand method calls as messages is most important because method names and terminology in Ruby revolve around these ideas.

3.5 Implementing Interfaces with Mixins

Interfaces are an area of object-oriented programming where Ruby deviates from the approaches used in PHP and Java programming practices. Let us start by taking a look at a common usage of an interface in PHP.

If we were to model a dinosaur park application in PHP, one of the first classes we might build is a TRex. This is the first of many carnivores we'll add to our park (because we're asking for trouble). Since an object in PHP can have only a single superclass, we can't define a TRex class that inherits from both Dinosaur and Carnivore. The solution in PHP for this is to make TRex inherit from the most obvious class (Dinosaur) and have it implement a Carnivore interface.

PHP   ruby_philosophy/php/interfaces.php

```php
class Dinosaur {
    public $vertebrate = true;
}

interface Carnivore {
    public function hunt();
}

// we have to implement hunt() for this to be valid
class TRex extends Dinosaur implements Carnivore {
    public function hunt() {
        print get_class($this)." is hunting!\n";
    }
}

// we have to implement hunt() for this to be valid
class Raptor extends Dinosaur implements Carnivore {
    public function hunt() {
        print get_class($this)." is hunting!\n";
    }
}
```

Here we've made both the TRex and Raptor classes implement the Carnivore interface. We can now use a type hint to make sure that we add only carnivores to our park.

PHP   ruby_philosophy/php/type_hint.php

```php
class DinosaurPark {
    protected $dinosaurs = array();

    public function add(Carnivore $dinosaur) {
        $this->dinosaurs[] = $dinosaur;
    }

    public function run() {
        foreach ($this->dinosaurs as $dino) {
            $dino->hunt();
        }
    }
}

$park = new DinosaurPark;
$park->add(new TRex);
$park->add(new Raptor);
```

```
$park->run();
// => TRex is hunting!
// => Raptor is hunting!
```

You've probably noticed that we've repeated ourselves while implementing the hunt method on both classes. Although it wasn't too bad repeating a single method, you can imagine that it would get worse as we added more. The problem with interfaces is that even if all of the carnivore methods are the same in every class definition that uses the interface, we must rewrite the method implementations in each class.

Ruby takes a unique approach to implementing class interfaces by using modules. A module can contain methods, constants, and instance variables just like a Ruby class. Modules are very similar to classes. The biggest difference between a class and module is that a module cannot be instantiated.

In Ruby, we implement the hunt method for our dinosaurs in a Carnivore module. We can then use the include keyword to add all the Carnivore methods to our TRex and Raptor classes. We often refer to this use of modules as *mixins* since the module defines a set of methods that we mix in to our class definition. If we take a look at Figure 3.1, on the next page, we see that mixins are not part of the normal single-inheritance class hierarchy.

Ruby   ruby_philosophy/ruby/interfaces.rb

```ruby
class Dinosaur
  def initialize
    @vertebrate = true
  end
end

module Carnivore
  def hunt
    puts "#{self.class} is hunting!"
  end
end

class TRex < Dinosaur
  include Carnivore
end

class Raptor < Dinosaur
  include Carnivore
end
```

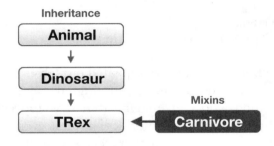

Figure 3.1: METHOD ORGANIZATION

The Carnivore module is started using the module keyword followed by a constant name. It finishes with the end keyword. Be aware that the include keyword in Ruby is nothing like the include statement in PHP. In Ruby, include pulls all the methods from the specified module into the current scope.

Including this module essentially solves the issue we ran into with repeated code in our PHP Carnivore implementations. Once we have mixed in the methods from Carnivore, Ruby doesn't care about the class of the dinos added to the park. Ruby cares only that these objects respond to a message named hunt.

Ruby   ruby_philosophy/ruby/type_hint.rb

```ruby
class DinosaurPark
  def initialize
    @dinosaurs = []
  end

  def add(dinosaur)
    @dinosaurs << dinosaur
  end

  def run
    @dinosaurs.each {|dino| dino.hunt }
  end
end

park = DinosaurPark.new
park.add(TRex.new)
park.add(Raptor.new)
park.run
# => TRex is hunting!
#    Raptor is hunting!
```

You may wonder at this point what happens when we have conflicts in method names or instance variables. Ruby simply overrides any existing methods with the last one added. It is a good idea to create unique method names when including multiple modules in a class.

`Ruby` `ruby_philosophy/ruby/module_conflicts.rb`

```ruby
module Ninja
  def attack
    puts 'throw shuriken'
  end
end

module Pirate
  def attack
    puts 'slash sword'
  end
end

class Person
  include Ninja
  include Pirate
end

person = Person.new
person.attack
# => slash sword
```

Modules are a versatile tool in Ruby and allow us to extract and share common behavior in objects. Next we'll take a look at a different use of modules—code organization.

3.6 Organizing Code with Namespaces

Organizing user-defined PHP classes and functions is somewhat ad hoc because no constructs are provided by the language to avoid clashes in class or function names. While adding namespaces to PHP has been a popular discussion among its developers for years, PHP 5 does not support namespaces at the time of writing.

Some developers have worked around this by adopting a convention of separating different class package names with underscores. This solution solves the immediate problem and also works conveniently with autoloading in PHP. It can, however, leave us with some really long class names.

Ruby creates namespaces using modules. A module is simply a container for objects, methods, constants, and instance variables. Placing this data in a module allows us to create a unique identifier for names that might otherwise conflict. Let's say that we had two different libraries that defined a Document class. In PHP, we would typically prefix each class with the name of the class package.

PHP   ruby_philosophy/php/module_namespaces.php

```php
class XML_Document {
    public function __construct() {
        print "new xml document\n";
    }
}

class PDF_Document {
    public function __construct() {
        print "new pdf document\n";
    }
}

$xml = new XML_Document;
$pdf = new PDF_Document;
```

Ruby takes a different approach by encapsulating each Document class in a module that defines the base package with which we are working.

Ruby   ruby_philosophy/ruby/module_namespaces.rb

```ruby
module XML
  class Document
    def initialize
      puts 'new xml document'
    end
  end
end

module PDF
  class Document
    def initialize
      puts 'new pdf document'
    end
  end
end

xml = XML::Document.new
pdf = PDF::Document.new
```

We can then differentiate between Document classes by prefixing Document with the module name and a double colon (::). Although it may not seem like we saved much typing when referring to the Ruby class, there are a couple ways to benefit from this namespace. When organizing our classes using underscores in PHP, we always need to reference a class using the full class name.

`PHP`
`ruby_philosophy/php/module_qualified.php`

```php
class XML_Document {
    public function __construct() {
        print "new xml document\n";
    }
}

class XML_Parser {
    public function __construct($source) {
        new XML_Document($source);
    }
}
```

Here we instantiate a new XML_Document from within XML_Parser. One of advantages of using namespaces is implicit qualification of the namespace from within the module. This means that all code within the context of the XML module can refer to the class as simply Document instead of XML::Document.

`Ruby`
`ruby_philosophy/ruby/module_qualified.rb`

```ruby
module XML
  class Parser(source)
    def initialize
      Document.new(source)
    end
  end

  class Document
    def initialize
      puts 'new xml document'
    end
  end
end
```

Another approach that lets us take advantage of the namespace is to import the objects of that namespace into the current scope. This can be done using the include keyword. Once again this pulls all the module objects into the current scope.

`Ruby`
`ruby_philosophy/ruby/module_include.rb`

```ruby
module XML
  class Document
    def initialize
      puts 'new xml document'
    end
  end
end
```

```
include XML
```

```
Document.new
```

The Document object no longer needs to be prefixed with XML:: when we
reference it. Most Ruby libraries and packages use a base namespace to
prevent conflicts with other libraries. This logically separates libraries
to make them much easier to manage in the context of a large project
with multiple dependencies.

3.7 Overriding Operators

Most operators are unique in Ruby because they're actually methods on
the receiving object. Ruby uses a special syntax to make these methods
appear like the normal operators we would see in PHP.

Ruby ruby_philosophy/ruby/operator_syntax.rb

```
# full method name with parentheses
1.+(2)

# method without parentheses
1.+ 2

# Ruby uses a syntax to make this method call look just like PHP
1 + 2
```

You'll rarely see Ruby developers write an expression like 1.+(2) in real
code. The cleaner 1 + 2 syntax is the preferred syntax usage, but you
can begin to see the power of Ruby operators in this example. Each
class can implement the same operator differently. A good example of
this is how the addition sign (+) performs addition with numbers but
concatenation with strings.

Ruby ruby_philosophy/ruby/operator_plus.rb

```
puts 1 + 2     # => 3
puts 'a' + 'b' # => ab
```

Overriding operators is possible in PHP but requires the operator PECL
extension written by Sara Goleman.[1] This plug-in is a nice addition
to PHP but is rarely included in standard configurations. Let's take
a look at defining operators for a custom class using Sara's operator
extension.

---

1. http://pecl.php.net/package/operator

`ruby_philosophy/php/operator_definition.php`

```php
// this syntax is only available in PHP using the operator extension
class MyClass {
    public function __add($value) {
        return "MyClass + $value";
    }

    public function __div($value) {
        return "MyClass / $value";
    }

}
$a = new MyClass;

print $a + 2;
// => MyClass + 2

print $a / 2;
// => MyClass / 2
```

We've used the extension to add both an addition operator (+) and a division operator (/) to this class. We have done this using two magic methods added by the extension. Implementing these same operators for a Ruby class does not require any plug-in and is very straightforward. We can implement a method named directly after each operator we wish to implement.

`ruby_philosophy/ruby/operator_definition.rb`

```ruby
class MyClass
  def +(value)
    "MyClass + #{value}"
  end

  def /(value)
    "MyClass / #{value}"
  end
end
a = MyClass.new

puts a + 2
# => MyClass + 2

puts a / 2
# => MyClass / 2
```

We can override all the common arithmetic and comparison operators and even the unary + and - operators. Overriding these, however, requires us to define methods named +@ and -@, respectively, to differentiate from addition and subtraction operators. There are a few operators that we cannot override since they cannot be reproduced with a method and are actually language constructs. These are as follows.

= .. ... ! **not** && **and** || **or** != !~ ::

Operators aren't the only thing we can redefine. In Ruby, we can add and change any existing method on all objects.

3.8 Reopening Classes

If you've ever accidentally redefined a class or function in PHP, you've probably been thrown a nasty fatal error.

`PHP` `ruby_philosophy/php/reopen_class.php`

```php
class Person {
    public function greeting() {
        return 'Hi!';
    }
}

class Person {
    public function greeting() {
        return 'Hello there!';
    }
}

// => PHP Fatal error: Cannot redeclare class Person
```

PHP simply doesn't allow this, and it seems to make a lot of sense for PHP to prevent this from happening. Ruby treats the situation much differently and will redefine the first method with the new one defined directly after.

`Ruby` `ruby_philosophy/ruby/reopen_class.rb`

```ruby
class Person
  def greeting
    'Hi!'
  end
end

class Person
  def greeting
    'Hello there!'
  end
end

p = Person.new
puts p.greeting

# => Hello there!
```

Although this may seem like a bug in Ruby, it is actually a feature of the language. In Ruby this is referred to as "reopening a class" and can be extremely useful for extending and redefining methods at runtime. Part of Ruby's philosophy is to give developers the power to do what they want, trusting that they'll use that power wisely. This type of feature may seem like it would lead to elusive bugs and general chaos, but it is actually quite manageable in practice.

Reopening classes gives new meaning to the Open/Closed principle, which states that a class should be open for extension but closed for modification. In Ruby we can extend a class by externally modifying it, preventing the need for inheritance. This is very powerful, and it often leads to a much more manageable code than large extension hierarchies.

Another interesting feature of Ruby is that we are not limited to extending our own classes. We can extend any base Ruby class as well. This is often critically referred to as *monkey patching*, since it's not very wise to be overriding base Ruby methods. It is a best practice to leave existing Ruby base methods alone, but this doesn't mean that we can't extend the base classes with bonus functionality for our application. For example, let's say we want a method on Integer to check whether an integer is an odd number. Before adding this method, trying to use the odd? method will result in a NoMethodError.

```
irb> 3.odd?
NoMethodError: undefined method `odd?' for 3:Fixnum
        from (irb):1
```

We can dynamically add this method by defining the Integer class with the odd? method implementation. This will not redefine Integer in its entirety but will simply reopen the class to add our new method. All previous Integer methods will continue to exist after the definition.

```
irb> class Integer
irb>   def odd?
irb>     self % 2 == 1
irb>   end
irb> end
=> nil
```

Now we can use our new method, just as we would with any other integer method.

```
irb> 3.odd?
=> true
```

Rails extends Ruby base classes substantially with a library called ActiveSupport, which reopens String, Integer, Array, and many further classes to add some very useful functionality. The odd? method is actually part of ActiveSupport along with a corresponding even? method.

One of the most powerful uses of reopening classes is the plug-in system available in Rails. We can use Rails plug-ins to extend and override nearly every part of Rails. We'll discuss plug-ins more in Section 13.13, *Rails Plug-Ins*, on page 392.

3.9 Chapter Review

In this chapter, we learned a lot about the unique language features that differentiate Ruby from PHP. This will give you a much better understanding of how Rails works by giving you the tools to decode what Rails is doing under the hood.

Let's review what else we learned in this chapter:

- We now see how objects manipulate data in a more sophisticated way than simple functions. We also learned that Ruby is not concerned with enforcing object types.
- We learned about the versatility of Ruby modules and how they can be used to create both namespaces and mixins.
- We looked at how object operators and attributes in Ruby differ from those in PHP and how we can use this to our advantage.
- We learned how Ruby classes can be reopened at any time to give us some really amazing flexibility with the language at runtime.

3.10 Exercises

Here are some extra exercises that you can try on your own:

- We already reopened Fixnum to add the odd? method. Try reopening this class again to add the even? method.
- Create a Person class that defines the == operator to compare object instances of people by comparing their names.
- Create a module named SoftwareDeveloper to extend the functionality of the Person class from the previous example. Make this module implement the debug method, and include it as a mixin to the Person class.

Part II

Building a Rails Application

Chapter 4

Modeling the Domain

Now that we have seen some high-level differences between PHP and Rails in Part I, it's time to put our experiences into action and get hands-on by building a Rails application. In this part, we'll build a Rails app from start to finish; along the way we will see in context how building an application in Rails is different from how we'd go about the task using PHP.

We'll offer an imaginary scenario here of a typical application development situation. Our friend Joe has called us with a plea. Joe is an experienced PHP programmer but has heard enough buzz about Rails to finally pique his interest. He has started a new Rails user group in his area but just doesn't have the time to create a decent website for it. He wants this group to be a success, and he knows that a website with only the date and location of meetings just won't cut it. He has asked for our help in creating an application to help plan and organize the group meetings. Since Joe is a good friend of ours, we'll help him build a killer app for his group.

The application we build will cover many of the features that Rails offers and will help us get a good idea of how to build a typical application using Rails. Creating a user group site will be a great introduction to hands-on coding with Rails because it contains enough objects to exercise the use of various ActiveRecord methods and associations. Giving Joe the ability to manage the application's data will require us to build a simple authentication system. Finally, all of this will need to be nicely wrapped up in a presentable public interface. When the application is finished, you should have a solid understanding of how Rails code is organized and have a good grasp on the practical uses of the various Rails components. Meanwhile, we'll continue to relate these development practices to those typically used in PHP.

Requirement	Feature
1. Describe the group	Display prominent description of group goals.
2. Inform of meeting details	Present information on past and future meetings.
3. Share coder knowledge	Display presentations and encourage members to present.
4. Show off coder projects	Create list of members with breif description of their work.
5. Get people talking	Use a mailing list to get people together outside of meetings.
6. Keep information current	Equip application with an easy-to-use administrative interface.

Figure 4.1: REQUIREMENTS AND FEATURES

To follow along as we build the application, you'll probably want to download the code examples for this application. The example source code is available online.[1]

4.1 Defining Requirements

We'll start the same way we might for any application, whether it be PHP or otherwise. We need to figure out the goals we want to accomplish and how our application can help us achieve them. Joe is as opinionated as any client and comes up with a solid list of requirements, as shown in Figure 4.1. We've taken this a little further, and we've assigned a feature to each of his requirements.

Our next step is to create some simple mock-ups of how the application might look. The interface needs to manage meetings, presentations, and users in our application. Joe tells us that he wants the meetings to include a date, a location, and a short description. He also wants to be able to add presentations to each meeting along with the person presenting.

---

1. http://www.pragprog.com/titles/ndphpr/source_code

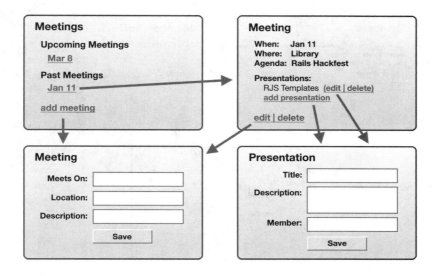

Figure 4.2: MEETINGS PAGE FLOW

Let's first concentrate on how we will need to manage these resources, and then we can begin coding them. To map out how we want this to work, we sit down with Joe to create some page flow diagrams. The drawing in Figure 4.2 shows a series of pages representing a typical web application. This includes the display of our meetings along with the ability to add, edit, and delete meetings and their associated presentations.

Our member pages (shown in Figure 4.3, on the next page) are much simpler, consisting of the ability to view and change user profiles. These page flow diagrams should provide us with enough material to start writing code.

At this point, we have a fair idea about how the application will look. If we were building this application in PHP, it would be tempting to simply make a PHP file for each one of these pages. First, we'd spend a bit of time working out the directory structure of our little application, figure out how to connect the PHP files, and probably gather up our favorite libraries from PEAR and other repositories to do tasks such as form handling. If we had chosen some PHP framework, we'd have fewer decisions, but we'd also have to start with the huge decision of which of the dozens of PHP frameworks to choose.

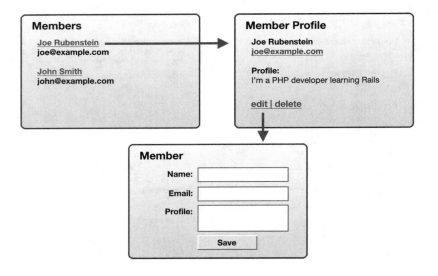

Figure 4.3: USERS PAGE FLOW

We could then dip into the home page and start fleshing it out in real PHP code and have a nonfunctioning mock-up of the home page to show Joe a couple of hours later. Joe would probably be impressed we threw it together so quickly. Once that was out of the way, we could start building the other pages and some code to deal with the database.

This isn't PHP, though; it's Rails. One of the big wins of adopting Rails is that it frees your mind of almost all the up-front decisions such as where to put things or what libraries to use. For our application, we'll do it "the Rails way" and follow whatever methods and tools that Rails has given us to use. By making this conscious decision to worry less about the innards of our application, we can simply concentrate on solving Joe's problems and trust that Rails will have the facilities available to let us do that efficiently.

We called this chapter *Modeling the Domain* instead of *Building the Website* because a Rails application has a different focus and workflow than a usual PHP website. Where plain PHP lets us start any place we'd like and build whatever we'd like, Rails has a strongly defined workflow for us to follow. That workflow starts by making us examine our problem domain—Joe's user group meetings—and modeling the data and interactions around that.

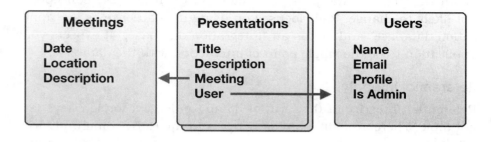

Figure 4.4: MODELING THE APPLICATION DATA

Through our interviews with Joe and creating these page flow diagrams, we should be able to identify the basic data that our application is dealing with and determine what our domain model will look like. Looking through our diagrams, let's create a list of the data we'll need to represent in our application. It seems right now that we have three sets of data to represent the resources in our application. If we take a look at Figure 4.4, we see that each meeting needs an association with one or more presentations, and each presentation will be associated with a user. Before we actually model this data into Ruby classes in our application, it's important to learn a little more about Rails' opinion of databases.

4.2 Using the Database

Rails rejects the idea of putting business logic in the database in the form of in-database constraints, referential integrity, or stored procedures. While the database is seen as a way to store relational data, all business logic for that data belongs in the domain model of our application.

If you've primarily worked with MySQL in the past, this is a pretty standard approach. Although MySQL supports many these features, they are not terribly commonplace in PHP applications that use MySQL.

If you're accustomed to using things such as referential integrity and stored procedures in your databases, this approach may seem ignorant or controversial at the very least. There have been many discussions about this topic in the past, and Rails' rejection of these concepts is not likely to change. Rails focuses on using the database as an "application database" and not as an "integration database." It expects your application to be the single point of interaction with the database.

Referential Integrity

Referential integrity in the form of database-defined foreign keys is a hot topic. There are still many developers in the Ruby community who think this is an oversight and that these constraints should have better native support in Rails. One of the great aspects of Rails is the plug-in environment that allows us to disagree with the Rails core by simply installing a plug-in to add the features we want. Although using database foreign keys is unconventional and discouraged in a typical Rails application, there is a plug-in to help make them less painful to use; it's available on the Red Hill Consulting website.[2]

You can find more information about installing Rails plug-ins within your application in Section 13.13, *Rails Plug-Ins*, on page 392.

Using a Single Primary Key

Another intensely debated opinion in Rails is the rejection of composite keys in favor of all tables using a single primary key named id. The core team believes the cost of supporting composite keys outweighs the benefits. The cost in this case is the immense and ugly increase in the complexity of the Rails code. The ripple effect of supporting composite keys would have too many implications in the simplicity and beauty of Rails code.

Another reason is that there is usually not a tangible benefit to using composite keys over a single unique key. This is even truer when we're using a simplified Rails syntax for performing much of our database interactions. Like support for foreign key constraints, there is a Rails plug-in to add composite key support if your application requires them. The composite keys plug-in was written by Dr. Nic Williams; you can find it in RubyForge.[3]

Stored Procedures

Stored procedures are another database feature that is not recommended in Rails applications. Rails is attached to the idea of having a

---

2. http://www.redhillonrails.org/
3. http://compositekeys.rubyforge.org/

single layer of domain logic and complexity and having that logic written in Ruby. The typical need for stored procedures is in heavy "integration database–style" environments where multiple applications and people need to interact with a single database. Rails favors using web services to talk to the integration database through the Rails application itself.

Avoiding stored procedures generally makes it easier to keep revision history on your domain logic and makes application code easier to unit test. We realize that not all organizations have a choice of avoiding stored procedures, especially in an Oracle or SQL Server environment. There is a page that further details working with stored procedures on the Rails wiki.[4]

Model and Database Naming Conventions

Coming from PHP, we know that different developers have vastly different PHP coding styles. Some developers like to use CamelCase names like getFoo(), while others prefer underscore names like get_foo(). PHP itself is a big mix of different styles, so it provides little guidance on how our code should look. Ruby, on the other hand, provides a solid foundation of standards. Features of the Ruby language even help enforce these standards. As a result, most Ruby code looks quite similar. This is great for us because it keeps code readable, and mixing code from different sources doesn't end up looking like a hodgepodge of different coding styles.

In every way, Rails is an extension of Ruby. Although Ruby provides guidance for how to name our classes and methods, Rails takes this further and even gives us conventions for naming database tables and columns. In PHP, there are no such rules, and many developers like it this way. This may require a little shift in thinking.

As we said earlier, Rails is largely about removing the burden of decision about how to structure all the little details of our applications. This allows us to focus more on our application itself and less on its gritty implementation details. By following the Rails conventions for naming things in the database, Rails will implicitly connect the database tables to their corresponding model objects without us needing to do any configuration to map them together. These conventions also help keep Rails applications easily readable.

---

4. http://wiki.rubyonrails.org/rails/pages/StoredProcedures

Model Naming Conventions	
Table:	`software_projects`
Class:	`SoftwareProject`
File:	`app/model/software_project.rb`
Test File:	`test/unit/software_project_test.rb`

Figure 4.5: MODEL NAMING CONVENTIONS

While Ruby's well-defined conventions keep classes and methods in check, Rails' conventions keep application structure in check. This is a big help for application maintenance as well. If the next developer who maintains the application understands Rails and our application is built with all the Rails standards, then that developer will come in already having some understanding of the application.

By taking a look at Figure 4.5, we can see that database tables are expected to be named using a plural form of whatever we are storing, formatted with underscores. Each database table in our application will have an associated model, which is named using the singular form of the table name formatted using CamelCase. Finally, the filename will be based on the name of the model but in an underscore format.

This might seem like quite a few rules to follow when creating files and classes, but Rails does most of the work for you. When you run the generate script, Rails will automatically create the correct files and filenames according to conventions.

4.3 Creating the Application

Before we create our models, we need to set up a new Rails application. This means creating a new Rails project along with the MySQL database needed for development. We'll name this application user_group, and once again use MySQL for our database.

Joe Asks...

What's This "rake" Command?

We briefly mentioned Rake in Section 1.2, *The Components of Rails*, on page 4, and we'll use this tool often as part of our development process. Rake is "Ruby Make," a great system for gluing together all of your Ruby command-line tasks. Rails uses Rake extensively and even supports making your own special automation tasks!

There is also a somewhat similar system for PHP called Phing, but it has had limited adoption by PHP developers. By contrast, almost all Rails developers use and love Rake.

```
derek> cd work
work> rails -d mysql user_group
```

The development database for this project will be named, by Rails conventions, user_group_development. We'll use a Ruby tool called Rake to create this database for our application. Navigate to your application's root directory to run db:create.

```
work> cd user_group
user_group> rake db:create
(in /Users/derek/work/user_group)
```

If we want to change the username and password used to connect to this database, we need to edit our config/database.yml configuration, as discussed in Section 1.6, *Configuring the Database*, on page 12. Other than that, we should now have a new Rails application ready to go. Let's start WEBrick to get the application running on localhost.

```
user_group> ruby script/server
```

At this point in a typical PHP application, we would most likely create a relational database schema using a tool such as phpMyAdmin or even straight SQL create statements. Although we created our table with plain old SQL for our newsletter application in Chapter 1, *Getting Started with Rails*, on page 3, we'll take a different approach this time.

Rails *migrations* are a higher-level way of creating and modifying database tables using Ruby code instead of SQL. In this application, we'll create and modify all of our tables using migrations. A migration file will be created automatically for each model we generate.

4.4 Generating the First Model

We'll start constructing our application by creating a model to represent
a user in our application. Our conventions state that for a table named
users, we'll create a model named User. Let's use script/generate to create
this.

```
user_group> ruby script/generate model User
exists   app/models/
exists   test/unit/
exists   test/fixtures/
create   app/models/user.rb
create   test/unit/user_test.rb
create   test/fixtures/users.yml
create   db/migrate
create   db/migrate/001_create_users.rb
```

We can now see all our naming conventions fall into place. The generate script has already created our model and test file. It has even
created the migration file we'll be using to create the database table.
If we open the model file app/model/user.rb, we can see that the class
has correctly been named User. Likewise, opening the migration file
db/migrate/001_create_users.rb shows us that we'll execute create_table
:users, which is the plural underscore version of our model name.

You might be wondering how Rails determines the plural version of a
word. Rails includes an inflection component to convert words to their
plural or singular forms. To see this in action, we'll use another utility
script that comes with Rails. This script starts an IRB session but also
loads our Rails environment and code. This lets us interactively play
with our application through the command line.

```
user_group> ruby script/console
Loading development environment
>> 'user'.pluralize
=> "users"
>> 'users'.singularize
=> "user"
```

We can see that the pluralize and singularize methods are added to all
strings and that our user string is converting as expected. Most of the
time, Rails' default inflection engine will handle our models as expected.
Rails will successfully convert most irregular words as well but doesn't
catch absolutely everything. Let's try something a little less expected.

```
>> 'bacon'.pluralize
=> "bacons"
```

Joe Asks...
Is Pluralization Worth the Hassle?

There have been many heated discussions over the pluralization conventions in Rails. The reason pluralization was added to Rails was to make the language more natural when referring to data and classes. A database table contains plural users, while a User class represents a single user. This follows in line with the principle of least surprise. It is possible to turn off pluralization by adding the following to your configuration block in config/environment.rb.

```
config.active_record.pluralize_table_names = false
```

This option is most useful for legacy database schemas that can't be changed to use Rails conventions. We highly suggest you stick with the conventional approach for all new projects.

If we were building a meaty application that needed a bacon table, we would want to refer to our bacon in plural as simply bacon. Rails seems to be adding a trailing *s* where it isn't warranted. We can fix this by adding custom inflection rules to an initializer that runs as Rails starts. Open the file config/initializes/inflections.rb, and at the bottom we'll see some sample code on how to modify inflections. Below the sample code, we'll add bacon as an uncountable word similar to fish and sheep, since the word remains the same in both singular and plural form.

```
Inflector.inflections do |inflect|
  inflect.uncountable %w( fish sheep bacon )
end
```

Now if we exit and reload our interactive console to reinitialize the Rails environment, the pluralization of *bacon* will behave as expected.

```
>> exit

user_group> ruby script/console
Loading development environment
>> 'bacon'.pluralize
=> "bacon"
```

4.5 Building Database Tables

When we generated our User model, the generator also created our users migration file. All migrations are stored within the db/migrate/ directory of our application and keep a version history of database changes within the source tree. We'll see that the migration file for our users table has a numbered prefix of 001, which designates it as version 1 of our database history.

This gives us a powerful tool for applying and rolling back any changes we make to the database. This is especially useful for teams that need to keep in sync with each other's database changes. Migrations are written in Ruby, which lets you easily make applications that are more platform and database independent. It requires you to know some Ruby, but that is what we are here for, right?

To get a better idea of how this works, let's fill in our users migration. If we open the db/migrate/001_create_users.rb file, we can see the up and down methods. These will instruct our migration what to do when migrating *up* to revision number 1 of our database or reverting *back* down to revision number 0.

`Ruby` `building_a_rails_app/user_group_1/db/migrate/001_create_users.rb`

```ruby
def self.up
  create_table :users do |t|
    t.string  :email
    t.string  :password, :limit => 40
    t.string  :name
    t.text    :profile,  :text
    t.boolean :admin,    :default => false
    t.timestamps
  end
end
```

When we migrate up in this migration, we'll be creating the users table. We determined earlier that this table needs to store the email, password, name, profile information, and whether the user has admin privileges. We'll also add a couple special columns to store the date and time of when the user record was created or updated. The t.timestamps method does this by adding columns named created_at and updated_at. ActiveRecord will automatically insert the current time into these columns when we insert or update user records. We'll typically add these columns to all tables that have data being modified by the application.

Each line within the create_table :users block specifies a column for the table we are creating. Taking a look at Figure 4.6, on the facing page,

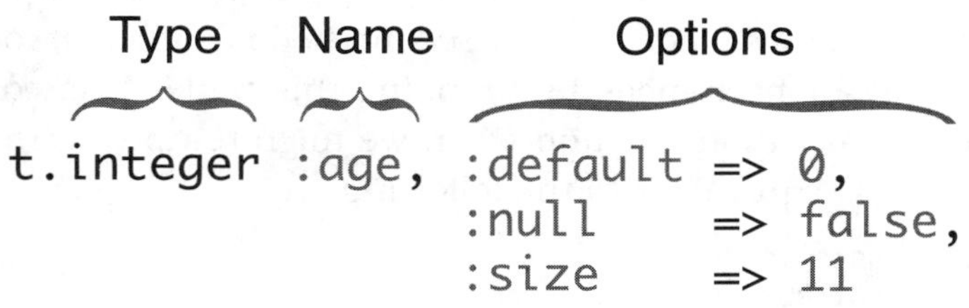

Type   Name   Options

```
t.integer :age, :default => 0,
                 :null    => false,
                 :size    => 11
```

Figure 4.6: ADDING MIGRATION COLUMNS

Joe Asks...

Isn't PDO Database Independent?

In PHP, PDO provides database access independence to your applications. This is great because it allows you to perform queries across different database platforms with a single, consistent interface. However, the problem still exists that creating and modifying tables requires different SQL syntax for different databases. This typically results in PHP applications having different SQL load files for each database on which they run. Migrations simplify this by using a single database definition written in Ruby to abstract out platform-specific differences.

---

we see that the first argument is the name of the column. The data type of the column is determined by the method name we use. Since column type keywords vary across different database platforms, Rails uses a database-independent syntax to specify the type of column we are creating. The valid types are binary, boolean, date, datetime, decimal, float, integer, string, text, time, and timestamp.

The second argument to the column creation method is a hash of options for the column. This is where we can specify whether this column uses a null constraint, default value, or character limit. We've taken advantage of these options to limit our password column to 40 characters and add a default value of false to the admin column.

Rails will automatically create a primary key column named id for us, and the drop_table :users code in the down method is sufficient for rolling back these migration changes by dropping this table. This completes our User model migration file, and when we migrate up to version 1, it will create a table equivalent to the following.

```
CREATE TABLE `users` (
  `id` int(11) NOT NULL auto_increment,
  `email` varchar(255) default NULL,
  `password` varchar(40) default NULL,
  `name` varchar(255) default NULL,
  `profile` text,
  `admin` tinyint(1) default '0',
  `created_at` datetime default NULL,
  PRIMARY KEY (`id`)
) ENGINE=InnoDB DEFAULT CHARSET=latin1
```

Now we'll use rake again to run our migration. Navigate to your application's root directory to run db:migrate.

```
user_group> rake db:migrate
(in /Users/derek/work/user_group)
== 1 CreateUsers: migrating =======================================
-- create_table(:users)
   -> 0.0043s
== 1 CreateUsers: migrated (0.0045s) ==============================
```

Running this task will migrate to the newest version of your database schema, which in our case has successfully updated us to version 1. It will determine the newest version by scanning the filenames of the files in db/migrate/ to find the highest sequentially numbered migration. To instruct the task to migrate to a specific version, we can add the VERSION= argument to the task.

```
user_group> rake db:migrate VERSION=0
(in /Users/derek/work/user_group)
== 1 CreateUsers: reverting =======================================
-- drop_table(:users)
   -> 0.0388s
== 1 CreateUsers: reverted (0.0391s) ==============================
```

Here we have specified in the migrate command to revert to VERSION=0. When executed, the migration drops the user table we had specified in the down method of this migration. Rails keeps track of the migration version we are on by automatically creating a table named schema_info the first time we run a migration. This table use a single column named version to remember the version number.

```
mysql> use user_group_development;
Database changed
```

```
mysql> select * from schema_info;
+---------+
| version |
+---------+
|       0 |
+---------+
1 row in set (0.00 sec)
```

We can check the current migration version at any time using the db:version Rake task.

```
rake db:version
(in /Users/derek/work/user_group)
Current version: 0
```

Now that we know how to write migrations, let's create them for each of the other database tables we need in this application. To do this, we'll use script/generate again to create the Meeting and Presentation models.

```
user_group> ruby script/generate model Meeting
...
create   app/models/meeting.rb
create   test/unit/meeting_test.rb
create   test/fixtures/meetings.yml
create   db/migrate/002_create_meetings.rb

user_group> ruby script/generate model Presentation
...
create   app/models/presentation.rb
create   test/unit/presentation_test.rb
create   test/fixtures/presentations.yml
create   db/migrate/003_create_presentations.rb
```

Things are pretty straightforward for our meeting migration. Joe tells us that all meetings need to start at 7 p.m. This means we don't need to store a separate time for each meeting and can stick with a date column. We'll then add a string column for the location and a text column for our meeting's description.

Ruby | building_a_rails_app/user_group_1/db/migrate/002_create_meetings.rb

```ruby
def self.up
  create_table :meetings do |t|
    t.date    :meets_on
    t.string :location
    t.text    :description
    t.timestamps
  end
end
```

The Presentation migration presents a new problem. We know that a presentation should be associated with both a meeting and a user. This

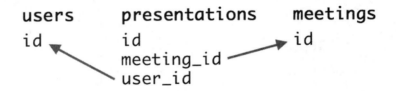

Figure 4.7: Foreign key conventions

means we need to create a foreign key to each of those tables. Rails has a convention it uses when creating foreign keys to associated tables. The foreign key is named using a singular version of the associated table name with an _id suffix. Taking a look at Figure 4.7, we see that for this situation we'll be using foreign keys named meeting_id and user_id.

A column used as a foreign key will most likely need an index to prevent a full table scan during queries. Adding an index can also be done in our migration using the add_index method. Looking at Figure 4.8, on the facing page, we see two different approaches. The first example demonstrates a unique index on a single column named url. The second shows us how we would go about adding an index on multiple columns.

`Ruby` building_a_rails_app/user_group_1/db/migrate/003_create_presentations.rb

```ruby
def self.up
  create_table :presentations do |t|
    t.integer :meeting_id
    t.integer :user_id
    t.string  :title
    t.text    :description
    t.timestamps
  end

  # add index to columns used in joins
  add_index :presentations, :meeting_id
  add_index :presentations, :user_id
end
```

We've used the simplest form of add_index to create an index on the necessary columns. This finishes up the migrations for our models. Let's now use rake to create our schema.

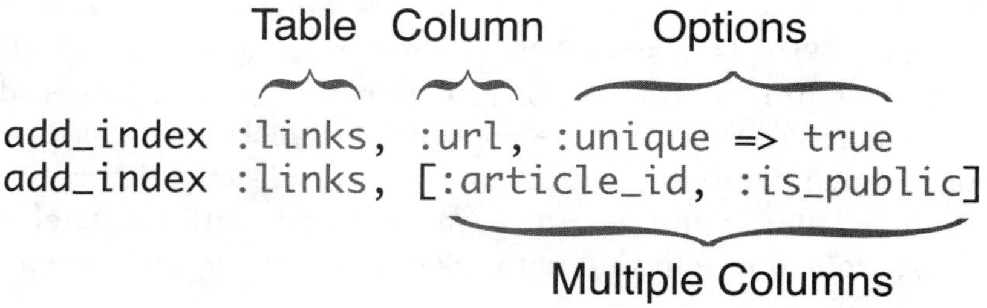

Table   Column   Options

add_index :links, :url, :unique => true
add_index :links, [:article_id, :is_public]

Multiple Columns

Figure 4.8: ADDING AN INDEX USING MIGRATIONS

```
user_group> rake db:migrate
(in /Users/derek/work/user_group)
== 1 CreateUsers: migrating ==========================================
-- create_table(:users)
   -> 0.0039s
== 1 CreateUsers: migrated (0.0040s) =================================

== 2 CreateMeetings: migrating ======================================
-- create_table(:meetings)
   -> 0.0524s
== 2 CreateMeetings: migrated (0.0526s) =============================

== 3 CreatePresentations: migrating =================================
-- create_table(:presentations)
   -> 0.0039s
-- add_index(:presentations, :meeting_id)
   -> 0.0083s
-- add_index(:presentations, :user_id)
   -> 0.0077s
== 3 CreatePresentations: migrated (0.0208s) =======================
```

We told you that following conventions would pay off, but the proof is in the pudding. Now that we have our database tables and models created, we can take a closer look at the power ActiveRecord gives us for manipulating data in these tables.

4.6 Employing ActiveRecord

Rails is a high-level development framework focused on programmer productivity. Rails applications are heavily focused on data, and that data is stored in relational databases.

The most common way to deal with databases, and the way you would typically do it in PHP, is to write SQL. However, writing SQL statements is not nearly as fun, convenient, or productive as writing Ruby code. The Rails answer to this, and the core of the Rails framework itself, is a sophisticated database abstraction layer called ActiveRecord. It is intended to provide a high-level, Ruby way of dealing with the database for the most common, mind-numbing SQL tasks we do daily such as SELECT or UPDATE statements.

In ActiveRecord, a class is a representation of a table, and properties of that class translate to columns in that table. To get an idea of how this works, let's create a new meeting record using our Meeting class. We'll once again use the console script to perform this.

```
user_group> ruby script/console
Loading development environment
>> meeting = Meeting.new(:meets_on     => '2007-12-06',
                         :location     => 'The Library',
                         :description => 'Rails Hackfest')
=> #<Meeting:...>
```

Here we have created a new meeting object by passing a hash of the data we want to insert into the constructor method of the Meeting class. You'll notice that the keys for the hash are based directly on the name of the columns for this table. ActiveRecord inspects the database structure for the meetings table and dynamically adds new properties to the Meeting class based on the table's column names. This stores the record in memory only, and to insert this data to the database, we'll use the save method.

```
>> meeting.save
=> true
>> meeting.id
=> 1
```

ActiveRecord automatically fills in the primary key for the inserted record, and we can verify the newly inserted ID by reading the id method. There is not a verbatim copy of ActiveRecord in PHP yet. To get an idea of what the equivalent PHP for this code would look like, here's a hypothetical PHP implementation of the previous syntax.

PHP building_a_rails_app/php/active_record/new_object.php

```php
$meeting = new Meeting(array('meets_on'    => '2007-12-06',
                             'location'    => 'The Library',
                             'description' => 'Rails Hackfest'));
$meeting->save();
$meeting->id();
```

> ### Joe Asks...
> #### Is ActiveRecord Slow?
>
> Some PHP developers seem to think that using a high-level way of accessing the database (ActiveRecord) instead of raw SQL means that it has to be slow or the purpose is to hide away the underlying SQL. This is misinformed.
>
> ActiveRecord always allows you to drop down to straight SQL whenever you need it. Most Rails applications will end up using some handwritten SQL, so the MySQL skills that using PHP taught you will carry over well.
>
> In the early stages of our application, we should worry much more about the application's functionality and less about any micro-optimizations we could gain by hand-tuning our SQL for every SELECT or UPDATE. We can always do that later—if we find some place where we actually have a performance issue.

A more likely scenario in PHP is that we would perform this operation by creating a SQL INSERT statement. We would execute the SQL using PDO's exec method, getting the inserted ID with lastInsertId.

`PHP` building_a_rails_app/php/active_record/new_meeting.php

```php
$dbh = new PDO('mysql:host=localhost;dbname=user_group_development',
               'root', '');

$sql = "INSERT INTO meetings (
           meets_on, location, description
        ) VALUES (
           '2007-12-06', 'The Library', 'Rails Hackfest'
        )";
$dbh->exec($sql);
print $dbh->lastInsertId();
```

Retrieving records from the database in Rails is done using the Meeting.find method:

```
>> meeting = Meeting.find(:first)
=> #<Meeting:...>
>> meeting.location
=> "The Library"
```

This usage of the find method performs a query for the first record in the meetings table and returns a Meeting object loaded up with the data from that row. We can now access the values for the row using the properties of this object. The equivalent PHP code would execute a SQL statement that limited the results to one record.

`PHP`   building_a_rails_app/php/active_record/find_first_meeting.php

```php
$dbh = new PDO('mysql:host=localhost;dbname=user_group_development',
               'root', '');

$sql = 'SELECT * FROM meetings LIMIT 1';
$result = $dbh->query($sql);
$row = $result->fetch();

print $row['location']."\n";
```

Often we will want to find a record by its primary key in the database. In this case, we can simply replace :first with the specific ID of the record we want to find. Let's try this by using the primary key we obtained earlier by calling the id method.

```
>> meeting = Meeting.find(1)
=> #<Meeting:...>
```

Here we have retrieved the record with a primary key value of 1. To do the same thing in PHP, we would once again write SQL to select the data using a WHERE condition to restrict the ID to a specific value.

`PHP`   building_a_rails_app/php/active_record/find_pk_meeting.php

```php
$dbh = new PDO('mysql:host=localhost;dbname=user_group_development',
               'root', '');

$sql = "SELECT * FROM meetings WHERE id='1'";
$result = $dbh->query($sql);
$row = $result->fetch();
```

The find method is versatile and has enough options to replace most of the SELECT operations you'll need to do in your application. We'll discuss them more in depth as we get further along in our application.

Taking a look back at our meeting data, we realize that we should probably be more specific about our meeting location. Let's update this detail by setting the location column data directly through our object.

```
>> meeting.location = 'University Library'
=> "University Library"
>> meeting.save
=> true
```

Here we see that we can also assign values directly to the ActiveRecord attributes.

> ⌇⌇ **Joe Asks...**
>
> **Couldn't We Just Write ActiveRecord in PHP?**
>
> It is certainly possible to write an object relational mapper in PHP, and many of the newer PHP frameworks have done this in response to Rails. You'll however find that some of the features, and much of the elegance of ActiveRecord, cannot be reproduced in PHP because of some technical limitations. But PHP is gaining ground, and we might yet see something emerge. It is worth playing around with if you have the time; you'll probably learn a new thing or two about both Rails and PHP doing so.

In this case, updating the location does not save to the database until we call the save method. The update performed would be similar to what the following PHP code executes.

PHP

`building_a_rails_app/php/active_record/update_meeting.php`

```php
$dbh = new PDO('mysql:host=localhost;dbname=user_group_development',
               'root', '');

$sql = "UPDATE meetings
        SET location='University Library'
      WHERE id='1'";
$dbh->exec($sql);
```

As you can see, this way of dealing with data through a proxy object is straightforward, and it's a whole lot nicer than writing SQL statements. There are quite a few more features and benefits that we'll discuss while building our application. For now, we'll add one more meeting to the database for the November meeting we had. This time we'll use the create method, which is nearly identical to the new method used earlier. It will however perform the save method behind the scenes so that we can avoid that additional step.

```ruby
>> Meeting.create(:meets_on    => '2007-11-08',
                  :location    => 'University Library',
                  :description => 'Lightning Talks')
=> #<Meeting:...>
```

At this point we have our database schema figured out and all of our model files up and running. We also have a few records inserted so that we have some sample data to work with. This allows us to move on to the next step, which is creating an interface for our application data through the use of Rails controllers and views.

4.7 Chapter Review

Congratulations! We made it through, and we laid a foundation of models for us to build a real application on. We've come a long way in a short time, and things are starting to take shape. Joe's user group will be online in no time.

The concepts presented in this chapter are important to every Rails project we will undertake. The model layer is the center of a Rails application. All the business logic is encapsulated in the models. The rest of the application—controllers and views—are built around the models.

It's important to have a firm understanding of the concepts presented in this chapter. If you didn't fully grasp some of the examples, take some time to go back through now. In the next chapter, we'll continue building up our application with the controllers and views.

We've learned some important concepts about Rails in this chapter:

- We started off by learning a domain-centered workflow to follow. This begins by working closely with the client to define the initial requirements and then working iteratively to model our domain objects (models) around them.

- We discovered that by simply accepting the Rails conventions for developing our application, we can free our minds from many of the little implementation details that often distract us from solving our client's actual problems.

- We learned that the heart of a Rails application are its models. In Rails, form generally follows function. Although we sketched out our user interface early on to get a grasp on the initial requirements, putting the user interface to code isn't where we start in a Rails application.

- Finally, we got our first taste of interacting with our domain via the models we created, instead of poking directly inside the database. We learned that ActiveRecord's place isn't to hide SQL. Its purpose is to give us a higher-level way of thinking about and interacting with the data while always dropping back down to the SQL when we need it.

4.8 Exercises

Here are some extra exercises that you can try on your own:

- Take another look inside the migrations we created and how our data will fit together. Compare the migrations to the generated model files. Review the model naming conventions.

- Explore some of the new Ruby syntax we showed in this chapter. For example, type %w(fish sheep bacon) on its own line in the Ruby console, and see what it really does.

- While you're in the Ruby console, play with the models we've created. Instead of a Meeting, create a new Presentation. Change its attributes, and save it again.

- Try using the MySQL console or a tool such as phpMyAdmin to get another view of what you've done to the database through the migrations and interacting with models.

## Chapter 5

Working with Controllers and Views

In this chapter we'll learn the conventions Rails uses to help organize our controllers and views. We'll cover how Rails uses the idea of resources on the Web to organize our applications and how to map a URL to a resource in our application. Once we get these basics down, we can begin to create all the pages to display and modify the meetings in our application.

5.1 Identifying Resources

One of the most important concepts to grasp when dealing with Rails controllers is the idea of resources. Once you have a grasp on how to identify resources and actions in your application, you'll have a lot better idea of how to build your controllers.

A common view of the Web is that we are navigating through a series of pages. We type in a URL or follow a link to a location where the browser requests a page and renders HTML as a response. This document or page-centric view of the Web remains from the days in which the Web consisted nearly entirely of documents. A document was the primary resource on the Web, and HTTP was a way of requesting those documents.

The Web has evolved significantly, but this page-centric view of the Web remains popular because many tools used to build websites and applications still revolve around the idea of a page.

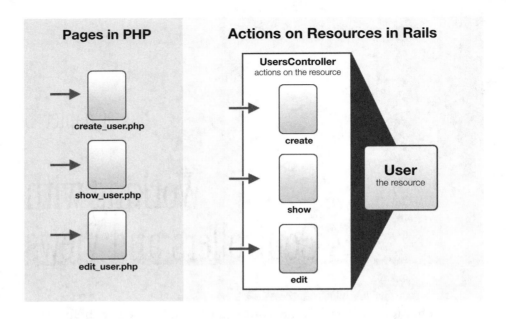

Figure 5.1: PAGES AND RESOURCES

PHP applications often consist of a single PHP file to represent each page. Rails takes a different perspective on this primarily because of its embrace of the MVC pattern and the object-oriented nature of Ruby.

Instead of seeing pages, we should identify objects in our application and build around those objects. We've already identified the objects in our own application as meetings, presentations, and users. By taking a look at some other applications, we can start to identify objects in other people's domains as well. The objects found at http://flickr.com are photographs, comments, photo sets, and contacts. Even a site as simple as http://google.com has websites as its primary objects.

Objects are the resources in our application, and we typically want to perform some type of action on them. We want to *create*, *edit*, *delete*, and *show* them to the users of our application. The diagram in Figure 5.1 shows how in a typical PHP application we might create three different pages to create, show, and edit a user. On the other side, Rails controllers help organize our actions by combining all the actions that relate to users into a single UsersController. If objects such as User are the nouns in our application, the controllers will handle all the verbs associated with that noun.

Each action in our controller will return some type of response to the browser when it has completed, just as our PHP page would. Most of the time this will be a 200 OK HTTP response along with some HTML, while other actions may redirect to a different action. In public websites and applications, the primary actions performed are usually to list or show a resource to the end user.

Although the browser prefers to receive information about these resources in HTML, there are various reasons why you might want to retrieve the resource in a variety of different formats. Flickr's primary display of its resources is in HTML, but you can also request to view the same resources represented in REST, XML-RPC, SOAP, JSON, or PHP. They provide a multitude of formats to retrieve and modify their data because they know that browsers aren't the only device being used to request or modify their resources.

In reality, organizing our application around resources won't necessarily change the way our application looks to the end user. It should, however, get you thinking a little differently about code organization and help you understand the importance of controllers in MVC.

5.2 Creating Controllers

Similar to that with models and databases, Rails enforces a series of conventions for controllers and views. These rules help Rails map URLs to an action in our application and determine which templates to render for that action.

By looking at Figure 5.2, on the following page, we can see that controller class names are suffixed with *Controller*. Each controller has an associated subdirectory in app/views/ to store related template files. View template names are derived from their corresponding action in the controller. Rails will handle most of these details for us when we use the generate script to create a controller.

The big question now is what to name the controllers needed for this application. The first resource we are dealing with is meetings. Usually when building an interface around a resource such as this, we run into a similar set of actions. The most common actions are shown in Figure 5.3, on page 113.

Controller Naming Conventions

Class:	UsersController
File:	app/controllers/users_controller.rb
Views:	app/views/users/
Tests:	test/functional/users_controller_test.rb

View Naming Conventions

Method:	UsersController#new
File:	app/views/new.html.erb
URL:	http://example.com/users/new
Helpers:	app/helpers/users_helper.rb

Figure 5.2: CONTROLLER NAMING CONVENTIONS

There are of course additional operations we may need to perform on meetings, but these seven actions tend to show up as a reoccurring pattern in applications. Taking a look at our initial page flow diagrams, we see that we indeed want to perform each of these actions on our meetings. To group all the actions that we'll be performing on meetings, we'll use a MeetingsController. You will often name your controllers after the model they are managing, such as Meeting in this case. Controllers can also exist that aren't directly associated with a model. We'll get into an example of this when we write the authentication part of our application in Chapter 7, *Authenticating Users*, on page 163.

We'll use the generate script to create our new controller. This will help make sure everything is named correctly and is in the correct location. We can view documentation for this generator by running it without a controller name specified.

Common Actions	
index	Display a page that indexes or lists a collection of meetings.
show	Display a page that shows the details on an existing meeting.
new	Display a page with a form to create a new meeting.
create	Create a new meeting.
edit	Display a page with a form to modify an existing meeting.
update	Update an existing meeting.
destroy	Delete an existing meeting.

Figure 5.3: COMMON ACTIONS

```
user_group> ruby script/generate controller
...
Example:
  ./script/generate controller CreditCard open debit credit close
...
```

In the middle of all the output is an example of how to use the controller generator. It gives us an example of creating a CreditCard controller and has four additional arguments. These are names of actions added to the generated controller. Adding a list of actions is not required, and we can always add more later. In this case, we'll take advantage of the feature. Since our first order of business is to create a listing of meetings, we'll add an additional index argument after the name of our Meetings controller.

```
user_group> ruby script/generate controller Meetings index
exists  app/controllers/
exists  app/helpers/
create  app/views/meetings
exists  test/functional/
create  app/controllers/meetings_controller.rb
create  test/functional/meetings_controller_test.rb
create  app/helpers/meetings_helper.rb
create  app/views/meetings/index.html.erb
```

This has successfully created all our controller-related files, along with the index template for our first view. To see what we have going, let's fire up the server to check out how this looks in the browser.

> \\// Joe Asks...
>
> ### Are All Methods Considered Actions?
>
> A controller is a class, and an action is simply a method defined in that class. We refer to these methods as *actions* to distinguish that these methods are executed as part of the MVC cycle. Usually, this means that a URL points to them.
>
> Most actions will either render a template or redirect to a different action. Controllers can have other methods that are not actions—and these are good. Organizing larger sections of code into smaller methods of singular responsibility promotes better readability and less repetition. This is especially encouraged in object-oriented programming.

Make sure that your WEBrick server is still running in the background, and point your browser to http://localhost:3000/meetings/index. When you request this page, an HTTP request gets sent through Rails to our application. Rails knows from a default convention that you want to run code in the index action of the MeetingsController. This action will look for a view template of the same base name and will find and render the view template in app/views/meetings/index.html.erb.

The resulting page (shown in Figure 5.4, on the next page) doesn't do much yet but is helpful in showing us the power of conventions in Rails. We didn't have to map which code to run when we visited the URL, and we didn't need to tell the controller which view to render. Rails ties all of this together to work seamlessly based on the default naming conventions we have used. URLs will inevitably become more complex than the current scenario depending on the type of data we are working with. To remain flexible, Rails allows the customization of the URL parsing rules using a component called *Routing*.

5.3 Routing Requests

A typical usage of PHP is to request a script or page directly from the server by name. The best indication of this practice is seeing the extension of your PHP file directly in the URL such as http://example. com/list_meetings.php. Although this is an extremely simple approach

Figure 5.4: THE MEETINGS INDEX PAGE

to executing scripts on the server, it also has its drawbacks. The first of which is that your URL is tied directly to your file structure. Let's say you had an impulse to organize your application a little and wanted to logically separate your scripts by putting them in subdirectories such as /meetings/list.php. Making this change would make the URL for this page change to http://example.com/meetings/list.php. This would require you to go through and fix any links to this page in your own application and would still break any outside links that pointed to this page. After building up inbound links for a page over a period of time, you might determine that organizing your code was not worth users following the old URL to a 404 page.

More advanced PHP techniques exist to solve this problem using Apache rewrite rules and other similar measures. If you are familiar with this idea, then the idea of routing in Rails will make a lot of sense to you.

Rails completely separates the filesystem from the URL through its routing component. Routing adds a configurable mapping layer that defines how a URL is parsed and determines what code in our Rails application will execute for that particular URL. The configuration to set up these mappings for your application is in config/routes.rb. Ignoring all of the comments for now, let's take a look at the default routes defined near the bottom of this file. There are two routes defined here, and for now we'll focus on the first.

```
http://example.com/meetings/show/10

map.connect ":controller/:action/:id"
```

Figure 5.5: THE DEFAULT ROUTING RULE

`Ruby` `building_a_rails_app/user_group_1/config/routes.rb`

```ruby
ActionController::Routing::Routes.draw do |map|
  # Install the default routes as the lowest priority.
  map.connect ':controller/:action/:id'
  map.connect ':controller/:action/:id.:format'
end
```

New routes are set up in this file in a few different ways. The most basic way to define a route is done using the map.connect method we see used here. The first argument is a pattern that we'll use to match the incoming URL. The pattern is composed of a number of components (three in this case) separated by forward slashes.

When a request gets sent to our application for a resource, the path section of the URL is compared against each pattern from the top of the list down until it matches a route. As you can see in Figure 5.5, the URL http://example.com/meetings/show/10 matches our route pattern since it is composed of three different components: meetings, show, and 10. These components match up with :controller, :action, and :id in our route.

When the URL is matched to a specific route, Rails creates a hash by pairing the URL components with the values supplied in the URL. In this case, it would result in the following.

```ruby
params = { :controller => "meetings",
           :action     => "show",
           :id         => "10" }
```

Each component of a route can be described in one of three ways:

- :name
- *name
- name

If the component name is in the style of :name as in the default route example, it will match the associated component of the URL.

If the component is in the style of *name, it will match all the remaining components in the URL. It will collect this list of matched components into an array in the params hash.

```
# match all requests
map.connect '*all', :controller => "errors", :action => "show"

# http://example.com/test/this/route
params = { :all => ['test', 'this', 'route'] }
```

The *all component of this route matched all three segments of the URL and combined them into an array that can be referenced using params[:all]. Since each route requires a :controller and :action, we've included additional arguments to explicitly identify them in this route. This is necessary since they were not interpreted from the URL as they were in the default route.

Finally, if a component is in the style of name, it will need to match literally the corresponding component of the URL to be considered a match.

```
# Only match URL if the path begins with 'photos'
map.connect 'photos/:action/:slug', :controller => "photos"

# http://example.com/photos/edit/a1e32fa4
params = { :slug => 'a1e32fa4' }
```

In this example, the route will match only if the URL begins with the string *photos*. Once again we need to explicitly identify the controller since it is not inferred from the URL.

The :controller and :action parameters are special in that Rails uses these to determine the controller and action executed for this request. These components are required to be in every route in one way or another. In this example, Rails will execute the show action in MeetingsController based on the values gathered. All of these parameter values become accessible within our controller action so that we can use them just as we would with GET or POST variables.

At this point, you may be wondering how the URL http://localhost:3000/meetings/index matched any route. It has only two components and does not have a corresponding component for the :id component in our defined route. The answer is that the :action and :id components of routes are a little special in that they have implicit default values. The default value of :action is index, and the default for :id is nil. This makes sense when you think that most servers will use a file such as index.html or index.php as the default. Rails does the same by assuming

Figure 5.6: ROUTING ERROR

the default action is to index the data. With this in mind, you could visit http://localhost:3000/meetings and see that it does indeed still display the index action.

Rails will throw an error (such as that shown in Figure 5.6) when an incoming URL does not match a route pattern or Rails cannot find an adequate match for the given :controller or :action parameters of the route.

This error, and other exception pages you see in Rails, aren't very pretty. However, they do serve their purpose in helping you identify problems with your code. Lucky for us, these errors display only in the development environment in our application. We'll typically display a nicer-looking page to the user when an error occurs in a production environment. We'll talk more about this when we learn how to deploy our application in Section 10.2, *The Production Environment*, on page 238.

Routing is a quite complex topic, and this is only a cursory look at how routing works. At the moment, the default routes work for us. We'll revisit routes as we encounter situations that require more complex routes.

5.4 Retrieving Meeting Data

Now that we have an idea of how http://localhost:3000/meetings/index maps to execute the MeetingsController#index method, let's get back to our application. To display the list of meetings in app/views/meetings/ index.html.erb, we need to query the database for meeting data. We'd also like to be able to display a user-friendly name for each meeting based on its date.

Looking back at our diagrams shows us that Joe wants to have two different sections for this page, separating past and upcoming meetings. This means we need the data in two different sets. We don't want to maintain this application for Joe forever, so we'll do our best to make it maintainable for Joe. To do this, we've decided to add a few new methods in our Meetings class. We'll add two new class methods named upcoming_meetings and past_meetings to retrieve our meeting data. While we're in here, we'll also create an additional name method to give our meetings a nicer-looking version of the meeting date.

Ruby   building_a_rails_app/user_group_1/app/models/meeting.rb

```
Line 1   class Meeting < ActiveRecord::Base
   -       # class methods
   -       def self.upcoming_meetings
   -         find(:all, :conditions => "meets_on > CURRENT_TIMESTAMP()",
   5                    :order      => "meets_on")
   -       end
   -
   -       def self.past_meetings
   -         find(:all, :conditions => "meets_on <= CURRENT_TIMESTAMP()",
   10                   :order      => "meets_on")
   -       end
   -
   -       # formatted name based on date
   -       def name
   15        meets_on.to_s(:long)
   -       end
   -     end
```

To implement the name method, we've converted the date on line 15 to a nicely formatted string using to_s. This allows us to convert the date to a string using either a :short option or a :long option. Let's take a look at the result of this new method using the console script.

```
user_group> ruby script/console
Loading development environment
>> meeting = Meeting.find(1)
=> #<Meeting:...>
>> meeting.name
=> "December  6, 2007"
```

This looks much nicer than the default date and works well for our purposes. The two class methods we added will be used as custom

> ### ⟋⟍ Joe Asks...
> #### Aren't We Avoiding SQL?
>
> Rails tries hard to steer away from complexity in favor of simplicity. Most of Rails ActiveRecord methods reflect this in that they make queries to the database much easier than writing straight SQL. They continue to embrace SQL when it is the most concise way to find or modify our data. This is apparent in things such as the :order and :conditions options to find. By adding an option such as :order => "name DESC, id ASC", we can clearly order our results without resorting to a complex abstraction where SQL works just fine.

finder methods that separate our past and upcoming meetings. We've used the familiar find method to retrieve the data. This time we'd like to query for more than a single meeting. By changing the first argument to :all, ActiveRecord will retrieve the entire collection of meetings that matches our criteria. It will return these as an array of Meeting objects instead of a single object.

The second argument to find is a hash of options to use when finding our data. We'll order the results using the :order string value. This will compose the ORDER BY fragment of our SQL statement. Likewise, we will filter our results by implementing the :conditions option to append to the WHERE clause of the SQL statement.

5.5 Viewing Meetings

We can now use our new Meeting class methods within our controller's index action to retrieve the lists of meetings we want.

`Ruby` building_a_rails_app/user_group_1/app/controllers/meetings_controller.rb

```ruby
class MeetingsController < ApplicationController
  def index
    @upcoming_meetings = Meeting.upcoming_meetings
    @past_meetings     = Meeting.past_meetings
  end
end
```

You'll notice that we've used Ruby instance variables here. All data sets in this type of variable get passed into our views. We can now open our associated view at app/views/meetings/index.html.erb and use this data to iterate through our meetings.

`Ruby` building_a_rails_app/user_group_1/app/views/meetings/index.html.erb

```
Line 1   <h1>Meetings</h1>

         <div class="meeting_list">
           <h2>Upcoming Meetings</h2>
5          <ul>
             <% for meeting in @upcoming_meetings %>
             <li><%=h meeting.name %> </li>
             <% end %>
           </ul>
10       </div>

         <div class="meeting_list">
           <h2>Past Meetings</h2>
           <ul>
15           <% for meeting in @past_meetings %>
             <li><%=h meeting.name %> </li>
             <% end %>
           </ul>
         </div>
```

On line 7 we've used the built-in h helper method used to escape HTML entities in our output. As a shortcut, we'll often leave the parentheses off this method and write it in a more readable fashion like this: <%=h @variable %>.

We're making a little progress now, so let's take a look at our view's progress so far by refreshing our browser pointed to http://localhost:3000/meetings/index. This will give us a page that looks like Figure 5.7, on the next page, where we can see that our meetings have been split up into upcoming and past dates. Our next step is to add links to a detailed view of each meeting.

5.6 Adding Links

Rails has a unique way of adding hyperlinks that is different from how we'd typically do it in PHP. Similar to what we discussed earlier with routes, hard-coding our own hyperlink would make a coupling between a certain URL in the HTML and the controller and action. This might be a headache later if we decide to restructure the links, forcing us to go back and change the hyperlink manually. To use a more agile

Figure 5.7: PAST AND UPCOMING MEETINGS

approach, Rails generates URLs for us based on our routing rules. This helps us create less fragile links to other resources or pages.

Generating URLs

URL generation is essentially routing in reverse. We start with a hash of parameters that Rails uses to build the original URL based on our defined routes in config/routes.rb.

When working in our views, the url_for method will perform the most basic URL generation. In this case, we can build the desired URL string by specifying the :controller, :action, and :id parameters.

```
url_for(:controller => "meetings",
        :action    => "show",
        :id        => "10")
```

This will produce the following string.

```
"/meetings/show/10"
```

Rails will do its best to build the shortest URL possible to link to the resource and will append any additional arguments as GET parameters on the link. In this example, we'll add a page option.

```
url_for(:controller => "meetings",
        :action    => "index",
        :page      => "2")
```

Rails adds page as a GET variable since our routing rule does not include this option. It also will drop the index value since it is implicitly defined as the default action. This is the final result.

```
"/meetings?page=2"
```

Using Rails Helpers

View templates in Rails allow our HTML to be intermixed with display logic. Although this is convenient in most cases, we usually want to keep the amount of logic in our templates to a bare minimum. This means simple conditional statements or loops for the most part. Rails uses the idea of helper methods to handle more complex view logic. If you are familiar with the Smarty templating library for PHP, this is similar to using variable modifiers.

Helper methods are defined in a separate file to aid in the creation and display of your view code. This makes our templates easier to read and our complex view logic easier to test. Rails comes with a large set of built-in helpers as part of the framework and makes creating your own custom helpers easy.

While url_for generates the basic URL for us, the link_to built-in helper will create the actual anchor tag for us as well.

```
link_to(meeting.name, :controller => "meetings",
                      :action     => "show",
                      :id         => meeting.id)
```

This code produces a string such as the following:

```
<a href="/meetings/show/1">December 6, 2007</a>
```

The first argument in link_to determines the content or clickable text of the link. In this case, we've used the name of the meeting as the hyper-link. The second argument defines the link URL using a hash. This hash is usually composed of at least a :controller and :action component to specify where we want the link to lead us. When we're linking to an action in the same controller, we can omit the :controller option. Rails will assume that when the :controller value is missing, we're linking to an action in the current controller.

Let's use the link_to helper method to add hyperlinks from each of our meetings to the show action for that specific meeting. We'll also add a link to the new action that we'll use to create new meetings.

`building_a_rails_app/user_group_2/app/views/meetings/index.html.erb`

```erb
Line 1  <h1>Meetings</h1>
   -
   -    <div class="meeting_list">
   -      <h2>Upcoming Meetings</h2>
   5      <ul>
   -        <% for meeting in @upcoming_meetings %>
   -        <li>
   -          <%= link_to h(meeting.name), :controller => "meetings",
   -                                       :action     => "show",
  10                                       :id         => meeting.id %>
   -        </li>
   -        <% end %>
   -      </ul>
   -      <p class="add">
  15        <%= link_to "add meeting", :controller => "meetings",
   -                                   :action     => "new" %>
   -      </p>
   -    </div>
   -
  20    <div class="meeting_list">
   -      <h2>Past Meetings</h2>
   -      <ul>
   -        <% for meeting in @past_meetings %>
   -        <li>
  25          <%= link_to h(meeting.name), :controller => "meetings",
   -                                       :action     => "show",
   -                                       :id         => meeting.id %>
   -        </li>
   -        <% end %>
  30      </ul>
   -    </div>
```

Factoring out the hard-coded hyperlink with link_to is good. We can do even better, though, with the aid of some new routes in our application.

This time we'll take a look at a new way of defining routes using *named routes*.

Named Routes

Named routes are a way of creating a label to specific links in our application. We create explicit routes to locations within our application to give us shortcut methods to use when referring to these locations. Let's open our config/routes.rb file again to add two named routes.

Joe Asks...

What Is map.resources?

You may notice instructions about using map.resources within the comments of your route's source file. This is an advanced type of routing that automatically maps a resource in our application to the most common actions we'll perform on that resource. This also maps a named route to each of these actions. This style of routing can be powerful, but we'll stick with explicit named routes while still learning.

Ruby | building_a_rails_app/user_group_2/config/routes.rb

```ruby
ActionController::Routing::Routes.draw do |map|
  # meetings routes
  map.meeting '/meetings/show/:id', :controller => "meetings",
                                    :action     => "show"
  map.new_meeting '/meetings/new', :controller => "meetings",
                                   :action     => "new"

  # Install the default route as the lowest priority.
  map.connect ':controller/:action/:id'
  map.connect ':controller/:action/:id.:format'
end
```

Instead of calling map.connect in these routes, we've replaced the connect method with a custom name for the route. In this case we've used meeting to link to a single meeting and new_meeting to link to an action for creating a new meeting.

Rails uses these new routing rules to dynamically add helper methods for generating links to these actions. We can use *route_name*_url to generate the URL of the link, or we can use *route_name*_path to generate the path:

```ruby
meeting_path(:id => meeting.id)
# => /meetings/show/6

meeting_url(:id => meeting.id)
# => http://localhost:3000/meetings/show/6
```

We no longer have to specify the :controller and :action components of this URL, since they are explicitly defined in the named route. We do, however, need to specify the :id component to link to a specific meeting. When generating a URL for a new meeting, we don't need to specify any of the components.

```
new_meeting_path
# => /meetings/new

new_meeting_url
# => http://localhost:3000/meetings/new
```

We can see how using these helpers could clean up our code a bit. Let's swap out our previous hashes to use the new helpers generated by our named routes. This will help us clean up some of the duplication that is happening here. We typically stick with using the generated _path when employing these methods in our views.

Ruby building_a_rails_app/user_group_3/app/views/meetings/index.html.erb

```erb
<h1>Meetings</h1>

<div class="meeting_list">
  <h2>Upcoming Meetings</h2>
  <ul>
    <% for meeting in @upcoming_meetings %>
    <li>
      <%= link_to h(meeting.name), meeting_path(:id => meeting.id) %>
    </li>
    <% end %>
  </ul>
  <p class="add"><%= link_to "add meeting", new_meeting_path %></p>
</div>

<div class="meeting_list">
  <h2>Past Meetings</h2>
  <ul>
    <% for meeting in @past_meetings %>
    <li>
      <%= link_to h(meeting.name), meeting_path(:id => meeting.id) %>
    </li>
    <% end %>
  </ul>
</div>
```

Writing Custom Helper Methods

There is one last thing we'd like to do with this view before we continue. When either the upcoming or past meetings list is empty, the interface just displays a blank area. It would be much nicer to display a short message that says "No Meetings" when none are available. We'll go ahead and create a custom helper to do this so that we can share the same logic between upcoming and past meetings. Let's open the file helpers/meetings_helper.rb. This is where we'll write custom helper methods that are shared between all of the views for our MeetingsController.

`Ruby` building_a_rails_app/user_group_4/app/helpers/meetings_helper.rb

```ruby
module MeetingsHelper
  def no_meetings(meetings)
    content_tag('li', "No Meetings") if meetings.empty?
  end
end
```

To display our message, we've used the content_tag standard Rails helper method. In this case we've specified that we want to return an HTML li tag, with "New Meeting" as the tag content. This completes our small but helpful method. We can now add it into our view to make empty lists a little nicer.

`Ruby` building_a_rails_app/user_group_4/app/views/meetings/index.html.erb

```ruby
<% for meeting in @upcoming_meetings %>
<li>
  <%= link_to h(meeting.name), meeting_path(:id => meeting.id) %>
</li>
<% end %>
<%= no_meetings(@upcoming_meetings) %>
```

We can use custom helpers whenever we need to share snippets of logic between different areas of the template. Although this type of refactoring may seem unnecessarily small, it is a good way to keep our code clean and readable. Templates can quickly become unwieldy when too much repetition creeps in.

With these links in, our meetings index view should look like Figure 5.8, on the following page. It is starting to shape up into something! We now need a way to create new meetings in our application. We already created a hyperlink to add a new meeting. It's about time we implement the new action.

5.7 Creating New Meetings

To start creating new meetings, we need to create an HTML form to submit the meeting details. We'll create this in an action named new in our MeetingsController. Let's add this method, along with an associated view named app/views/meetings/new.html.erb.

Figure 5.8: PAST AND UPCOMING MEETINGS

Ruby `building_a_rails_app/user_group_3/app/controllers/meetings_controller.rb`

```ruby
def new
  @meeting = Meeting.new
end
```

In this action, we have created a Meeting instance variable that we'll use to help build our form in the view. Rails comes with a group of built-in helper methods designed to make building HTML forms easier. There is one to create the form and an additional collection of helpers used to build each form element tag we need.

Ruby `building_a_rails_app/user_group_3/app/views/meetings/new.html.erb`

```erb
Line 1  <h1>Create a New Meeting</h1>
   -
   -    <div class="form">
   -      <%= error_messages_for :meeting -%>
   5
   -      <fieldset>
   -      <legend>Enter Meeting Details</legend>
   -      <% form_for :meeting, :url => { :action => "create" } do |form| %>
   -        <div>
  10          <%= form.label :meets_on %>:<br />
   -          <%= form.date_select :meets_on %>
   -        </div>
   -        <div>
   -          <%= form.label :location %>:<br />
  15          <%= form.text_field :location, :size => 35, :class => "text" %>
   -        </div>
```

```
       <div>
         <%= form.label :description %>:<br />
         <%= form.text_area :description, :rows => 4, :class => "text" %>
20     </div>

         <%= submit_tag "Create", :class => "submit" %>  
         <%= link_to "cancel", { :action => "index" }, :class => "cancel" %>
       <% end %>
25     </fieldset>
     </div>
```

There is a lot of markup packed in here, so we'll take it step by step. The form_for helper on line 8 creates our form tag. Taking a look at Figure 5.9, on the next page, we see that the first argument to form_for is a symbol based on the name of the instance variable we assigned in our controller. In this case, the @meeting variable translates to :meeting. In the second argument, we've specified the :url option to generate our action attribute based on our routes.

We discussed blocks back in Section 2.9, *Understanding Blocks*, on page 51, and this is a perfect example of their usefulness. The form_for helper uses a block that yields a form builder. We use the block argument named form to create the content of our form. Let's take a closer look at how we create an individual input element.

`Ruby`   building_a_rails_app/user_group_3/app/views/meetings/new.html.erb

```
<div>
  <%= form.label :location %>:<br />
  <%= form.text_field :location, :size => 35, :class => "text" %>
</div>
```

Here we've created a text input tag for the meeting location using the text_field method. We've paired this with a label tag for the input. The first argument of each method is the name of a meeting attribute. We can add more attributes to our form elements using the optional second argument. If you view the source of the generated HTML, you'll get an idea of what the helpers are building here.

building_a_rails_app/html/form_helper.html

```
<div>
  <label for="meeting_location">Location</label>:<br />
  <input class="text" id="meeting_location" name="meeting[location]"
         size="35" type="text" />
</div>
```

The date_select helper handles the rather tedious task of creating three different select boxes to fill in our meets_on date attribute.

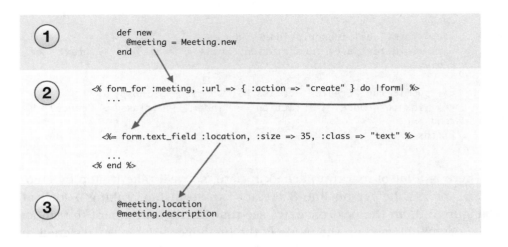

Figure 5.9: USING THE FORM_FOR HELPER

`Ruby` `building_a_rails_app/user_group_3/app/views/meetings/new.html.erb`

```
<div>
  <%= form.label :meets_on %>:<br />
  <%= form.date_select :meets_on %>
</div>
```

The markup generated by this helper is a little more complex than other attributes since the single date value needs to be split into three separate components to fill the form. These different elements are later reassembled to a single date to save to the database.

The good news is that Rails handles these details behind the scenes, and all we have to remember is the simple helper syntax. If we visit http://localhost:3000/meetings/new, we should now have the complete meeting form displayed in Figure 5.10, on the next page.

On line 8, we've set our form to post to the create action. This action won't need a template file, because it will be processing form submission only, not actually rendering any new HTML. Let's add a new method in our controller for this action.

Figure 5.10: THE FORM TO CREATE A MEETING

Ruby

building_a_rails_app/user_group_3/app/controllers/meetings_controller.rb

```ruby
def create
  @meeting = Meeting.new(params[:meeting])
  if @meeting.save
    flash[:notice] = 'Meeting successfully created.'
    redirect_to :action => "index"
  else
    render :action => "new"
  end
end
```

In PHP, we access submitted form data by using the $_GET and $_POST superglobals. Rails makes this same data available within the Rails controllers in a single hash named params containing both GET and POST data similar to the $_REQUEST array in PHP. In PHP, the data submitted from this HTML form would be structured similar to this.

PHP

building_a_rails_app/php/post/post_data.php

```php
$_POST = array(
  'meeting' => array(
    'location'    => 'University Library',
    'description' => 'Rails Hackfest',
  )
);
```

In a similar way, when the form is submitted to the create action in Rails, it will pass along all the POST variables for our meeting data in a hash named :meeting nested within params. In Ruby we could think of the params data like this:

Ruby · building_a_rails_app/ruby/post/post_data.rb
```ruby
params = {
  :meeting => {
    :location    => "University Library",
    :description => "Rails Hackfest"
  }
}
```

With the data in a hash like this, we can pass the meeting data from the params hash to a new instance of Meeting. This will assign the values from the form submission to create a new meeting.

Ruby · building_a_rails_app/ruby/post/post_data_assignment.rb
```ruby
Meeting.new(params[:meeting])
```

This has the same effect as when we created our meetings earlier from the console and is synonymous with doing this:

Ruby · building_a_rails_app/ruby/post/post_data_new.rb
```ruby
Meeting.new(:location    => "University Library",
            :description => "Rails Hackfest")
```

Once we have assigned the values, we place the @meeting.save statement within a conditional. The save method will return false if the meeting doesn't save for some reason. The most common reason this might happen is from a violation of validation rules that the meeting must pass in order to properly save. We'll cover validations in more depth in Chapter 6, *Validating and Testing Models*, on page 151.

5.8 Redirection and Flash Data

When a new meeting inserts correctly in our create action, we'll redirect the user to the meetings index page.

Ruby · building_a_rails_app/user_group_3/app/controllers/meetings_controller.rb
```ruby
if @meeting.save
  flash[:notice] = 'Meeting successfully created.'
  redirect_to :action => "index"
else
  render :action => "new"
end
```

> ### Joe Asks...
> #### Does Flash Have Anything to Do with Adobe Flash?
>
> Although it confusingly shares the same name, flash data in Rails has no relation to Adobe Flash or Adobe Flex. Flash in Rails is a way of temporarily storing a message in a session so that we can "flash" this message to the user on the next request.

Although in PHP we use header("Location:...") to perform redirects, Rails performs a redirect from the controller using the redirect_to method. We'll once again use URL generation to create a location string based on a hash of parameters.

Here we redirect to the index action. The redirect_to method also accepts a string as the redirection location, but passing a hash is preferred when linking to other actions within our application.

In this particular action, we are redirecting to a completely new HTTP request. Rails uses the same "shared nothing" architecture as PHP, which means any variables set in the create method will be gone once this request is over. Before our redirection, however, we set a *flash message* to notify the user of the success of our operation.

The flash method is accessed like a hash, but it is special in how it persists in our application. Any data that we set using this method remains available in the next request. This allows us to pass messages from one request to the next using session storage to keep this message persistent. Remember, however, that this data will be available only on the next immediate request for this user and will be gone thereafter.

Now that we're passing this flash notice to the index action, we need to render the message it contains in that action's view. We'll add a simple div tag at the top of this page to display the message when there is flash data available. We access the flash data from our view using the flash method. We'll use this to get the :notice message assigned in the previous request.

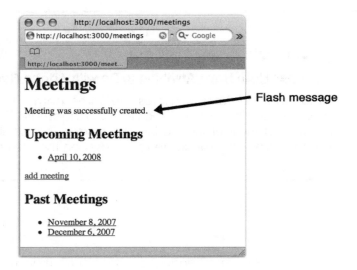

Figure 5.11: FLASH MESSAGE ON INDEX PAGE

`Ruby` `building_a_rails_app/user_group_4/app/views/meetings/index.html.erb`

```
<h1>Meetings</h1>

<% if flash[:notice] %>
<div id="flash_notice"><%=h flash[:notice] %></div>
<% end %>

<div class="meeting_list">
```

Let's now add another meeting with our form to make sure it works as we expect. We'll add the next upcoming meeting as the first Thursday of next month at the usual location. When we submit it, we'll be redirected to the index page. Here we'll see a message (such as the one in Figure 5.11) that tells us that the creation was successful. Remember that this message is available for only a single request and will vanish when you hit your browser's Refresh button.

5.9 Administrating Meetings

We can now create and view the list of meetings, but Joe tells us he wants the ability to edit and delete these meetings from the application as well. At this point we'll go ahead and implement a more detailed view of each meeting. This is typically done using a show action in our controller.

Viewing Meeting Details

We've already added a link to the show action from our index page, but at this point the link leads nowhere. It's about time to create a show method for this action in our controller.

`Ruby` `building_a_rails_app/user_group_4/app/controllers/meetings_controller.rb`

```ruby
def show
  @meeting = Meeting.find(params[:id])
end
```

When we follow a link from our meetings index to a specific meeting, we'll end up at a location such as http://localhost:3000/meetings/show/1. When this URL gets parsed through our default route, the 1 will match up with :id route component to become available in our controller as params[:id]. We'll use this primary key to retrieve this page's meeting using the find method. Next we'll use this object in our view to display the meeting details. We'll create this view in a template named app/views/meetings/show.html.erb.

`Ruby` `building_a_rails_app/user_group_4/app/views/meetings/show.html.erb`

```erb
Line 1  <h1><%= link_to "Meetings", :action => "index" %>
          &rarr; <%=h @meeting.name %>
        </h1>

     5  <div class="details">
          <dl>
            <dt>When:</dt><dd><%=h @meeting.name %> @ 7:00pm</dd>
            <dt>Where:</dt><dd><%=h @meeting.location %></dd>
            <dt>Agenda:</dt><dd><%=h @meeting.description %></dd>
    10    </dl>

          <h2>Presentations</h2>
          <ul id="presentations"></ul>

    15    <p class="modify">
            <%= link_to "edit", :action => "edit", :id => @meeting.id %>  |
            <%= link_to "destroy", { :action => "destroy", :id => @meeting.id },
                                   :confirm => 'Are you sure?',
                                   :method => :delete %>
    20    </p>
        </div>
```

In our view, we use the @meeting variable to show all the details for this meeting. We've also added a placeholder for where we'll add presentations for the meeting later. On lines 16 and 17, we've placed links to edit and destroy this meeting. Our link to destroy the meeting is particularly unique. In addition to the hash specifying the URL of where this link goes, we've also added a third argument with the :confirm and

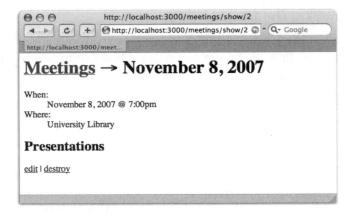

Figure 5.12: SHOWING A MEETING

:method options. The :confirm option will add a JavaScript dialog box that prompts us with "Are you sure?" before deleting a meeting. This should provide a nice little safeguard to prevent the accidental deletion of meetings. The end result of this view should be the page shown in Figure 5.12.

Generally we don't want to link to a destructive action in our views, and these type of actions are best put behind a form that submits a POST request. This is so that crawlers and tools that prefetch web pages do not unintentionally delete our data by following these links. Plus, putting this type of operation behind a POST request follows closer with the idea of how HTTP should work in general. Rails is all about convenience, and it provides us with the quite simple :method option that we can add to our link_to helper. When we add :method => :delete, Rails will generate JavaScript that will dynamically build a form and submit it using a POST request instead of following the actual link.

Reusing Code with Partials

Now we have a nice listing of the meeting details, but Joe wants to edit these meetings as well. Let's add the edit action to our controller. We will once again use the params[:id] value to fetch our meeting object by its primary key.

Ruby   building_a_rails_app/user_group_4/app/controllers/meetings_controller.rb

```ruby
def edit
  @meeting = Meeting.find(params[:id])
end
```

The form in our view will have a significant amount in markup in common with our new view. As always, we'll try to reduce the duplication in our code. Rails provides a nifty way for us to extract our common form elements to a different template so that we can share it between our two different views.

Partials in Rails are snippets of HTML code that you can share between different views. They are stored in your views/ directory just like normal view templates, but they are prefixed with an underscore. This helps us easily recognize which view files aren't associated directly with an action. For this partial, we want to extract the form markup shared between the new and edit views. Since we're extracting common code for our *form*, we'll name this partial app/views/meetings/_form.html.erb.

Ruby   building_a_rails_app/user_group_4/app/views/meetings/_form.html.erb

```erb
<div>
  <%= form.label :meets_on %>:<br />
  <%= form.date_select :meets_on %>
</div>
<div>
  <%= form.label :location %>:<br />
  <%= form.text_field :location, :size => 35, :class => "text" %>
</div>
<div>
  <%= form.label :description %>:<br />
  <%= form.text_area :description, :rows => 4, :class => "text" %>
</div>
```

We've separated only the parts that are common to each view, which are the individual inputs for the form. We can now remove this code from our new.html.erb view and replace it with a call to render our _form.html.erb partial template.

Ruby   building_a_rails_app/user_group_4/app/views/meetings/new.html.erb

```erb
<% form_for :meeting, :url => { :action => "create" } do |form| %>

  <%= render :partial => 'form', :locals => { :form => form } %>

  <%= submit_tag "Create", :class => "submit" %>  
  <%= link_to "cancel", { :action => "index" }, :class => "cancel" %>
<% end %>
```

The render method takes the name of the partial file without the leading underscore or extension. So in this case we'll use :partial => 'form' to render the _form.html.erb file. This is actually quite similar to performing an include on a file in PHP.

One of the trickier parts of using partials is variable scope. Our form variable in new.html.erb is not a global variable and is available only in the scope of the new.html.erb template. Since the partial template is in a separate file, we need to pass our local variable into the partial file using the :locals option. Here we pass our form builder object into the partial to be used by the same name. Although local variables need to be passed into partials using :locals, instance variables such as @meeting will automatically be shared. Since we're passing only a single object to the partial, we can refactor this partial to use a nice shortcut. Instead of using the :locals hash to pass the variable into our partial, we'll use the :object option to pass the form builder object into our partial.

`Ruby` `building_a_rails_app/user_group_5/app/views/meetings/new.html.erb`

```
<%= render :partial => 'form', :object => form %>
```

The object will become accessible in the partial by the same name as the partial file (without the underscore). In this example, the variable name will be form since the partial name is _form. Remember that this will work only for a single variable. It is most appropriately used when the data in this variable is the object represented by the partial, as the form is in this case.

Editing Meetings

With our form partially created, the edit view is quite simple now. This will be similar to the new template, but with a few small changes. When we submit an edit, we'll want the form to submit to the update action instead of create. The cancel link will also change slightly to lead us back to the show action.

`Ruby` `building_a_rails_app/user_group_4/app/views/meetings/edit.html.erb`

```
Line 1   <h1>Edit Meeting</h1>
     -
     -   <div class="form">
     -     <%= error_messages_for :meeting -%>
     5
     -     <fieldset>
     -     <legend>Enter Meeting Details</legend>
     -     <% form_for :meeting, :url => { :action => "update",
     -                                    :id => @meeting.id } do |form| %>
    10
```

```
-              <%= render :partial => 'form', :object => form %>
-
-              <%= submit_tag "Save", :class => "submit" %>  
-              <%= link_to "cancel", { :action => "show", :id => @meeting.id },
15                                       :class => "cancel" %>
-          <% end %>
-          </fieldset>
-      </div>
```

The edit page (shown in Figure 5.13, on the next page) takes full advantage of our form helpers to prepopulate the data for the form based on the @meeting object.

To actually update data in the database, we need to build an update action in our controller. This is similar to the create action and will not render anything new. Instead, it will either redirect or render the edit template.

`Ruby` `building_a_rails_app/user_group_4/app/controllers/meetings_controller.rb`

```
Line 1   def update
-          @meeting = Meeting.find(params[:id])
-
-          if @meeting.update_attributes(params[:meeting])
5            flash[:notice] = 'Meeting successfully updated.'
-            redirect_to :action => "show", :id => params[:id]
-          else
-            render :action => "edit"
-          end
10       end
```

The update_attributes method shown on line 4 assigns all the values for our object using the submitted form values in params[:meeting]. It will then attempt to save the resulting object to the database. Just like the create action, it will set a flash message and redirect us when it succeeds. If it fails, it will redisplay the edit form along with the associated errors.

Once again, we need to display flash data in the next request. This is the second, and probably not the last, time we need to display a flash message on a page. Instead of copying and pasting the same code in our show view, let's extract this flash code to a custom helper method. The helper will likely be used in other controllers within our application, so we'll define it in app/helpers/application_helper.rb. Any custom helpers we add to this module will immediately become available in all views within our application instead of being limited to a specific controller.

Figure 5.13: EDITING A MEETING

building_a_rails_app/user_group_5/app/helpers/application_helper.rb

```ruby
module ApplicationHelper
  def flash_notice
    if flash[:notice]
      content_tag('div', h(flash[:notice]), {:id => "flash_notice"})
    end
  end
end
```

To display our flash notice from the custom helper, we've used the content_tag helper again. In this case we've created a div tag, with our flash data as the tag content. We've also used an additional hash of attributes to add an id="flash_notice" attribute to this div. Now we can replace the flash code usage in both our index and show views with this new helper.

building_a_rails_app/user_group_5/app/views/meetings/index.html.erb

```ruby
<h1>Meetings</h1>

<%= flash_notice %>
```

building_a_rails_app/user_group_5/app/views/meetings/show.html.erb

```ruby
<h1><%= link_to "Meetings", :action => "index" %>
  &rarr; <%=h @meeting.name %>
</h1>

<%= flash_notice %>
```

Destroying Meetings

The last action we'll add to our MeetingsController will implement the destroy action we linked to while showing the meeting details. This action is simple, and once again instantiates our meeting from the primary key given. It then uses the destroy method on the object to delete the meeting record from the database.

`Ruby` building_a_rails_app/user_group_5/app/controllers/meetings_controller.rb

```ruby
def destroy
  @meeting = Meeting.find(params[:id])
  @meeting.destroy

  flash[:notice] = 'Meeting successfully destroyed.'
  redirect_to :action => "index"
end
```

Taking a step back to look at our controllers, we can see that we've definitely been repeating ourselves through our actions. Four of our actions start by finding the Meeting object for the given primary key. Let's add a new method to our MeetingsController to handle this operation in a single location. We'll put this at the bottom of our controller class in app/controllers/meetings_controller.rb, and we'll make it private so it doesn't get confused with our action methods. Making this method private prevents it from being accessed as an action in the controller. To see the important differences in method visibility between PHP and Ruby, check out Section 12.3, *Visibility*, on page 328.

`Ruby` building_a_rails_app/user_group_5/app/controllers/meetings_controller.rb

```ruby
private

def find_meeting
  @meeting = Meeting.find(params[:id])
end
```

We could go and replace all these finds with our new method find_meeting, but Rails has an even better way of doing this. We can add this method as a filter to be executed before actions in our controller.

`Ruby` building_a_rails_app/user_group_5/app/controllers/meetings_controller.rb

```ruby
class MeetingsController < ApplicationController
  before_filter :find_meeting, :except => [:index, :new, :create]
```

Adding this before_filter using the name of our new method will instruct the controller to execute find_meeting before every action in this controller. We of course want to do this only for the actions that have an :id parameter passed in. The method allows for an additional :except

> ### Joe Asks...
> #### Should My Action Method Be Empty?
>
> If an action method is empty, we technically don't even need to define it in our controller. Rails will render the associated view automatically even when the action is not explicitly defined in the controller. It is a better practice, however, to keep these empty methods around so that we can easily glance at our controller and get a better idea of what is happening.

option to instruct Rails that it should perform the method before all except the given list of actions. Now we can go and remove the repeat code we've used in our actions to find our meetings.

This finishes up all the methods we need for our first controller, and we finally have the application doing something useful. By now you should have a good understanding of the conventions Rails uses to glue together the controller with its associated views. Our remaining controllers will build on this knowledge and will also expand upon the idea of using controllers to access and modify resources within your application.

Joe plays around with our administration interface and is impressed. It didn't take us long at all to get this up and running, and he's excited to see more. He points out that the pages lack flair, and of course he's right. We haven't gotten around to adding any images or styles, and these aren't even valid HTML pages yet. It's time to get cracking on a design and some images for our application.

5.10 Separating Public Files

Rails is different from PHP in how it serves files on the server. As mentioned earlier, PHP files are often requested directly by their filename on the server. We would even speculate that most PHP applications are fully accessible from the web server so that you could point your browser's URL directly at any file in that application.

The directory structure example in Figure 5.14, on the next page shows us a typical PHP setup where the my_application/ is completely accessible from the Web.

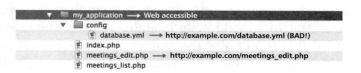

Figure 5.14: WEB-ACCESSIBLE AREAS OF PHP

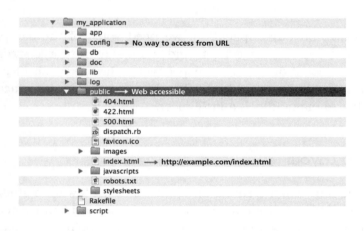

Figure 5.15: WEB-ACCESSIBLE AREAS OF RAILS

Notice that we go to pages in our application by navigating our browser directly to the PHP files. Here we have a potential security hole, because any file put in this application's structure can be navigated to from a browser. If we were to store database credentials in a format other than PHP such as the YAML file shown, users could download this file directly from the server by just pointing to its location.

If we take a look at Figure 5.15, we can see that Rails uses a single directory named public to store all web-accessible files. When we send a request to our Rails application, it will first look for the resource in this public directory and return it if found. When we request something such as http://example.com/meetings/, Rails will first look for that resource in user_group/public/meetings/. When it doesn't find anything, the URL will then be parsed and routed through our Rails application code. We will likely never put any actual Ruby code into the public/ directory.

We can, of course, structure our PHP code in a similar way using something such as Apache's mod_rewrite module. Many of the modern PHP frameworks do this to address the same security concerns. However, this is not the norm in PHP applications because it is not nearly as simple as the previously mentioned approach to serving PHP files.

So, what do we put in the Rails public directory? For starters, this is where we'll put our images, JavaScript, and CSS files. We can also create custom 404 (page not found) or 500 (server error) pages to display to the user when things go wrong.

To put a face on our application, we need some of the sample code from online.[1] Copy the stylesheet[2] and images[3] to the public/stylesheeets/ and public/images/ directories, respectively. Having these files in our public directory gets us ready to add a layout and user interface to our application to make it look a little nicer.

5.11 Adding a Layout

Most of the time when creating an application, we'll want a similar look and feel to our application along with some standard header and footer markup. In our PHP scripts we might thus have included a header and footer file that we could share between different pages.

`PHP` `building_a_rails_app/php/layout/index.php`

```php
<?php
require_once 'header.php';
?>

    <h1>Meetings</h1>
    <h2>Upcoming Meetings</h2>
    <ul>
      <li>...</li>
    </ul>

<?php
require_once 'footer.php';
?>
```

---

1. http://www.pragprog.com/titles/ndphpr/source_code
2. http://media.pragprog.com/titles/ndphpr/code/building_a_rails_app/user_group_6/public/stylesheets/
3. http://media.pragprog.com/titles/ndphpr/code/building_a_rails_app/user_group_6/public/images

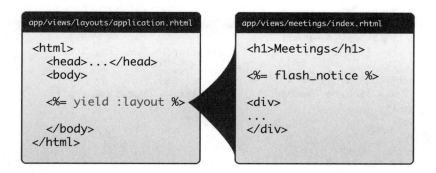

Figure 5.16: LAYOUT TEMPLATE PARSING

Rails has a similar way of doing this using something called *layout templates*. We'll use a single layout for all the pages in our application. This layout will include both the header and footer and will insert the markup from our individual actions into the layout at a specific point, as displayed in Figure 5.16.

Layout files are stored in the app/views/layouts/ directory of our application and are written using ERB just like our other view templates. By naming this file application.html.erb, Rails knows to automatically wrap it around every action's output in our application. If we take a look at our layout file, we'll see we have a few new things going on here.

`Ruby`   building_a_rails_app/user_group_6/app/views/layouts/application.html.erb

```
Line 1  <!DOCTYPE html PUBLIC "-//W3C//DTD XHTML 1.0 Transitional//EN"
   -       "http://www.w3.org/TR/xhtml1/DTD/xhtml1-transitional.dtd">
   -    <html>
   -    <head>
   5      <meta http-equiv="Content-type" content="text/html; charset=utf-8">
   -      <title>TucsonRails <%= ": #{@title} " if @title %></title>
   -      <%= stylesheet_link_tag "screen", :media => "screen" %>
   -    </head>
   -
   10   <body class="<%= controller.controller_name %>">
   -    <div id="wrapper">
   -      <div id="logo">
   -        <img src="/images/logo.gif" alt="Tucson Rails" />
   -      </div>
   15
```

```
  -        <div id="nav">
  -          <ul>
  -            <li id="nav_meetings">
  -              <%= link_to "Meetings", :controller => "meetings" %>
 20          </li>
  -            <li id="nav_users">
  -              <%= link_to "Members", :controller => "users" %>
  -            </li>
  -          </ul>
 25        </div>
  -
  -        <div id="content">
  -          <%= yield :layout %>
  -        </div>
 30
  -        <div id="footer"> </div>
  -      </div>
  -      </body>
  -      </html>
```

Let's break this down to see what parts of this are noteworthy outside of regular HTML markup. The first thing we may notice is a couple things we've done in the header.

> **Ruby**   building_a_rails_app/user_group_7/app/views/layouts/application.html.erb

```
Line 1  <title>TucsonRails <%= ": #{@title} " if @title %></title>
  -     <%= stylesheet_link_tag "screen", :media => "screen" %>
```

We've set a default title for our page but have also added some logic to add a subtitle if the @title instance variable is set. Instance variables we set in our specific actions or templates are also available in our layout file. This allows us to change sections of the header or footer through variables in the action we're dealing with. In this case, we can set the @title variable in any one of our specific action views to create a title specific to that page.

We have also used a built-in helper to include our style sheet. The stylesheet_link_tag helper method will generate the markup to include our CSS file in the layout when passed the name of our external CSS file. We'll see some the benefits of using this helper when we deploy the application in Chapter 10, *Deploying the Application*, on page 235.

> **Ruby**   building_a_rails_app/user_group_6/app/views/layouts/application.html.erb

```
<body class="<%= controller.controller_name %>">
```

In the body we've added a little snippet to add a class name to our body tag based on the name of the current controller.

We've done this by accessing an instance of the controller and calling the controller_name method. This technique helps us highlight the correct navigation link in our CSS by setting a unique class for every controller in our application.

`Ruby`   building_a_rails_app/user_group_6/app/views/layouts/application.html.erb

```
<div id="content">
  <%= yield :layout %>
</div>
```

The last bit of new stuff here is where we see the yield :layout statement. This statement will instruct the layout to render the contents of our action's view. Rails will render and insert our action's output into this area to create our final combined HTML. This statement can also be written as simply yield, omitting the :layout parameter. You will often see it written as such, but we prefer to pass in :layout to make it easier for us to read what the code is doing.

If we now refresh our meetings index page, we'll be presented with Figure 5.17, on the next page. Now our application is starting to look a little nicer than the plain-Jane layout we previously had.

At this point, we're pretty excited to show Joe our progress. We take him aside and show him how we can view and add new meetings to the application. He seems pretty excited but is a little worried about how reliable our code is. He asks to take a look at our tests, and we smile embarrassingly. There is obviously a lot more to do. It's about time to start validating the data being entered and get a few tests written to make sure things are working as expected.

5.12 Chapter Review

This chapter was intense, but we managed to build a functioning controller with Rails! We're moving along quickly, and we even have a face and layout to our application. And we've met some of the major requirements we defined earlier with Joe.

Let's review the highlights of what we've learned:

- We can now think in terms of "resources." We saw that most Rails controllers look similar and share a convention of common actions such as create, edit, update, and destroy. We structured our application's resources the same way.

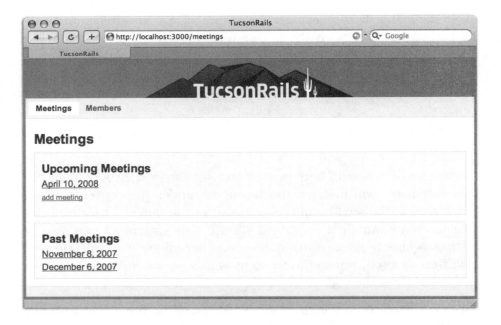

Figure 5.17: STYLED MEETINGS

- We learned how Rails routes requests and the flow through controller actions. We wrote actions to show views, redirect to other actions, and even pass data to the next request with flashing.

- We wrote our first views, and they looked a lot like PHP! The main difference was that Ruby saved us some typing with its built-in helper methods. We used these helpers to save us from the repetitive tasks of linking and building forms. We also learned to write our own custom helpers.

- We started building a simple administration interface that we'll expand on in upcoming chapters.

Before moving on to the next chapter, you might want to spend some time reviewing this one. We covered a lot of material, and as an aspiring Rails developer, you'll want to have a good handle on all of it.

5.13 Exercises

Here's some exercises for you to try on your own:

- Look inside the Meeting model and the custom finder methods we created such as upcoming_meetings that help decouple our controllers from the insides of our models. Play around with these, and see the effects. For bonus points, write your own custom finder.

- Go back to the Ruby console, and interact with the Meeting model. Use the custom finders to find meetings. Practice creating, editing, and destroying models from the console. Interact with your domain model outside of the user interface.

- Write named routes to link to the meeting index and edit actions. Try using the new *_url method to generate the URL for our redirect_to method instead of using a hash.

- Poke around inside the views. Get comfortable with their syntax and the Rails helpers. If you're using a Rails-friendly editor such as TextMate, now is a great time to learn the keyboard shortcuts for working with Rails views.

Good luck with the exercises. If you decide to modify the views, back up your work, and restore the originals before continuing. In the next chapter, we'll dive back into our models to validate the data coming in and test that everything works correctly.

## Chapter 6

Validating and Testing Models

After poking around our application, Joe tries to create a new meeting without any data entered. Unfortunately, our application isn't smart enough to stop him at this point. Validating data in our application is also part of the domain logic. Validations help describe our model requirements and behavior.

In this chapter, we'll see how to add simple validation rules to our meetings to prevent the end user from entering invalid data. We'll also start testing our Rails code to verify that existing functionality doesn't break as we add features. We'll learn how we can use execution environments in Rails to help us set up our test environment.

6.1 Validating Model Data

Talking with Joe a little more, he comes up with some simple rules that he would like our application to enforce before the meeting data can be saved. He wants to require that the meeting date be assigned and require that the meeting location is a minimum of four characters long. Fortunately for us, Rails has an easy way of declaring validation rules on our Meeting class. Placing these rules in the model class ensures that they are enforced regardless of where we create or modify a meeting in our application.

We will use two different validation rules to enforce these validations. To require that the meeting date is present, we need to use the validates_presence_of method. To ensure that the location is a certain length, we'll use the validates_length_of method.

Ruby   building_a_rails_app/user_group_3/app/models/meeting.rb

```ruby
class Meeting < ActiveRecord::Base
  validates_presence_of :meets_on
  validates_length_of   :location, :minimum => 4
```

It may seem strange that we're requiring that the meeting's meets_on column be present. Our HTML form doesn't seem to even give us the option of setting an empty date. We can, however, still change this data from the console or future web services that don't use the HTML form to create meetings.

When we try to insert a record that fails one of our rules, the validation will intercept the save operation and return false. If we take a look back at the create method in our MeetingsController, we can see that when this happens, we'll instruct the controller to render the :new action's view.

Ruby   building_a_rails_app/user_group_4/app/controllers/meetings_controller.rb

```ruby
def create
  @meeting = Meeting.new(params[:meeting])

  if @meeting.save
    flash[:notice] = 'Meeting successfully created.'
    redirect_to :action => "index"
  else
    render :action => "new"
  end
end
```

We can now see an additional benefit of using the Rails form helper methods. If a validation error occurs and the meeting doesn't save, the @meeting instance variable still holds the user-submitted data from our form. When rendering our form back to the user, the form_for and associated helpers in the template will use this data to repopulate the form with the values from the last submission.

When a model fails to save because of a validation error, the model is flagged with a list of errors that occurred. The errors are contained in our @meeting object, which makes it easy to access and display them in our view. To see an example of this, let's fire up the console script.

```
user_group> ruby script/console
Loading development environment
>> meeting = Meeting.new(:location => "")
=> #<Meeting:...>
>> meeting.valid?
=> false
>> meeting.errors.on(:location)
=> "is too short (minimum is 4 characters)"
```

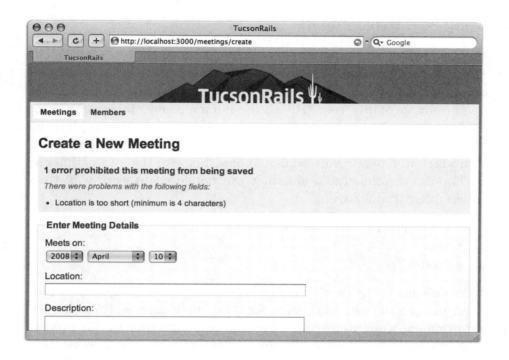

Figure 6.1: VALIDATION ERRORS

ActiveRecord objects have a method named errors, which is a list of errors encountered during validation. We usually don't deal with this object directly because Rails provides a convenient helper method to take care of displaying this data for us in our application.

Ruby building_a_rails_app/user_group_3/app/views/meetings/new.html.erb

```ruby
<div class="form">
  <%= error_messages_for :meeting -%>
```

Using the error_messages_for method at the top of the form in app/views/ meetings/new.html.erb renders a chunk of HTML displaying the validation errors on the :meeting object. If we now try to insert a location that is too short, we'll be presented with the page shown in Figure 6.1.

Joe is pretty impressed with how fast we were able to add this with only a couple lines of code. However, he is still a little disappointed by our lack of unit tests thus far. After all, Rails is supposed to make testing easy, right? I guess it is time to add a few tests to verify our code is behaving as expected, but first we'll learn a thing or two about how environments work in Rails.

6.2 Using Rails Environments

Rails embraces the idea of different execution environments. We can use different environments to run our application with a unique set of configuration and debugging options depending on the situation. A good example of this from PHP is the common usage of the display_errors setting. It is convenient to display errors during development, but this setting should always be turned off when the application is deployed to a production environment. Rails handles this with the idea of different execution environments and comes preconfigured to work with three different environments.

- Development
- Test
- Production

Rails defaults to the development environment, which is where we have been doing all of our work thus far. The application will use the test environment when we perform any unit tests and will use the production environment when we finally deploy our code. We'll learn more about running our code in different environments when we tackle deployment in Chapter 10, *Deploying the Application*, on page 235.

Rails loads the common config/environment.rb file for all environments. It then loads a configuration file that is specific to the current environment from the config/environments/ directory. For example, when we're running in development mode, Rails loads and executes the code in config/environments/development.rb. Rails will also connect to a different database depending on the current environment. You probably noticed this when we set up the database connection for our application in config/database.yml.

Having a different configuration file for each environment is useful. A good example of this is how Rails caches Ruby code. In a typical development environment, you want an immediate feedback cycle. When you change application code, you want to be able to hit Refresh in your browser and see the changes immediately.

The problem with this is that Rails reloads the Rails framework on each request. Once we deploy our application to a production environment, we shouldn't be changing the live code. In this case we can gain performance by caching the Ruby objects in memory. If we take a look at both config/environments/development.rb and config/environments/production.rb, we can see that Rails is set up to do just this. In the development mode, we don't cache classes.

`Ruby` `building_a_rails_app/user_group_3/config/environments/development.rb`

```ruby
config.cache_classes = false
```

While in our live application, we will cache the Ruby classes.

`Ruby` `building_a_rails_app/user_group_3/config/environments/production.rb`

```ruby
config.cache_classes = true
```

Rails sets smart default configuration options so that you don't need to change much to get started. You can browse many of the configuration options for our application by viewing the various configuration files mentioned. There are comments throughout these files to explain many of the available options. We'll go over some of these in more detail when we deploy our application in Chapter 10, *Deploying the Application*, on page 235.

The idea of environments frees us from having to perform any changes to our code to test or deploy our applications. It also allows us to keep all of our data separate so that we can develop and test without fear of affecting production data. This concept is especially important when testing our application.

6.3 Testing Our Models

Tests are extremely important in our application, and not only to satisfy Joe. They will keep our application maintainable as we get further along in development. It's likely that we'll come back to refactor and update our code as we learn new Rails tips and tricks. Having tests makes it much less stressful to make these changes because we will be able to track and easily find regression bugs that pop up.

Preparing the Test Environment

Tests in Rails are stored in three different subdirectories within test/.

unit/
> Tests for our model classes.

functional/
> Tests for our controller classes.

integration/
> Higher-level application integration tests.

Tests in Rails use the *Test::Unit* Ruby library, which is a member of the xUnit-style family of testing frameworks. This style of code will look quite familiar if you have used PHPUnit for unit testing in PHP. Tests run in the test environment and use a completely separate database than our current development environment. To get started, let's create our test database. We'll once again use the db:create Rake task to do this, but this time we'll add an argument to the script. We can change the environment in which we execute the task by adding a RAILS_ENV argument. In this case, we want to temporarily switch to the test environment to create the user_group_test database.

```
rake db:create RAILS_ENV=test
(in /Users/derek/work/user_group)
```

We might additionally need to open config/database.yml to modify our credentials to the user_group_test database. Once we've done this, we need to create the tables needed to perform our tests. The schema for our test database will be identical to the current development schema. We could use the RAILS_ENV=test argument to migrate our database from scratch on this database, but Rails actually provides a Rake task to make this a bit easier. The db:test:prepare task will automatically copy our entire development structure to our test database.

```
user_group> rake db:test:prepare
(in /Users/derek/work/user_group)
```

Writing Test Methods

We should now have our database up and ready for testing. We'll start by adding tests for our Meeting model. Our generator has already created an associated test file for us in test/unit/meeting_test.rb. We'll first verify that our custom find methods we created work as expected. Let's replace the test_truth method with some useful tests to verify that our custom class methods are working as expected.

`Ruby` `building_a_rails_app/user_group_3/test/unit/meeting_test.rb`

```ruby
require File.dirname(__FILE__) + '/../test_helper'

class MeetingTest < Test::Unit::TestCase

  def test_should_find_upcoming_meetings
    meetings = Meeting.upcoming_meetings
    assert meetings.size > 0

    for meeting in meetings
      assert meeting.meets_on > Time.now.to_date
    end
  end
```

```
  def test_should_find_past_meetings
    meetings = Meeting.past_meetings
    assert meetings.size > 0

    for meeting in meetings
      assert meeting.meets_on <= Time.now.to_date
    end
  end
end
```

Any method prefixed with test_ is considered a test and will be executed when we run these tests. We often like to think of our tests as a specification of what our model should do. If we use nice descriptive method names, this actually becomes a useful form of documentation for your application. When Joe views our tests, he can see what the application is expected to do. In this case, a meeting model "should find upcoming meetings" and "should find past meetings."

In each test we start out by using our custom method to find the list of meetings. We then check whether the methods return a collection of meetings and whether each meeting's date is the expected range. We'll use the closest equivalent of PHPUnit's assertTrue, which is named assert in Ruby. This will confirm that the statements we are making return some type of value that is not false or nil.

Running Tests

We'll use the ruby command to run our tests from the command line. Let's execute this test case we've written so far.

```
user_group> ruby test/unit/meeting_test.rb
Loaded suite test/unit/meeting_test
Started
FF
Finished in 0.209111 seconds.

  1) Failure:
test_should_find_past_meetings(MeetingTest)
[test/unit/meeting_test.rb:15]:
<false> is not true.

  2) Failure:
test_should_find_upcoming_meetings(MeetingTest)
[test/unit/meeting_test.rb:7]:
<false> is not true.

2 tests, 2 assertions, 2 failures, 0 errors
```

It appears that both of our tests failed. If we take a look at the line number from the failure message, we can see that both trip up on the assertion that meetings.size > 0. This has happened because we don't have any data in our testing database to run against. We need to load some sample data for these tests to work with.

Using Fixtures

Rails uses *fixture* files to load this data for us. Fixtures are used in unit tests to set up a test environment into an expected state before the test begins. To accomplish this for database-dependent tests, Rails has a way of storing sample data in YAML format. These files are stored in test/fixtures/ and are named based on the table in which they load their data. In our unit test file we load this data by using the fixtures method.

Ruby | building_a_rails_app/user_group_4/test/unit/meeting_test.rb

```ruby
class MeetingTest < Test::Unit::TestCase
  fixtures :meetings
```

This method will clear existing data from this table and load the fresh fixture data before every test. Rails uses transactions to speed up this process if our database supports them. To accurately perform these tests, we need to add some fixture data for our meetings.

building_a_rails_app/user_group_4/test/fixtures/meetings.yml

```yaml
last_months_meeting:
  meets_on:     <%= 1.month.ago.to_s(:db) %>
  location:     University Library
  description:  Rails Hackfest

todays_meeting:
  meets_on:     <%= Time.now.to_s(:db) %>
  location:     University Library
  description:  Rails Hackfest

next_months_meeting:
  meets_on:     <%= 1.month.from_now.to_s(:db) %>
  location:     University Library
  description:  Rails Hackfest
```

We've added a mix of meeting dates to test our methods. We have a meeting in the past, one for today, and one in the future. Notice that we've named each meeting fixture record with a label such as todays_meeting, which is meaningful to the data it contains. This is important because it allows us to reference these records in our tests using a readable name instead of by using a meaningless ID. ERB can be used here similarly to how we've done in view templates.

In this example we dynamically change the date of the meetings to be in relation to the current date. This will allow the data remain valid as time passes.

There are a couple really neat examples of the power of Ruby here. Since Ruby classes are always open for modification, Rails actually extends quite a few classes to create a suite of additional functionality to Ruby's standard library. In this example, we see how the Ruby Numeric class has been extended to add some readable methods that allow us to convert numbers to dates. We also see a custom to_s implementation on Ruby's Date class that takes :db as a parameter to convert it to a MySQL-formatted date string such as 2007-12-06.

Now that we have our meetings fixtures populated, let's run our tests again:

```
user_group> ruby test/unit/meeting_test.rb
Loaded suite test/unit/meeting_test
Started
..
Finished in 0.068613 seconds.

2 tests, 5 assertions, 0 failures, 0 errors
```

It appears that the YAML data is loading now and our tests pass.

Adding More Tests

Let's now add a test to verify our name method works as expected. This one is a little trickier since it's hard to know exactly what to expect with the data being dynamic. We've decided to use a regular expression to assert that the format is correct.

Ruby

building_a_rails_app/user_group_4/test/unit/meeting_test.rb

```ruby
def test_should_format_date_as_name
  meeting = meetings(:todays_meeting)
  assert_match /\w* \d{1,2}, \d{4}/i, meeting.name
end
```

When a fixture is loaded for our test, we have the ability to reference the data in that fixture using a method after the same name. Remember how we named each fixture record with a meaningful name? Now we can retrieve the record by calling meetings(:todays_meeting) to reference the fixture record we named todays_meeting in meetings.yml. Rails will use the data for this fixture to create and return a Meeting object. This is the preferred way to reference a record in the fixture file. By naming our fixtures after their purpose, they become much less cryptic when we revisit them a month from now. We'll know exactly the nature of the data that we're accessing from the fixture, and we'll have fewer questions from Joe.

Rerunning our tests show that everything passes. This is great, but now Joe is also hounding us about testing the validation methods we added. Let's take a look at the tests that we come up with.

`Ruby` `building_a_rails_app/user_group_4/test/unit/meeting_test.rb`

```ruby
Line 1  def test_should_create_meeting
    -     assert_difference 'Meeting.count', 1 do
    -       meeting = create_meeting
    -       assert !meeting.new_record?
    5     end
    -   end
    -
    -   def test_should_require_meets_on
    -     m = create_meeting(:meets_on => nil)
   10     assert m.errors.invalid?(:meets_on)
    -   end
    -
    -   def test_should_have_a_location_with_four_char_minimum
    -     m = create_meeting(:location => 'boo')
   15     assert m.errors.invalid?(:location)
    -   end
    -
    -   protected
    -     def create_meeting(options = {})
   20       attrs = { :meets_on    => "2008-01-01",
    -                 :location    => "University Library",
    -                 :description => "Lightning Talks" }.merge(options)
    -       Meeting.create(attrs)
    -     end
```

We've added three new tests here to our model, along with a protected method to help us factor out common code. We use the create_meeting method on line 19 as a way of creating a new Meeting record for our tests. The merge method works the same as the array_merge function in PHP and will override any attributes with those passed in to the method using the options hash.

We start by testing that a meeting that has valid data is actually created in test_should_create_meeting. We use a new assertion here that is quite useful. The assert_difference assertion checks that a change takes place in our code. In this case, we're creating a meeting and want to assert that the number of meetings increases by one when the code is executed.

The first argument is an expression (Meeting.count in this case). The second argument is the difference that we expect the argument to produce when compared before and after code execution. This is actually a shortcut for performing something similar to the following code.

Ruby `building_a_rails_app/ruby/assert_difference.rb`

```ruby
def test_should_create_meeting
  before_count = Meeting.count

  meeting = create_meeting
  assert !meeting.new_record?

  after_count = Meeting.count
  assert_equal 1, after_count - before_count
end
```

The other two tests check that our two different validation rules are set up correctly. In one case, we set the meets_on attribute to nil to verify that an error is added to the model when we try to save without a value. We then have another test to verify that the location indeed cannot be fewer than four characters long. Testing for this invalid input is sometimes referred to as *negative testing*. Let's run these tests one more time.

```
user_group> ruby test/unit/meeting_test.rb
Loaded suite test/unit/meeting_test
Started
......
Finished in 0.07934 seconds.

6 tests, 9 assertions, 0 failures, 0 errors
```

Now that we've written these tests, Joe seems a bit more at ease. He reminds us that our application is far from done. We need to be able to add presentations to the meetings and deal with users.

6.4 Chapter Review

In this chapter we've learned two important aspects of Rails. Here's what we've done:

- We added validations to our models and saw the Rails stack funnel our validation errors all the way up to the view.

- We learned an easy way to display errors to the end user without a whole lot of work. We also saw how nice the Rails form helpers can be when validation fails, because they repopulate our form automatically!

- We wrote our first tests to verify the business logic in our models. These tests will ensure that this functionality continues to work as we continue making changes to the application.

- We also started to build a specification of our Meeting model functionality through some strategically named test methods.

6.5 Exercises

Here are some exercises for you to try on your own:

- Try to add a validation condition that will validate the maximum length of the meeting location.

- Practice running the unit tests we wrote. What extra tests can you add? Try playing around with tests as a way of experimenting with the different ActiveRecord functionality on your models. What happens when you call Meetings.count() with a :conditions argument similar to find's?

Chapter 7

Authenticating Users

Users are a pretty important part of our application. In this chapter, we'll build a registration form for new users to register as members of our group. We'll also build a secure authentication system for Joe and others to log in to the application.

We need three different roles for users in our app. There will be guest users, members, and administrators. A guest user is restricted from modifying any information on the site. Members will be able to edit their own profile information. An administrator like Joe can modify any resource in the application, including all meetings, presentations, and users.

7.1 Migrating to a More Secure User

Before we get into creating users, we have a little problem with our users table. We hadn't initially thought about how we needed to store passwords or authenticate users. This was fine at the moment, and it allowed us to get going on the application instead of pouring over every detail up front. We'd like to change this table a bit now to use a more secure authentication setup for our users. Luckily, Rails is agile enough that making these types of changes isn't a big deal.

It's a really bad idea to store plain-text passwords for our users. If anyone were to gain unauthorized access to our database, they would be able to read the stored password data. A much more secure approach is to store the passwords using a *salted hash*. For each user created in our application, we will generate a random string that is unique to that user. This string is referred to as the *salt* and will be saved to the database with that user's record. When we encrypt the password for this user, we will prepend the salt to make it much harder for an attacker to use a single cracked password to decode other passwords in the system. This also means that two different users with the same password will always have a different password encryption stored in the database.

We'll use migrations to make updates to the users table to reflect these changes. Instead of a password column, we need to use two different columns: one for the encrypted password and another for the random salt string. We'll use the versatile generate script to create a fresh migration file. This time we'll use the migration argument along with the name of our migration. We can also specify additional arguments in the style of column-name:data-type to generate the method calls for adding new columns. We'll use this to add the salt column.

```
user_group> ruby script/generate migration AddSaltToUsers salt:string
exists  db/migrate
create  db/migrate/004_add_salt_to_users.rb
```

Let's take a look at db/migrate/004_add_salt_to_users.rb to see what was generated.

Ruby building_a_rails_app/user_group_5/db/migrate/004_add_salt_to_users.rb

```ruby
class AddSaltToUsers < ActiveRecord::Migration
  def self.up
    add_column :users, :salt, :string
  end

  def self.down
    remove_column :users, :salt
  end
end
```

The generator gives us a great start on this migration, but we need to add a few more things to finish it. The generated code adds the salt column using the add_column method. We'll also add a limit on this column to restrict it to forty characters. We'll use this same migration file to rename our password column to encrypted_password. In the down method, we'll perform the reverse by dropping the salt column and renaming our column to password.

Ruby building_a_rails_app/user_group_6/db/migrate/004_add_salt_to_users.rb

```ruby
class AddSaltToUsers < ActiveRecord::Migration
  def self.up
    rename_column :users, :password, :encrypted_password
    add_column :users, :salt, :string, :limit => 40
  end
```

```
  def self.down
    remove_column :users, :salt
    rename_column :users, :encrypted_password, :password
  end
end
```

These methods demonstrate some of the simple ways in which we can alter database tables. Renaming the password column will retain all the current properties of that column, including the data type and limit. Let's perform this new migration to get our database up-to-date.

```
user_group> rake db:migrate
(in /Users/derek/work/user_group)
== 4 AddSaltToUsers: migrating =========================================
-- rename_column(:users, :password, :encrypted_password)
   -> 0.5251s
-- add_column(:users, :salt, :string, {:limit=>40})
   -> 0.0268s
== 4 AddSaltToUsers: migrated (0.5525s) ===============================
```

Now that our database is structured correctly to store secure passwords, we can move on to building the user registration portion of our application.

7.2 User Registration

User registration is essentially the creation of a new user. Before we dive too deep into the code, let's first figure out how we'd like the authentication page flow to work.

As shown in Figure 7.1, on the next page, new members will initially be presented with the registration form. Upon completion of registration, a new session will be started for them, and they will be directed to their profile page. Users with existing accounts can go directly to the login page to create a new session. From their profile page they can edit the details of their profile and log out to invalidate their session.

Building the Registration Form

The resource we're dealing with now is the users in our application, and we need a brand-spanking-new controller to deal with them. This controller will have pretty similar actions to those used when creating our meetings. We'll add these action names as additional arguments to our controller generator.

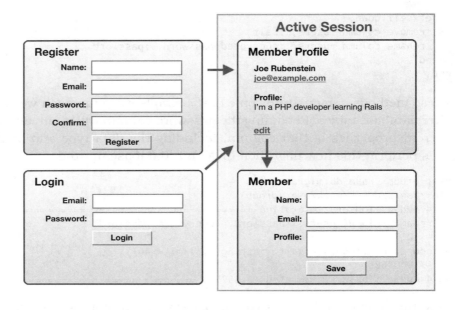

Figure 7.1: REGISTRATION PAGE FLOW

```
user_group> ruby script/generate controller Users index show new edit
exists   app/controllers/
exists   app/helpers/
create   app/views/users
exists   test/functional/
create   app/controllers/users_controller.rb
create   test/functional/users_controller_test.rb
create   app/helpers/users_helper.rb
create   app/views/users/index.html.erb
create   app/views/users/show.html.erb
create   app/views/users/new.html.erb
create   app/views/users/edit.html.erb
```

If we're doing things right, we'll notice that the UsersController will start to shape up like our MeetingsController. Controllers generally don't have a lot of unique logic in them. All domain logic should end up in the models, and all template logic is in the views and helpers. This leaves little left for most controllers to do except glue the two together.

We'll start our code with the new user registration form in app/views/ users/new.html.erb. We need once again to use the form_for helper to create our form, and this form will stylistically look pretty similar to what we've previously seen when creating our meetings.

`Ruby`   `building_a_rails_app/user_group_6/app/views/users/new.html.erb`

```
<h1>Register To Become a Member</h1>

<div class="form">
  <%= error_messages_for :user -%>

  <fieldset>
  <legend>Create a TucsonRails Account</legend>
  <% form_for :user, :url => { :action => "create" } do |form| %>
    <div>
      <%= form.label :name %>:<br />
      <%= form.text_field :name, :class => "short" %>
    </div>
    <div>
      <%= form.label :email %>:<br />
      <%= form.text_field :email, :class => "short" %>
    </div>
    <div>
      <%= form.label :password %>:<br />
      <%= form.password_field :password, :class => "short" %>
    </div>
    <div>
      <%= form.label :password_confirmation %>:<br />
      <%= form.password_field :password_confirmation,
                              :class => "short" %>
    </div>

    <%= submit_tag "Submit" %>
  <% end %>
  </fieldset>
</div>
```

You may have noticed that when creating a meeting, all the form fields were based directly on attributes of the Meeting model. In this case, we have two fields that aren't attributes for our user model yet. We don't have a field in our form that corresponds directly to the encrypted_password because the user is not typing in anything encrypted. The user will instead submit a plain-text version of their password in the password field. The encrypted version will be generated based on the plain-text password submitted.

We've also added a field named :password_confirmation to validate that the user hasn't mistyped their password. This is a special attribute that will work with our User validation when we add it later. The registration form should now look like that shown in Figure 7.2, on the following page.

Next we need to fill in the new and create actions to our UsersController. We'll have to manually add the create method since it does not require a

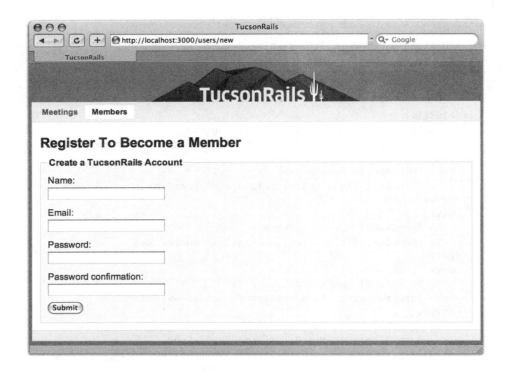

Figure 7.2: THE REGISTRATION FORM FOR NEW USERS

view and was not generated when we initially generated this controller. Although the new action is pretty standard, the create action has some important differences from our previous controller.

Ruby   building_a_rails_app/user_group_6/app/controllers/users_controller.rb

```ruby
Line 1   class UsersController < ApplicationController
  -        before_filter :find_user, :except => [:index, :new, :create]
  -
  -        def index
  5          @users = User.find(:all, :order => "name")
  -        end
  -
  -        def show
  -        end
  10
  -        def new
  -          @user = User.new
  -        end
  -
```

```
15    def create
  -      @user = User.new(params[:user])
  -
  -      if @user.save
  -        @current_user = @user
20        session[:user] = @user.id
  -
  -        flash[:notice] = "Successfully Signed up"
  -        redirect_to :action => "show", :id => @user.id
  -      else
25        render :action => "new"
  -      end
  -    end
  -
  -    def edit
30    end
  -
  -    def update
  -      if @user.update_attributes(params[:user])
  -        flash[:notice] = 'User successfully updated.'
35        redirect_to :action => "show", :id => @user.id
  -      else
  -        render :action => "edit"
  -      end
  -    end
40
  -    def destroy
  -      @user.destroy
  -      flash[:notice] = 'User successfully destroyed.'
  -      redirect_to :action => "index"
45    end
  -
  -    private
  -
  -    def find_user
50      @user = User.find(params[:id])
  -    end
  -  end
```

Once a user registers or logs in to our application, we need to remember
the user for future requests. We'll do this here using sessions. The most
popular way of doing this in PHP is using the session_start function along
with the $_SESSION superglobal array. Just as in PHP, Rails has various
ways to configure sessions depending on the demands of the application. The default storage mechanism in Rails is a cookie-based session
storage. This type of session will store our assigned session data in an
encrypted string saved to the client's computer in a browser cookie.

> ### ⚡ Joe Asks. . .
>
> #### What to Store in Sessions?
>
> Usually when creating a session, we store the minimal data needed to retain the state for the user. In most cases this is simply a unique identifier for the user. Once we have the user's ID, we can reinitialize that user at the beginning of each request and retrieve any other customizations for that user through the relational database.

Cookie session storage is quite fast but limits the amount of data we can store to the maximum size of a cookie (4KB). This typically isn't a problem when you are storing minimal session data as we are in our application.

When a user is successfully created from the submitted form data on line 18, we'll set the @current_user instance variable. This variable will help us easily identify the record for the current logged-in user in our application. We also need to set a session variable on line 20 so that we can remember the user's ID on subsequent requests. Session variables are stored in a hash-like data structure and can easily be assigned or retrieved using the sessions method. This is similar to using the $_SESSION array in PHP. In this case, we've assigned the :user session variable to store the authenticated user's ID. Once the session is active, we'll redirect the user over to what will become their member profile page (UsersController#show).

Processing User Creation

Most of the logic for the actual creation of the user has been left out of the controller. The password encryption logic is all in our User model and should work behind the scenes as we call User.new(params[:user]) and save. This enables us to create new users from different interfaces (such as the console), knowing full well that the creation logic will remain consistent.

Adding the Password Attribute

Our form in users/new.html.erb submitted an attribute named :password that actually doesn't exist in our User model. In order for our creation to work, we need to add this attribute to our model. We'll do this using the attr_accessor method, which will add both password and password= methods.

building_a_rails_app/user_group_4/app/models/user.rb

```ruby
class User < ActiveRecord::Base
  # unencrypted password
  attr_accessor :password
end
```

Now we can directly assign and retrieve the plain-text password for our model instance (although it will never be saved to the database). We'll see how this comes in handy a little later.

```
>> u = User.find :first
=> #<User:...>
>> u.password = 'chunkybacon'
=> "chunkybacon"
>> u.password
=> "chunkybacon"
```

Validating User Records

Our next step in filling out this model is to add a series of validation rules.

building_a_rails_app/user_group_5/app/models/user.rb

```ruby
Line 1  class User < ActiveRecord::Base
          # unencrypted password
          attr_accessor :password

    5     # validation
          validates_length_of       :email, :within => 3..100
          validates_uniqueness_of    :email, :case_sensitive => false
          validates_presence_of      :name
          validates_length_of        :password, :within => 4..40,
   10                                           :if => :password_required?
          validates_confirmation_of :password, :if => :password_required?

          # no encrypted password yet OR password attribute is set
          def password_required?
   15       encrypted_password.blank? || !password.blank?
          end
        end
```

We start by validating the email is within a given character length. This time we've used a Ruby Range object to specify both a minimum and maximum length for the email. We then verify that the email is unique so that we don't have members registering multiple times. The case_sensitive option will make sure Rails does not care about case when it compares the email to existing emails.

\|/ Joe Asks...

How Do Ranges Work?

A Range object in Ruby is just what it sounds like—a range of numbers or characters. This is a similar idea to using the range function in PHP but is quite different in implementation. A range in Ruby does not explicitly contain all the values within a set like the array returned in PHP. It is instead defined based on the beginning and end values but is smart enough to understand what falls in between.

```
irb> numbers = 1..4
=> 1..4
irb> numbers.include?(2)
=> true
irb> numbers.each {|num| print "#{num} " }
1 2 3 4 => 1..4
```

Ranges are a convenient syntax for referencing a set of values without explicitly storing the entire set.

Moving onto the password field, we verify that the length is within four to forty characters. We have then added the validates_confirmation_of method, which will make the model look for an additional attribute appended with _confirmation for comparison. In our case, this is the password_confirmation field from our form. When validation is performed, Rails will compare our two password fields and add an error if they don't match.

Since the plain-text password attribute is empty for all retrieved records, we don't want to always run the password validation rules. We want to run validation on these only when the user is trying to create a new password or change an existing one. We achieve this by adding the :if to our password validation on lines 9 and 11, along with the name of the method that must return true in order for them to run.

The password_required? method defined on line 14 will check either whether we don't have an encrypted version of the password yet or whether the password attribute isn't blank (it was submitted from the form). This effectively allows us to validate the password only when it's being changed. Let's fire up the console to get a better look at how this works. We'll start by finding an existing user. We can update any attribute, and as long as we don't change the password, the model will not try to validate the password.

```
>> user = User.find(1)
=> #<User:...>
>> user.admin = true
=> true
>> user.save  # don't validate the password
>> true
```

However, if we change the password attribute on this same user, Rails will now validate the new password when the user is saved.

```
>> user = User.find(1)
=> #<User:...>
>> user.password = 'chunkybacon'
=> "chunkybacon"
>> user.save  # validate the new password
=> true
```

Encrypting the Password

Now that we have the basic password assignment and validation working on our user, we can move on to the more complex task of actually encrypting the user's password.

`Ruby` `building_a_rails_app/user_group_6/app/models/user.rb`

```
Line 1  validates_confirmation_of :password, :if => :password_required?

        # callbacks
        before_save :encrypt_password
5
        # encrypts given password using salt
        def self.encrypt(pass, salt)
          Digest::SHA1.hexdigest("--#{salt}--#{pass}--")
        end
10
        protected


        # before save - create salt, encrypt password
        def encrypt_password
15        return if password.blank?
          if new_record?
            self.salt = Digest::SHA1.hexdigest("--#{Time.now}--#{email}--")
          end
          self.encrypted_password = User.encrypt(password, salt)
20      end

        # no encrypted password yet OR password attribute is set
        def password_required?
          encrypted_password.blank? || !password.blank?
25      end
      end
```

We have added a callback hook to our model on line 4 using the method before_save. This will intercept any save to our model and execute the given method before the save is performed. In our case, we want to call encrypt_password on the model before any save is done.

We'll be using the Digest::SHA1 Ruby library to encrypt both our random salt and password. This library allows us to generate a SHA1 hash similar to using the sha1 function in PHP. The first thing you'll notice in the encrypt_password method defined on line 14 is that we don't encrypt anything if the password attribute is blank. If a user has not been assigned a *new* password, we don't need to perform any encryption. We also need to assign a new salt value only for new users. Existing users will simply use their current salt value stored in the database. The new_record? method is an ActiveRecord feature that will let us know whether this user has not been saved to the database yet. Finally, in this method we assign our encrypted_password attribute.

We've added a class method named encrypt specifically for encrypting the password using the salt. Although it may not seem necessary for this to be a new method, this will help us reuse this logic during authentication and testing.

Registering a User

This wraps up creating new users for our application. Now that the form is ready to go, let's navigate to http://localhost:3000/users/new and add Joe to our application as a user.

Name:
   Joe Rubenstein

Email Address:
   joe@example.com

Password:
   chunkybacon

Creating our user brings us to an obvious realization of what we have to build next. We need to create the actions required to view the users in our application. To make sure that Joe inserted correctly, let's check out the data using the console.

```
user_group> ruby script/console
Loading development environment
>> joe = User.find :first
=> #<User:...>
>> joe.name
=> "Joe Rubenstein"
```

It looks like he is indeed in there. Let's make Joe an admin in our application through the console. This time we'll use a new method named update_attribute. This method will update a single attribute for a model and automatically save the associated record.

```
>> joe.update_attribute(:admin, true)
=> true
```

This is probably a good time to add tests for our user data. We'll first need to add some fixture data for users like we did with meetings in Chapter 5, *Working with Controllers and Views*, on page 109. When creating fixtures, it is good practice to insert only what is necessary to test the functionality of your application. Having small fixtures actually helps keep the data easy to reference and keeps the tests running fast. Our users fixture will need to use only a couple of records to accomplish what we need to test.

building_a_rails_app/user_group_6/test/fixtures/users.yml

```
admin_user:
  email:              joe@example.com
  name:               Joe Rubenstein
  admin:              true
  salt:               test_salt
  encrypted_password: <%= User.encrypt('chunkybacon', 'test_salt') %>

non_admin_user:
  email:              walter@example.com
  name:               Walter Sobchak
  admin:              false
  salt:               test_salt
  encrypted_password: <%= User.encrypt('nam', 'test_salt') %>
```

Notice that we've used the encrypt method in our fixtures to generate a sample encrypted password for our user records. We won't go into the actual tests here since they look similar to the unit tests we've already written for our meetings. It is, however, a good idea to keep on top of these as we progress in the application. Here are some test methods that you might want to implement.

- test_should_assign_new_password
- test_should_not_rehash_existing_password
- test_should_create_user
- test_should_verify_email_and_password_length
- test_should_have_unique_emails
- test_should_verify_password_confirmation
- test_should_require_name_email_and_password

If you are having troubles, check out the downloadable code examples online to see the final implementation of these tests.[1]

7.3 Viewing and Editing Users

Creating new users was the tricky part, and the rest of the UsersController implementation is fairly standard controller code. We'll be implementing all of the common actions we created in our last controller.

Listing Users

Before we continue adding actions to our controller, we'll add a private method named find_user at the bottom of our controller. This method serves the same purpose as the find_meeting method we created for our meetings controller. Again, we use a before_filter to fire off this method before every action that needs to instantiate the user object.

`Ruby` | building_a_rails_app/user_group_5/app/controllers/users_controller.rb

```ruby
class UsersController < ApplicationController
  before_filter :find_user, :except => [:index, :new, :create]

  def new
    @user = User.new
  end

  def create
    @user = User.new(params[:user])

    if @user.save
      @current_user = @user
      session[:user] = @user.id

      flash[:notice] = "Successfully Signed up"
      redirect_to :action => "show", :id => @user.id
    else
      render :action => "new"
    end
  end

  private

  def find_user
    @user = User.find(params[:id])
  end
end
```

---

1. http://www.pragprog.com/titles/ndphpr/source_code

Next we'll implement both the index and show actions in our controller. The index action will list all the users in our application. We'll find this list of users and sort them alphabetically by name. The show action doesn't need to explicitly do anything since we've already found the user record in the find_user method.

Ruby   building_a_rails_app/user_group_6/app/controllers/users_controller.rb

```ruby
def index
  @users = User.find(:all, :order => "name")
end

def show
end
```

Let's move on to the associated views for these actions. We already generated the view for the index action when we created the controller. Let's open app/views/users/index.html.erb, where we'll use the @users instance variable to loop through the user records.

Ruby   building_a_rails_app/user_group_6/app/views/users/index.html.erb

```erb
Line 1  <h1>Members</h1>

        <%= flash_notice %>

5       <div class="user_list">
        <ul>
          <% for user in @users %>
          <li class="<%= cycle('shade', '') %>">
            <%= link_to h(user.name), :action => "show", :id => user.id %>
10
            <% if user.admin? %>
              <%= image_tag("star.gif", :alt => "Admin", :size => "16x16") %>
            <% end %><br />

15          <span class="email"><%= h(user.email) %></span>
          </li>
          <% end %>
        </ul>
        </div>
```

We've introduced a couple new built-in Rails helpers here, with the first being the cycle method on line 8. This method will alternate output of the arguments given to it within its loop. In this case, we alternate the shade class on each user list item. We can use this class to add zebra stripes to the items in our list using CSS.

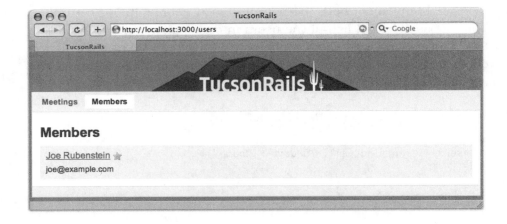

Figure 7.3: THE LIST OF USER GROUP MEMBERS

Joe also wanted a star next to the name of the users who are administrators of the application. We think he's a little nostalgic about his preschool days when he needed a gold star to feel special, but we'll humor him anyway.

We use the image_tag method on line 12 to create the markup for this. This method generates an img tag using the image name along with a hash of options. You may notice that we didn't need to specify the full path to the image. Rails knows that we store images in the images/ directory and takes care of this for us. In this example we've specified both the width and height in a single option named size. This will end up giving us a nice-looking list of users along with their emails, as shown in Figure 7.3.

Generating User Profiles

The show view in this controller will be the user profile page, where we can find more details on individual users. Here we realize that to display a gold star next to administrators on the show view, we'll be repeating our logic from the index view. It's time for some more refactoring. Let's extract the logic for displaying the admin status into a custom helper method named image_for_admin_status. We'll add this method to our UsersHelper module in app/helpers/users_helper.rb. This helper method will use the user object to determine whether it should render the star image.

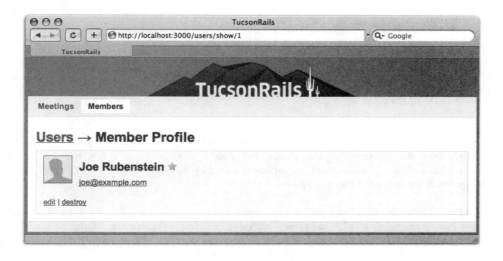

Figure 7.4: USER PROFILE PAGE

Ruby building_a_rails_app/user_group_6/app/helpers/users_helper.rb

```ruby
module UsersHelper
  def image_for_admin_status(user)
    if user.admin?
      image_tag("star.gif", :alt => "Admin", :size => "16x16")
    end
  end
end
```

Once we have this custom helper defined, we can replace the image_for
helper we used in the index view with this new custom helper.

Ruby building_a_rails_app/user_group_7/app/views/users/index.html.erb

```ruby
<li class="<%= cycle('shade', '') %>">
  <%= link_to h(user.name), :action => "show", :id => user.id %>
  <%= image_for_admin_status(user) %> <br />
  <span class="email"><%= h(user.email) %></span>
</li>
```

We'll also use this same helper to display the star in our show view now.
We generated this view template as well when we generated the controller. We just need to fill it in with the specific user's name, email, and
profile description. Joe is going to want to manage these user records,
so we'll also add a link to edit and destroy the user record. Let's open
app/views/users/show.html.erb.

`Ruby`   building_a_rails_app/user_group_6/app/views/users/show.html.erb

```
Line 1  <h1><%= link_to "Users", :action => "index" %>
    -      &rarr; Member Profile
    -    </h1>
    -
    5    <%= flash_notice %>
    -
    -    <div class="details">
    -      <%= image_tag "profile.gif", :alt => "profile", :class => "profile" %>
    -      <h2><%=h @user.name %> <%= image_for_admin_status(@user) %></h2>
   10      <p class="email"><%= mail_to h(@user.email) %></p>
    -      <p><%=h @user.profile %></p>
    -
    -      <div class="modify">
    -        <%= link_to "edit", :action => "edit", :id => @user.id %> |
   15        <%= link_to "destroy", { :action => "destroy", :id => @user.id },
    -                                :confirm => 'Are you sure?',
    -                                :method => :delete %>
    -      </div>
    -    </div>
```

To create an email hyperlink for each user, we've used the built-in mail_to helper method on line 10. Again, we use the image_tag to generate the markup for the image on this page. It may seem rather strange to be using a helper method on something as simple as an image tag.

The plain HTML markup is actually less typing than using the helper, so we're not saving any time. The real reason we use this helper is to give us options for where we choose to serve our images. By using this helper, we can later configure our application to download images from a different location than our application server. We'll discuss this strategy in more detail in Section 10.6, *Serving Assets*, on page 252.

After finishing our show action, the profile page should now look like Figure 7.4, on the preceding page. The only thing left is implementing the edit and destroy actions for the users. Let's go back into our Users-Controller.

Editing Users

The controller methods for editing and deleting users are nearly identical to that of our meetings.

`Ruby`   building_a_rails_app/user_group_6/app/controllers/users_controller.rb

```
def edit
end
```

```ruby
def update
  if @user.update_attributes(params[:user])
    flash[:notice] = 'User successfully updated.'
    redirect_to :action => "show", :id => @user.id
  else
    render :action => "edit"
  end
end

def destroy
  @user.destroy
  flash[:notice] = 'User successfully destroyed.'
  redirect_to :action => "index"
end
```

The edit view will once again use form helpers to help modify user data. This time we are unable to share the form between the new and edit views since they implement a different form.

Ruby | building_a_rails_app/user_group_6/app/views/users/edit.html.erb

```
Line 1   <h1>Edit User</h1>

         <div class="form">
           <%= error_messages_for :user -%>
5
           <fieldset>
           <legend>Edit User Details</legend>
           <% form_for :user, :url => { :action => "update",
                                        :id       => @user.id } do |form| %>
10             <div>
                 <%= form.label :name %>:<br />
                 <%= form.text_field :name, :size => 35, :class => "text" %>
               </div>
               <div>
15               <%= form.label :email %>:<br />
                 <%= form.text_field :email, :size => 35, :class => "text" %>
               </div>
               <div>
                 <%= form.label :profile %>:<br />
20               <%= form.text_area :profile, :rows => 4, :class => "text" %>
               </div>
               <div>
                 Administrator:
                 <%= form.radio_button :admin, true, :class => "radio" %>
25             <label for="user_admin_true">Yes</label>
                 <%= form.radio_button :admin, false, :class => "radio" %>
               <label for="user_admin_false">No</label>
               </div>
```

```
30      <%= submit_tag "Save", :class => "submit" %>  
  -     <%= link_to "cancel", :action => "index" %>
  -   <% end %>
  -   </fieldset>
  - </div>
```

The edit form uses the built-in text_area form helper to modify the user's profile and uses the radio_button helper method on line 24 to implement the boolean database column for admin.

This completes our users controller, and Joe asks us to update his profile information. He wants to be a nice host by introducing himself to his guests. We hit the edit link on his profile to view the edit page shown in Figure 7.5, on the next page.

Profile:

> I've been programming in PHP for the past four years and am excited to be learning Rails. I organize and host the Tucson Rails meetings and look forward to meeting up with others in the area who are excited about Rails.

7.4 Restoring Sessions

We set a session variable to remember this user. The question now is how to retrieve and restore that user's session during each new request. To accomplish this, we'll create a before_filter to initialize the user from the session data. This will set the @current_user instance variable if our user has an active session. We want this filter to run before every action, but we wouldn't be adhering to the DRY principle if we put it at the top of every controller. In Rails, all controllers inherit from the Application-Controller class. This means that anything we place in this class will apply to every subclass. Let's open app/controllers/application.rb to take a look at how this controller looks out of the box.

`Ruby` building_a_rails_app/user_group_5/app/controllers/application.rb

```ruby
# Filters added to this controller apply to all controllers in the
# application. Likewise, all the methods added will be available for
# all controllers.

class ApplicationController < ActionController::Base
  helper :all # include all helpers, all the time

  # See ActionController::RequestForgeryProtection for details
  # Uncomment the :secret if you're not using the cookie session store
  protect_from_forgery # :secret => 'b00ea36a03f524084b970c22f6f2ee7a'
end
```

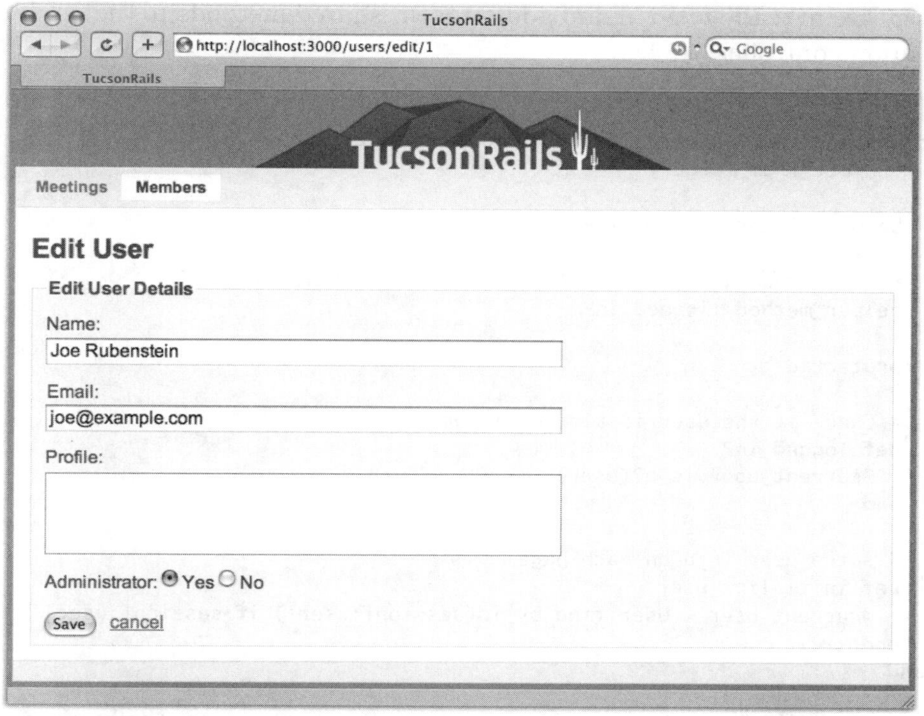

Figure 7.5: EDITING USERS

There are already a few lines of code for us in the application controller. The first uses helper :all to load all custom helper methods to be available all of the time. Although this is a convenient way of sharing helper methods between controllers, we prefer to leave this out unless we indeed do need to share helpers. In this application we've been sharing helpers between controllers by putting them in the application helper module, so we'll remove this.

The next line of code declares protect_from_forgery, which helps prevent cross-site request forgery attacks. Rails accomplishes this by automatically adding a unique token to forms that are created using built-in form helpers such as form_for and form_tag. When a user submits a POST request, Rails uses this token to validate that the session has not been hijacked. As commented near this method, we don't need to specify the :secret option unless we switch to a session storage other than the default cookie store.

Now we're ready to go in and add our own shared methods to the application controller.

`Ruby` `building_a_rails_app/user_group_6/app/controllers/application.rb`

```ruby
class ApplicationController < ActionController::Base
  protect_from_forgery

  before_filter :initialize_user

  # make these available as ActionView helper methods.
  helper_method :logged_in?

  protected

  # Check if the user is already logged in
  def logged_in?
    @current_user.is_a?(User)
  end

  # setup user info on each page
  def initialize_user
    @current_user = User.find_by_id(session[:user]) if session[:user]
  end
end
```

The logged_in? method defined on line 12 allows us to easily check whether the current user is logged in by checking whether the @current_user instance variable is set. We've also introduced a new controller method on line 7 named helper_method.

Back in Section 5.6, *Writing Custom Helper Methods*, on page 126, we introduced the idea of defining custom helpers within the modules in app/helpers/. The helper_method call gives us an alternate way of creating helpers. We can pass in a list of method names that we would like to make accessible in our views as custom helper methods. In this case we have made the logged_in? method available as a helper. We took this approach to creating the logged_in? helper because we're going to need the same logic for this in both the controller and the views.

Finally, we use a before_filter to execute the initialize_user method defined on line 17 before every action in our application. This will restore the user session when it is available. Notice here that we've used a new method named find_by_id. This method is called a *dynamic finder* and is defined at runtime based on the name of the attributes on our model. Rails will recognize when a method doesn't exist, and if it notices that the method begins with find_by_, it will attempt to find the column given based on the name of that method.

Joe Asks...

Why Use find_by_id Instead of find?

You may wonder why we would ever use the find_by_id(id) method instead of just using find(id). The difference comes down to exception handling. When we perform a find(id), Rails assumes that the ID given is a valid record and will throw an exception if it is not. At times we want to find the object by an ID but would rather have nil as a result if a record for the ID isn't found. This is exactly what find_by_id(id) will do.

```
user_group> ruby script/console
Loading development environment
>> User.find(100)
ActiveRecord::RecordNotFound: Couldn't find User with ID=100

>> User.find_by_id(100)
=> nil
```

We can even query by multiple columns by concatenating them together using _and_ in the method name.

```
user_group> ruby script/console
Loading development environment
>> meeting = Meeting.find_by_meets_on "2007-12-06"
=> #<Meeting:...>
>> meeting.location
=> "University Library"

>> meeting = Meeting.find_by_id_and_location(1, "University Library")
=> #<Meeting:...>
>> meeting.id
=> 1
```

Now we just need to work out a system for our users to log in and out of our application with their registered accounts.

7.5 Logging In

Our first challenge is figuring out how logging in and out of our application fits within the idea of resources in our application. When a user signs in to our application, we'll create a session to remember their state. Signing out of the application will subsequently destroy that session. It sounds like authentication revolves around the manipulation of sessions and that the resource in this scenario is the session itself. Let's create a new controller for sessions with a new view as our login template.

```
user_group> ruby script/generate controller Sessions new
exists   app/controllers/
exists   app/helpers/
create   app/views/sessions
exists   test/functional/
create   app/controllers/sessions_controller.rb
create   test/functional/sessions_controller_test.rb
create   app/helpers/sessions_helper.rb
create   app/views/sessions/new.html.erb
```

There is a Rails plug-in written by Rick Olson (a Rails core member) that implements an authentication system based on the idea of sessions as resources. The plug-in is called Restful Authentication, and we'll be creating a simplified spin-off version of this to implement our own authentication. We can find the original plug-in in Rick's SVN Repository.[2]

Our login form will be in app/views/sessions/new.html.erb and needs to use an email and password field. This controller does not associate directly with a model, and this form will not wrap a model as we did previously. Instead, we'll be using a different form helper that is around just for this type of situation. The form_tag helper method will create a form that doesn't wrap an object, and we'll pass the action location in as the first argument. In this case we'll be submitting to the :create action in the SessionsController.

Ruby   building_a_rails_app/user_group_6/app/views/sessions/new.html.erb

```
Line 1   <h1>Login</h1>

         <%= flash_notice %>

5        <div class="form">
           <fieldset>
           <legend>Enter email/password</legend>
           <% form_tag :action => "create" do %>
             <div>
10             <label for="email">Email: </label><br />
               <%= text_field_tag :email, params[:email], :class => "short" %>
             </div>
             <div>
               <label for="password">Password: </label><br />
15             <%= password_field_tag :password, params[:password],
                                      :class => "short" %>
             </div>
```

---

2. http://svn.techno-weenie.net/projects/plugins/restful_authentication/

```
     -       <%= submit_tag "Login" %>
     -     <% end %>
    20     </fieldset>
     -   </div>
```

The form element helpers are a little different as well. The text_field_tag on line 11 takes the name of our field and then the value of the field. Since we're not wrapping an object, we'll use the posted parameters to explicitly repopulate the form fields if the login happens to fail.

Now our login page should look like that in Figure 7.6, on the next page. Upon submission, the form will send our credentials to the SessionsController#create method in app/controllers/sessions_controller.rb.

`Ruby` building_a_rails_app/user_group_7/app/controllers/sessions_controller.rb

```ruby
Line 1   def new
     -   end
     -
     -   def create
    5      @current_user = User.authenticate(params[:email], params[:password])
     -     if @current_user
     -       session[:user]  = @current_user.id
     -       redirect_to :controller => "users", :action => "show",
     -                   :id => @current_user.id
    10     else
     -       flash[:notice] = "No user was found with this email/password"
     -       render :action => 'new'
     -     end
     -   end
```

Here we'll perform the user authentication to check whether their credentials are valid. If they authenticate, we'll remember their application state by setting the :user session. We'll then redirect to the user's profile page.

We can see on line 5 that we've pushed the actual authentication logic into a method on our User class. Let's open app/models/user.rb to see how this logic works.

`Ruby` building_a_rails_app/user_group_7/app/models/user.rb

```ruby
# encrypts given password using salt
def self.encrypt(pass, salt)
  Digest::SHA1.hexdigest("--#{salt}--#{pass}--")
end

# authenticate by email/password
def self.authenticate(email, pass)
  user = find_by_email(email)
  user && user.authenticated?(pass) ? user : nil
end
```

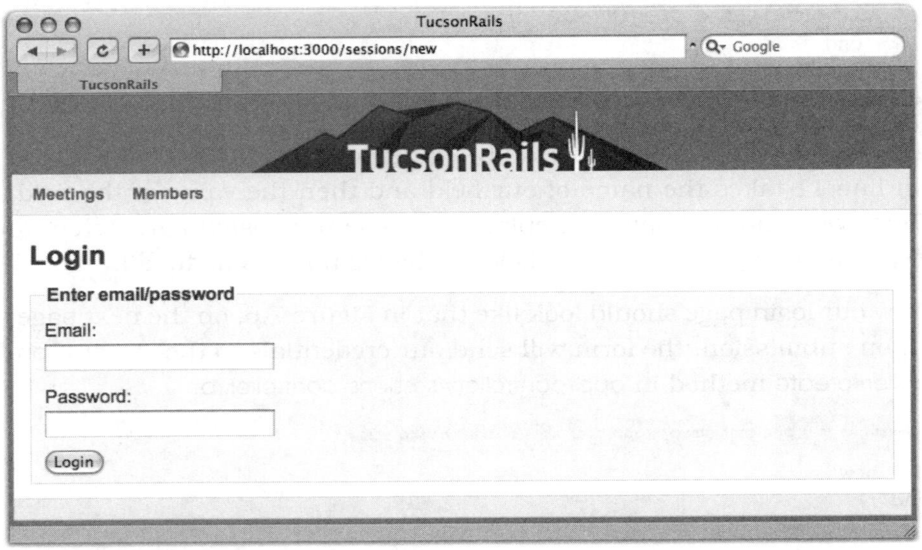

Figure 7.6: LOGIN FORM

```
# does the given password match the stored encrypted password
def authenticated?(pass)
  encrypted_password == User.encrypt(pass, salt)
end
```

We have added two new methods to this class under our encryption method. The User.authenticate method will first try to find a user with the submitted email. If we find the user, we'll compare their encrypted password with a fresh encryption of the submitted password using the authenticated? method. If the passwords match, we'll return the successfully authenticated user.

The final part of our session controller logic is to implement an action to log out from the application. Since logging in was creating a session, logging out will be the destroy action in our SessionsController. Destroying the session consists of calling reset_session to clear out all session data stored for this user. We will finish by redirecting the user back to the login page.

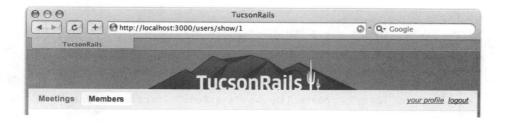

Figure 7.7: ADDING LOGIN/LOGOUT LINKS

Ruby   building_a_rails_app/user_group_7/app/controllers/sessions_controller.rb

```ruby
def destroy
  reset_session

  flash[:notice] = "Logged out successfully"
  redirect_to :action => "new"
end
```

This completes the guts of logging in and out of the application. At this point, however, we have no way for our users to get to these pages. It's about time we add some links to log in and log out of the application. We'll add these links to our layout view so that they're visible at the top of each page.

As shown in Figure 7.7, authenticated users will be shown a link to their profile along with a link to log out. Unauthenticated users will be presented with the login and registration links. We'll take advantage of the logged_in? helper that we created earlier in the application controller to determine the authentication status of our users.

Ruby   building_a_rails_app/user_group_7/app/views/layouts/application.html.erb

```erb
<ul>
  <li id="nav_meetings">
    <%= link_to "Meetings", :controller => "meetings" %>
  </li>
  <li id="nav_users">
    <%= link_to "Members", :controller => "users" %>
  </li>
</ul>
<div>
<% if logged_in? %>
  <%= link_to "your profile", :controller => "users",
                              :action    => "show",
                              :id        => @current_user.id %>
```

```
 
<%= link_to "logout", :controller => "sessions",
                      :action    => "destroy" %>
<% else %>
  <%= link_to "join us", :controller => "users", :action => "new" %>
   
  <%= link_to "login", :controller => "sessions", :action => "new" %>
<% end %>
</div>
```

The application is coming along quite well at this point. We've even finished a fully operational user authentication system. At this point, you should have a pretty good understanding of how controllers work and should begin to see similar patterns between how each is implemented.

7.6 Chapter Review

In this chapter, we implemented the user functionality into our application, and we added a great deal of functionality. Here's what we did:

- We updated our first table with a migration. Instead of creating a new table, we altered an existing one. In this case, we improved the security of our system by not storing the passwords of our users in plain text.

- We learned how to save and retrieve session data. This is an indispensable part of understanding how to maintain state in our Rails applications.

- We continued to evolve our application by building a complete user registration system, profiles for our users, and a form to let users log in and log out.

Joe's user group application is looking great! In the next chapter in this part, we'll add the ability for users to create and edit their presentations for the meetings. We'll see how ActiveRecord associations play an important role in this.

7.7 Exercises

Your Rails skills have advanced to the point where you now make an entire iteration of the application on your own. Unlike the previous chapters, try these exercises in the order shown here. You should now be able to add an entire feature—from the model, to its tests, to the controller, and finishing up with the view.

- Right now, the User model collects the name, email, and profile of the user. Create a new migration to add another column in the table. Try favorite_color or another piece of information that Joe might want to collect on his user group members.

- Add a validation rule for the new attribute you created on the User model. If you get stumped for what to validate, just use validates_presence_of.

- Write a unit test for the validation before trying it on the Ruby console or modifying the views. Make sure it performs as you expect by testing the validation behavior fully.

- Finally, modify the views in the application to show the new User attribute that you created. Make sure that the user can edit the attribute and that it's also shown on the profile page.

## Chapter 8

Defining Associations

Joe plays around with the application so far and is pretty happy with our authentication system. He reminds us that we still have to list the presentations given at each meeting. Doing this requires us to dive back into our model code to learn a little about associations in ActiveRecord. Associations in Rails are powerful and allow us to do some really complex data manipulations without having to write any SQL or joins for our tables. This helps tremendously in making our code clean and easy to read.

Each one of our meetings can have several presentations associated with it. Likewise, each user can also have multiple presentations. These association are actually relationships that we can define right in our models. Foreign keys in the database are usually indicative that you'll want to connect the two associated models' classes for those tables. Let's take a look at how we'll accomplish this.

8.1 Connecting Presentations

Associations between models are defined in a similar way to how we declared validation rules in our model classes. Our first goal is to create a link between our meeting and presentation objects. We'll do this by adding a declaration in our Meeting model using the has_many method.

Ruby | building_a_rails_app/user_group_7/app/models/meeting.rb

```ruby
class Meeting < ActiveRecord::Base
  has_many :presentations
```

The has_many method sets up a one-to-many association between these two objects. You'll notice that the declaration uses a plural underscored version of the associated object name (:presentations) so that the code reads naturally. When declaring this association, Rails assumes that our database tables have used correct foreign key naming conventions. The presentations table should (and does) have a meeting_id column. The presentations table also has a user_id column, indicating another association. A user in our application has_many presentations, so we'll add this relationship in the user model.

`Ruby` | building_a_rails_app/user_group_7/app/models/user.rb

```ruby
class User < ActiveRecord::Base
  # unencrypted password
  attr_accessor :password

  # associations
  has_many :presentations
```

This doesn't quite finish our associations, since we have yet to assign the reverse of each association for our Presentation model. Each presentation is associated with a single meeting and a single user. To declare these associations, we need to use the belongs_to method. Notice that this time we use the singular version of the associated object's name (:meeting and :user) so that the code reads naturally.

`Ruby` | building_a_rails_app/user_group_7/app/models/presentation.rb

```ruby
class Presentation < ActiveRecord::Base
  belongs_to :meeting
  belongs_to :user

  validates_presence_of :title, :user
end
```

The belongs_to methods here declare that a presentation object has both a parent meeting object and a parent user object. Almost all associations will be assigned in pairs like this. While in our model, we've also gone ahead and added some simple validation to ensure that data is present for presentation attributes.

Now that we've declared these relationships, let's use the console to create a few presentations. Joe tells us that he presented a talk at the November meeting titled "Creating Rake Tasks." We'll start by finding the user record for Joe.

```
user_group> ruby script/console
Loading development environment
>> joe = User.find_by_email "joe@example.com"
=> #<User:...>
```

Once we have Joe's record, we'll create our presentation. Instead of passing in a user_id attribute for the new presentation, we can directly assign the Joe's user object to the user attribute.

```
>> rake = Presentation.create(:title => "Creating Rake Tasks",
                               :user => joe)
=> #<Presentation:...>
```

This creates a valid presentation object, but the presentation is not associated with any meeting yet. Let's find the November meeting and then add this presentation to that meeting.

```
>> nov = Meeting.find_by_meets_on "2007-11-08"
=> #<Meeting:...>
>> nov.presentations << rake
=> [#<Presentation:...>]
```

The associations we defined have dynamically added a collection of new methods to our Meeting object to help create and access the meeting's associated presentations. One of these is the presentations method, which returns an array of all the presentations associated with the meeting. To add a new presentation, we used the standard << array method to push the new presentation onto the list.

This automatically assigns the presentation's foreign key to the primary key for this meeting and saves the presentation record in the presentations table. To retrieve and view the new array of presentations on our meeting, we can now use the presentations method on any meeting object.

```
>> nov.presentations
=> [#<Presentation:...>]
>> nov.presentations[0].title
=> "Creating Rake Tasks"
```

We can even directly access different elements of this array and access the properties of that presentation object. Here we have accessed the first presentation using the bracket syntax. We then view the title on the presentation returned.

Joe now tells us to add the "RJS Templates" presentation he gave at the December meeting. This time we'll use another dynamic method that Rails adds for our association that allows us to do the same thing a little more succinctly.

```
>> dec = Meeting.find_by_meets_on "2007-12-06"
=> #<Meeting:...>
>> dec.presentations.create(:title => "RJS Templates", :user => joe)
=> #<Presentation:...>
```

This allowed us to skip the building of an interim presentation object, and we directly created the associated presentation for the December meeting by using the presentations.create method. Now that we have hooked up some presentations, let's try viewing our association in reverse. This time we'll use the methods that are dynamically added to our presentation object by the belongs_to method.

```
>> presentation = Presentation.find(:first)
=> #<Presentation:...>
>> presentation.title
=> "Creating Rake Tasks"
>> presentation.meeting.location
=> "University Library"
```

Since a presentation belongs only to a single meeting, the association method meeting is named in the singular and returns the single meeting associated with the presentation.

8.2 Testing Associations

We know that before we show Joe anything, it's probably a good idea to add some more tests to make sure all our associations are working correctly. First we need some fixture data for our presentations. We'll add these to the fixtures/presentations.yml file.

building_a_rails_app/user_group_7/test/fixtures/presentations.yml

```
creating_rake_tasks:
  meeting:      todays_meeting
  user:         admin_user
  title:        Creating Rake Tasks
  description:  How to automate tasks in Rails

rjs_templates:
  meeting:      todays_meeting
  user:         admin_user
  title:        RJS Templates
  description:  How to write Javascript based templates in Ruby
```

In these fixtures, we see yet another benefit to creating appropriately named fixture records. In the fixture, we simply refer to the associated fixture records by their fixture name. In this case, we've associated these presentations to our todays_meeting meeting record from meetings.yml and the admin_user from users.yml.

Let's open test/unit/meeting_test.rb to add a test for an association with presentations. To use the presentation fixture data, we need to add :presentations to the list of fixtures we're loading for this test case.

Ruby
`building_a_rails_app/user_group_7/test/unit/meeting_test.rb`

```ruby
class MeetingTest < Test::Unit::TestCase
  fixtures :meetings, :presentations
```

Once we have both the meeting and presentation fixtures loading for each test, we can implement the test for this association.

Ruby
`building_a_rails_app/user_group_7/test/unit/meeting_test.rb`

```ruby
def test_should_have_many_presentations
  meeting = meetings(:todays_meeting)

  assert meeting.presentations.size > 0
  assert_kind_of Presentation, meeting.presentations.first
end
```

We first find the todays_meeting record. We then make sure our presentations data association is actually populated with presentations. Finally, we introduce the assert_kind_of method, which ensures that the result from the association is indeed a collection of Presentation objects.

Adding tests for our presentation association can be done in a similar way, except this time we're expecting only a single object returned by the association method.

Ruby
`building_a_rails_app/user_group_7/test/unit/presentation_test.rb`

```ruby
def test_should_belongs_to_meeting
  rjs = presentations(:rjs_templates)
  assert_kind_of Meeting, rjs.meeting
end
```

We'll once again assert that we get the correct object type back when we use our association. Instead of running each unit test manually, we'll use a Rake task included in Rails that allows us to run all of the unit tests at once. This task is called test:units.

```
user_group> rake test:units
(in /Users/derek/work/user_group)
/usr/local/bin/ruby -Ilib:test "/usr/local/bin"..."user_test.rb"
Loaded suite /usr/local/...
Started
................
Finished in 0.1611 seconds.

17 tests, 32 assertions, 0 failures, 0 errors
```

This task becomes particularly helpful as the number of unit test files increases.

At this point, it is a good idea on your own to add the additional tests
needed to make sure the other presentation and user associations are
working. Here are some test methods that you might want to implement
for presentations.

- test_should_belongs_to_user

- test_should_create_presentation

- test_should_require_title_and_user

8.3 Integrating Presentations into Meetings

Looking at our original diagrams, we know we need to be dealing with
presentations as a resource in the same way we were doing with meetings and users. Let's create a new controller for handling presentations.
According to our initial diagrams, we also need the new and edit views
for this controller.

```
user_group> ruby script/generate controller Presentations new edit
exists  app/controllers/
exists  app/helpers/
create  app/views/presentations
exists  test/functional/
create  app/controllers/presentations_controller.rb
create  test/functional/presentations_controller_test.rb
create  app/helpers/presentations_helper.rb
create  app/views/presentations/new.html.erb
create  app/views/presentations/edit.html.erb
```

We want these presentations to show up alongside their respective
meetings in our application. We left a placeholder earlier for where we
need to add these to our meetings. Now that we have the associations
set up, let's add them into our app/views/meetings/show.html.erb view.

Ruby   building_a_rails_app/user_group_7/app/views/meetings/show.html.erb

```
<h2>Presentations</h2>
<ul id="presentations">
  <% for presentation in @meeting.presentations %>
  <li id="presentation_<%=h presentation.id %>">
    <h3>
      <%=h presentation.title %> 
      <span class="modify">
      (<%= link_to "edit", :controller => "presentations",
                           :action     => "edit",
                           :meeting_id => presentation.meeting.id,
                           :id         => presentation.id %>  |
```

```
          <%= link_to "destroy", { :controller => "presentations",
                                    :action     => "destroy",
                                    :meeting_id => presentation.meeting.id,
                                    :id         => presentation.id },
                                  :confirm => 'Are you sure?',
                                  :method  => :delete %>)
      </span>
    </h3>
    <p class="user">By: <%=h presentation.user.name %></p>
    <p class="description"><%=h presentation.description %></p>
  </li>
  <% end %>
</ul>
```

We've put the full details for each presentation here, along with links to edit and destroy them. Joe asks whether we can also display a message when there are no presentations and add a link to create new presentations. We're happy to comply.

Ruby building_a_rails_app/user_group_7/app/views/meetings/show.html.erb

```
Line 1   <% if @meeting.presentations.size == 0 %>
    -    <p id="no_presentations">
    -      There are no presentations for this meeting.
    -    </p>
    5    <% end %>
    -
    -    <p class="add">
    -      <%= link_to "add presentation", :controller => "presentations",
    -                                      :action     => "new",
   10                                      :meeting_id => @meeting.id  %>
    -    </p>
```

The December meeting now should look like Figure 8.1, on the next page; it is starting to shape up rather quickly.

8.4 Routing Presentations

Presentations pose a challenge for us because when we work with them, we want to do so in the context of a meeting. You've probably noticed that we've added a meeting_id value to all the links to the presentation controller. If you take a look at the URL that is now generated by the link_to helper, you'll see something like http://localhost:3000/presentations/edit/1?meeting_id=2. This is definitely a little ugly, so let's see what we can do to make this URL look a little nicer. The default :controller/:action/:id route isn't going to cut it in this case, since we'll potentially have both meeting and presentation IDs in the URL.

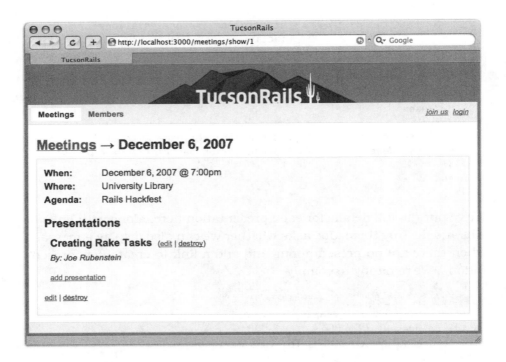

Figure 8.1: MEETINGS PRESENTATIONS

Let's add a route to handle this URL. Open config/routes.rb, and add the following route directly above the default route.

Ruby | building_a_rails_app/user_group_7/config/routes.rb

```ruby
map.presentation 'meetings/:meeting_id/presentations/:action/:id',
                 :controller => "presentations",
                 :action     => "show",
                 :meeting_id => /\d+/

# Install the default route as the lowest priority.
map.connect ':controller/:action/:id'
```

Here we've created another route named presentation. This route is composed of five different components, and we've adjusted the path pattern so that we can nest our presentations behind a meeting ID. We've also introduced a few features writing this route.

We can set default values for any component of the route in one of two ways. We can add a hash argument in the form of :name => "value", or we can add a hash of default values with the :defaults option. A default value will be assigned as the value for a component that is missing in the URL.

```
# :page component defaults to "1"
map.connect "users/index/:id/:page", :controller => "users",
                                      :action    => "index",
                                      :page      => "1"

# :page component defaults to "1"
map.connect "users/index/:id/:page", :controller => "users",
                                      :action    => "index",
                                      :defaults  => {:page => "1"}
```

Each component can also have a regexp requirement it must pass in order for the route to match. This is also done with two different approaches just like default values. We can assign a regular expression in the form of :name => /regexp/, or we can add a :requirements hash option.

```
# :page must be numeric
map.connect "users/index/:id/:page", :controller => "users",
                                      :action    => "index",
                                      :page      => /\d+/

# :page must be numeric
map.connect "users/index/:id/:page", :controller   => "users",
                                      :action       => "index",
                                      :requirements => {:page => /\d+/}
```

With these options in mind, let's dissect this route pattern a little more. In this route, we've set the default :action as show. We've also added a regular expression to the :meeting_id parameter to make sure it is a valid number for the route to match. Save the route file, and let's return to the browser. If we hit Refresh to take a look at the generated URL to edit a presentation, we'll see something nicer looking now, such as http://localhost:3000/meetings/2/presentations/edit/1.

8.5 The Presentation Controller

The presentation controller will look strikingly similar to the controller for our meetings. The biggest difference is that we don't need any show or index actions because these views are integrated right into our meeting's page. We'll start by writing before filters needed to find our objects from the parameters.

`Ruby` building_a_rails_app/user_group_6/app/controllers/presentations_controller.rb

```ruby
Line 1  class PresentationsController < ApplicationController
          before_filter :find_meeting
          before_filter :find_presentation, :except => [:new, :create]

     5    def new
            @presentation = Presentation.new
          end

          def edit
    10    end

          private

          def find_meeting
    15      @meeting = Meeting.find(params[:meeting_id])
          end

          def find_presentation
            @presentation = @meeting.presentations.find(params[:id])
    20      end
        end
```

Since we've been passed in meeting_id in all methods, we'll add a method named find_meeting, which is defined on line 14. This method will be used as a before filter to initialize the meeting object for every action.

In find_presentation, we want to make sure that the presentation we find belongs to the meeting returned in find_meeting. The most appropriate way to do this in Rails is to find our presentation through an association proxy. In this case, we chain a find call onto the meeting object's presentations method. This will limit our find to only the records that are associated with this specific meeting.

Now we can implement the create, update, and destroy actions.

`Ruby` building_a_rails_app/user_group_7/app/controllers/presentations_controller.rb

```ruby
Line 1  def create
          @presentation = Presentation.new(params[:presentation])

          if @meeting.presentations << @presentation
     5      redirect_to_meeting('Presentation successfully created.')
          else
            render :action => "new"
          end
        end
    10
        def update
          if @presentation.update_attributes(params[:presentation])
```

```
        redirect_to_meeting('Presentation successfully updated.')
      else
15       render :action => "edit"
      end
    end

    def destroy
20    @presentation.destroy
      redirect_to_meeting('Presentation successfully destroyed.')
    end

    private
25
    def redirect_to_meeting(notice)
      flash[:notice] = notice
      redirect_to :controller => "meetings",
                  :action     => "show",
30                :id         => @meeting.id
    end
```

We see only a few other differences here from what we did in our
meetings controller, starting with the create action. On line 2, we initialize the @presentation object from form parameters as usual, but
this time instead of saving the presentation directly, we assign it to
the current meeting object using the @meeting.presentations association method. Since we will be redirecting to MeetingController#show after
almost all these actions, we've extracted this logic to a separate method
named redirect_to_meeting that we've defined on line 26. We've even
moved our flash assignment to this method to cut down on repetition.

The new and edit templates are pretty familiar to us at this point. The
biggest difference in our views is that we now need to make sure that
both the form action and links include the meeting_id to ensure it gets
passed to our controller.

`Ruby` building_a_rails_app/user_group_7/app/views/presentations/new.html.erb

```
<h1>Create a New Presentation</h1>

<div class="form">
  <%= error_messages_for :presentation -%>

  <fieldset>
  <legend>Enter Presentation Details</legend>
  <% form_for :presentation,
              :url => { :action    => "create",
                        :meeting_id => @meeting.id } do |form| %>

    <%= render :partial => 'form', :object => form %>
```

```erb
    <%= submit_tag "Create", :class => "submit" %>  
    <%= link_to "cancel", { :controller => "meetings",
                            :action     => "show",
                            :id         => @meeting.id },
                          :class => "cancel" %>
  <% end %>
  </fieldset>
</div>
```

We'll also make sure our cancel links point back to the meeting for which this presentation is associated. Our edit page will end up looking like Figure 8.2, on the facing page.

Ruby   building_a_rails_app/user_group_7/app/views/presentations/edit.html.erb

```erb
<h1>Edit Presentation</h1>

<div class="form">
  <%= error_messages_for :presentation -%>

  <fieldset>
  <legend>Enter Presentation Details</legend>
  <% form_for :presentation,
              :url => { :action     => "update",
                        :meeting_id => @meeting.id,
                        :id         => @presentation.id } do |form| %>

    <%= render :partial => 'form', :object => form %>

    <%= submit_tag "Save", :class => "submit" %>  
    <%= link_to "cancel", { :controller => "meetings",
                            :action     => "show",
                            :id         => @meeting.id },
                          :class => "cancel" %>
  <% end %>
  </fieldset>
</div>
```

We once again need to share the common form info between the two views by creating a partial app/views/presentations/_form.html.erb.

Ruby   building_a_rails_app/user_group_7/app/views/presentations/_form.html.erb

```erb
Line 1  <div>
          <%= form.label :title %>:<br />
          <%= form.text_field :title, :size => 35, :class => "text" %>
        </div>
     5  <div>
          <%= form.label :description %>:<br />
          <%= form.text_area :description, :rows => 4, :class => "text" %>
        </div>
        <div>
    10    <%= form.label :user_id, "Presented by" %>:
```

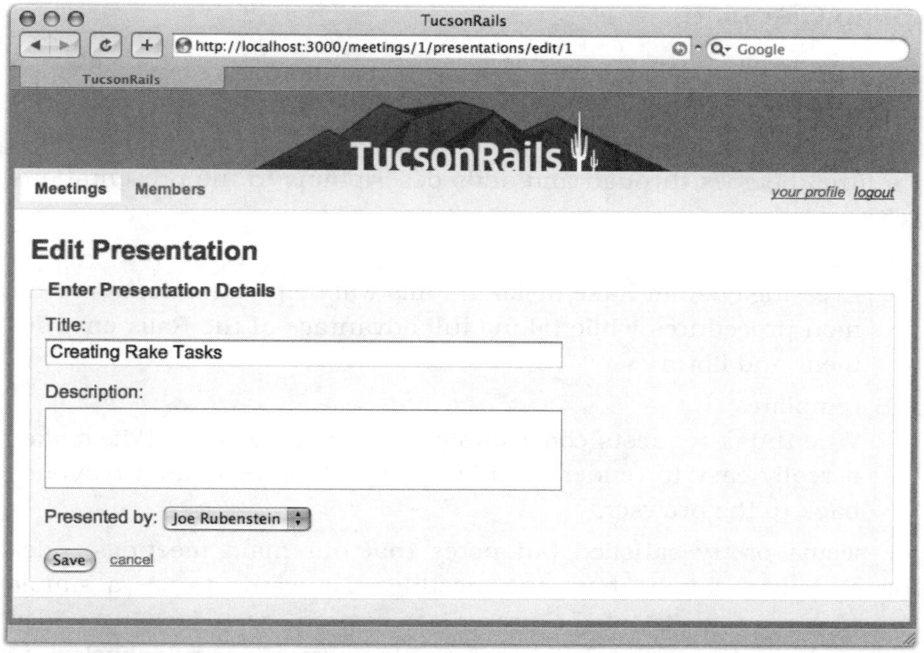

Figure 8.2: EDITING PRESENTATIONS

```
<%= form.collection_select(:user_id, User.find(:all), :id, :name) %>
</div>
```

On line 11 of our form, we use a new form helper. The collection_select method will build a select menu from a collection of objects. We pass in the collection along with the columns we want to be used as the value and label for each option. In this case, passing the :id and :name will result in Rails building something similar to the following.

building_a_rails_app/html/collection_select.html
```
<select id="presentation_user_id" name="presentation[user_id]">
  <option selected="selected" value="1">Joe Rubenstein</option>
  <option value="2">A Second User's Name</option>
</select>
```

8.6 Spring Cleaning

It's time to have a word with Joe again to make sure we're headed in the right direction with our progress. We can now add, edit, and remove presentations from our meetings. Joe plays around, and to test it a little, he goes through and adds descriptions to the presentations we've added.

Creating Rake Tasks

> Creating custom Rake tasks in Rails will help you automate common procedures while taking full advantage of the Rails environment and libraries.

RJS Templates

> When Ajax requests come into our Rails application, RJS makes it really easy to render JavaScript code fragments as a response back to the browser.

Joe seems pretty satisfied but notes that our main meetings index doesn't tell us much about the meetings. He wants to see a simple comma-separated list of the presentations from each meeting added near each meeting name. Let's open app/views/meetings/index.html.erb to see how we can help him with this.

Render Collections with Partials

Before we start implementing Joe's suggestion to add a list of presentations, it's time to do a little spring cleaning. We've ignored a couple things up to this point, but by now some of this repetition is starting to grate on us. We know that our application is supposed to adhere to the DRY principle, but taking a closer look at our index view reveals that we're repeating ourselves in the areas in which we list the meetings. It would probably be beneficial to extract these list items to a shared partial file so that we don't need to make modifications in two separate places.

`Ruby` `building_a_rails_app/user_group_7/app/views/meetings/index.html.erb`

```erb
<h1>Meetings</h1>

<%= flash_notice %>

<div class="meeting_list">
  <h2>Upcoming Meetings</h2>
  <ul>
    <%= render :partial    => "meeting",
               :collection => @upcoming_meetings %>
    <%= no_meetings(@upcoming_meetings) %>
  </ul>
```

```
  <p class="add"><%= link_to "add meeting", new_meeting_path %></p>
</div>

<div class="meeting_list">
  <h2>Past Meetings</h2>
  <ul>
    <%= render :partial => "meeting", :collection => @past_meetings %>
    <%= no_meetings(@past_meetings) %>
  </ul>
</div>
```

If we take a look at our index view again, we'll see that we've refactored this by replacing our meeting lists with partials. We've used a new technique for the render => :partial method here. This time we've added a :collection parameter to the second argument and assigned our array of meetings in each instance. As illustrated in Figure 8.3, on the next page, this approach will loop through each of our arrays and render the partial template for each item in the collection.

We've extracted our meetings to the meetings/_meeting.html.erb partial file. Now that the meeting is in a single location, we can add a call to the presentation_list method that Joe suggested. We'll add this new method in a moment.

Ruby | building_a_rails_app/user_group_7/app/views/meetings/_meeting.html.erb

```
<li>
  <%= link_to h(meeting.name), meeting_path(:id => meeting.id) %>
  <div class="presentation_list"><%= meeting.presentation_list %></div>
</li>
```

Each time we loop through this partial, a local variable will be assigned for the current element in the array. The variable will be named using the filename of the partial template we're working with. In this case, each loop will assign a meeting local variable since our partial is named _meeting. If we had named our partial _foo, we would have to call foo.presentation_list. This is Rails' way of nudging you to name your partials in a reasonable fashion.

We can refactor this even more since we're following Rails naming conventions with our partial files. Instead of passing the name of the partial and the :collection of items, we can simply pass the @upcoming_meetings as the partial.

Ruby | building_a_rails_app/user_group_8/app/views/meetings/index.html.erb

```
<%= render :partial => @upcoming_meetings %>
```

Rails will perform some reflection to determine that the elements in this array are Meeting objects. It will then assume that since these are

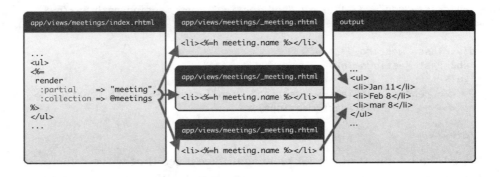

Figure 8.3: PARTIAL COLLECTIONS

meetings, the partial will be named _meeting (which it is). This works the same as using the :collection option, but it takes advantage of a convention to save us some typing.

Test-First Development

Of course our partial code in _meeting.html.erb isn't going to work yet. We haven't defined any presentation_list method for our meeting model yet. We're going to create this in what might seem like a slightly backward way of working. We'll write a test for this method before we write the actual method itself. This is often referred to as *test-first development* or *test-driven development*. Let's open test/unit/meeting_test.rb and add a single test to define the interface for how we want this new method to work.

`Ruby` `building_a_rails_app/user_group_7/test/unit/meeting_test.rb`

```ruby
def test_should_build_comma_separated_presentations
  m = meetings(:todays_meeting)
  assert_equal 'Creating Rake Tasks, RJS Templates',
               m.presentation_list

  m = meetings(:next_months_meeting)
  assert_equal 'no presentations', m.presentation_list
end
```

When we created our presentation fixtures, we assigned two sample presentations to the todays_meeting record. This means the presentation_list for this meeting should return a comma-separated list of the presentation titles. We start our test by finding this meeting and using the assert_equal method to ensure that the presentation_list method is equal to the expected string.

When no presentations are found for a meeting, we'd like this method to simply return "no presentations." We'll use the next_months_meeting meeting to test this since we didn't associate any presentations with this meeting.

To run our unit test this time, we need to run only the single test method that we're currently working with. We can do this by using the -n argument along with the name of the test.

```
user_group> ruby test/unit/meeting_test.rb -n \
            test_should_build_comma_separated_presentations
Loaded suite test/unit/meeting_test
Started
E
Finished in 0.387667 seconds.

  1) Error:
test_should_build_comma_separated_presentations(MeetingTest):
NoMethodError: undefined method `presentation_list' for
#<Meeting:0x241dcf8>
    ...

1 tests, 0 assertions, 0 failures, 1 errors
```

Our test acts as expected and raises an error. We obviously need to add this method for this test to work at all. If we go in and simply add an empty method named presentation_list to our Meeting model in app/models/meeting.rb, we'll get a little closer to our goal.

Ruby   building_a_rails_app/user_group_7/app/models/meeting.rb

```ruby
# comma separated list of presentations
def presentation_list
end
```

With this method defined, let's run our test again.

```
user_group> ruby test/unit/meeting_test.rb -n \
            test_should_build_comma_separated_presentations
Loaded suite test/unit/meeting_test
Started
F
Finished in 0.117175 seconds.

  1) Failure:
test_should_build_comma_separated_presentations(MeetingTest) \
  [test/unit/meeting_test.rb:49]:
```

```
<"Creating Rake Tasks, RJS Templates"> expected but was
<nil>.

1 tests, 1 assertions, 1 failures, 0 errors
```

Our test fails miserably, but at least it's not raising an error this time! It's pretty obvious from the failure message what is going wrong. Let's go in and fully implement this method now to pass our test.

Ruby | building_a_rails_app/user_group_8/app/models/meeting.rb

```ruby
# comma separated list of presentations
def presentation_list
  if presentations.size > 0
    presentations.collect {|p| p.title }.join(', ')
  else
    'no presentations'
  end
end
```

We've packed quite a bit of logic here into a small snippet of Ruby. If the associated presentation has any elements, we will iterate through them collecting the title of each presentation into a new array. We then use the join method to combine these titles together separated by a comma and space. The join method is similar to using the join function in PHP. When there are no presentations, we simply return a string saying so. This is an example of how this might look in PHP.

PHP | building_a_rails_app/php/presentation_list.php

```php
public function presentationList()
{
    if (count($this->presentations) > 0) {
        $titles = array();
        foreach ($this->presentations as $presentation) {
            $titles[] = $presentation->title;
        }
        return join(', ', $titles);
    } else {
        return 'no presentations';
    }
}
```

Now that we have the method defined and fully implemented, we can try to run our same test again.

```
user_group> ruby test/unit/meeting_test.rb -n \
            test_should_build_comma_separated_presentations
Loaded suite test/unit/meeting_test
Started
.
```

```
Finished in 0.059067 seconds.

1 tests, 2 assertions, 0 failures, 0 errors
```

It's a great feeling to see the test pass and know that our new method works without ever having to refresh our browser. The Rails community encourages this approach to development, and many developers get addicted and won't look back.

Reducing Queries

Using associations with Rails can sometimes be terribly inefficient. The first time we reference an association on each object, Rails will query the database to load the associated object. This means our meetings page needs to query once for meetings and then again for the presentations of each meeting.

Rails logs all these queries to log/development.log during each request. By viewing this log, we can see the queries that happen on a page. Let's take a look at what happens when we load the meetings index page.

```
Meeting Load (0.000457) ...
Meeting Load (0.000519) ...
SQL (0.000301) ...
Presentation Load (0.000311) ...
SQL (0.000493) ...
Presentation Load (0.000311) ...
SQL (0.000514) ...
```

Ignoring the SHOW FIELD FROM queries used to introspect our model attributes, we have seven queries that execute for this page. Each time we add a meeting, it looks like we'll have at least two more. Rails uses a feature called *eager loading* to help us alleviate this. When we are expecting an association will be called, we can tell Rails to combine the query for the presentation records into the same query we use to find the base meetings. Rails will perform an outer join to retrieve all the data needed and will sort the data to build the separate objects.

We can query for data this way by adding the :include option to the find method. In our case, we want to add eager loading to the find calls we use in both the upcoming_meetings and past_meetings methods. We'll add eager loading here to query for associated presentation objects as well when we hit the database.

Ruby | building_a_rails_app/user_group_8/app/models/meeting.rb

```ruby
def self.upcoming_meetings
  find(:all, :conditions => "meets_on > CURRENT_TIMESTAMP()",
             :order      => "meets_on",
             :include    => :presentations)
end

def self.past_meetings
  find(:all, :conditions => "meets_on <= CURRENT_TIMESTAMP()",
             :order      => "meets_on",
             :include    => :presentations)
end
```

If we now refresh watching the log, we'll see this.

```
Meeting Load Including Associations (0.000565) ...
Meeting Load Including Associations (0.000338) ...
```

We've reduced the number of queries down to two: one for the list of past meetings and presentations and one for the upcoming list. Unlike before, the number of queries won't increase as the number of meetings on the page increases. Although we could probably reduce this to a single query, we think that it is a little premature. Two queries isn't too bad, and we'll come back to further optimize only if this becomes a problem.

8.7 Chapter Review

In this chapter, we integrated presentations into our application, and we're starting to see some patterns emerge. Our controllers for meetings, users, and presentations look strikingly similar. When you identify the objects correctly in your application, the controllers seem to just fall into place around them.

Let's review what else we learned in this chapter:

- We learned how to link objects to one another using associations. Associations are a great way of creating compositional object relationships with a simple declaration. Joe should be able to easily figure out how our objects are related.

- We learned a little about how test-driven development works and how it can give us an immediate feedback cycle without a browser. This is a great way to work, and you'll always end up with great test coverage of your application working this way.

- We've learned how to add routes that nest a resource behind a parent resource. This is sometimes necessary when we need access to view and modify both of these resources in a controller.

We're getting close to being finished but are still missing one of the most important areas of our site. We'll finish up our application in the next chapter by adding a home page and securing administrative views and actions. We'll also learn a little about speeding up the performance of our application using caching.

8.8 Exercises

Here are some extra exercises that you can try on your own:

- Update the member profile pages to display the list of presentations done by that member. Add a presentations_list method to our User model to return that user's comma-separated list of presentations.

- Create a new model for locations so that we can add, edit, and remove new meeting locations from the application. Add an association that connects meeting objects to their associated location object.

- Add unit tests for our user's association with meetings and presentations. Are there any other tests that are missing? At this point, our application should have pretty good coverage of all the functionality in our models.

## Chapter 9

Preparing to Launch

Our application is coming along quite well, but it is missing one of the most obvious parts. Joe says he wants the home page to display a description of our group along with the date of the next meeting. He'd also like to add a link to the mailing list for the user group and a way to contact him via email.

In this chapter, we'll finally add the home page for Joe. We'll then work on securing areas of the site that require authentication. As we finish up the application, we'll look at some strategies for improving the application's performance.

9.1 Adding the Home Page

Our home page seems to be a collection of various data but in itself doesn't seem to focus on particular resource in our application. It is actually mostly static data, and we've decided that the easiest way to fit this into our application is to simply make a HomepageController. This controller will consist of only a single index method to display our home page.

```
user_group> ruby script/generate controller Homepage index
exists   app/controllers/
exists   app/helpers/
create   app/views/homepage
exists   test/functional/
create   app/controllers/homepage_controller.rb
create   test/functional/homepage_controller_test.rb
create   app/helpers/homepage_helper.rb
create   app/views/homepage/index.html.erb
```

The controller action for our home page simply needs to find the next
upcoming meeting to display on our page. The first method is the same
as using [0] to access the first element of the array.

Ruby `building_a_rails_app/user_group_8/app/controllers/homepage_controller.rb`

```ruby
class HomepageController < ApplicationController
  def index
    @meeting = Meeting.upcoming_meetings.first
  end
end
```

The view for our home page will display the next meeting and link to
the details for this meeting if it exists. Otherwise, we'll just display the
link to our mailing list.

Ruby `building_a_rails_app/user_group_8/app/views/homepage/index.html.erb`

```erb
<h1>Who We Are</h1>
<p>
  TucsonRails is a community interested in the <strong>Ruby and the
  Rails</strong> framework. We welcome all experience levels, and
  our goal is to promote and share our knowledge of Rails in and
  around the Tucson area.
</p>
<div class="highlight">
  <% if @meeting %>
  <div class="next_meeting">
    <h2>Up &amp; Coming</h2>
    <p>
      <span class="date">
        <%= link_to h("#{@meeting.name} @ 7:00pm"),
                      :controller => "meetings",
                      :action     => :show,
                      :id         => @meeting.id %>
      </span> : <span class="location"><%=h @meeting.location %></span>
    </p>
  </div>
  <% end %>
  <div class="join">
    <h2>Join the Mailing List</h2>
    <p>
      Start talking about Rails now in the
      <a href="http://groups.google.com/group/tucson-rails">
        tuscon-rails
      </a>
      Google Group.
    </p>
  </div>
</div>

<h3>Speakers Wanted</h3>
```

```
<p>
  <%= mail_to "joe@example.com", "Contact us" %> if you are
  interested in speaking at a future meeting.
</p>
```

The next order of business is to get this home page to show up at our base URL. Right now http://localhost:3000 still leads us to the Rails welcome page. To prevent Rails from displaying this page, we need to remove this page from the public directory. As we mentioned in Section 5.10, *Separating Public Files*, on page 142, Rails always will look in our public file for the resource before it routes the request through the entire application. Let's delete public/index.html from our application and hit Refresh.

Now we're confronted with the routing error shown in Figure 9.1, on the next page. It looks like we need to dive into our routes again to forward our base URL to our home page controller. Let's open config/routes.rb, where we'll add one last route to our application. We'll put this route at the very top of our list.

Ruby | building_a_rails_app/user_group_8/config/routes.rb

```
ActionController::Routing::Routes.draw do |map|
  map.root :controller => "homepage"
```

This route uses a special method named map.root, which defines a route for the base URL. In this case we'll direct it to the HomepageController. Since no action is specified, it will default to index. Hitting Refresh on our browser should now display our newly created home page.

Now let's open our application layout to add some links to our home page from the other pages in our application. It is pretty typical to have the logo in your application link to the home page. We would, however, prefer not to have the logo be a link when we're on the home page. Rails actually has a built-in helper method named link_to_unless_current that does exactly this for us.

Ruby | building_a_rails_app/user_group_8/app/views/layouts/application.html.erb

```
<div id="logo">
<%= link_to_unless_current(
      image_tag("logo.gif", :alt => "Tucson Rails"),
      :controller => "homepage") %>
</div>
```

While we're in our layout, let's also add a link to our home page in the navigation bar of our application. We'll place this to the left of our link to the meetings.

Figure 9.1: THE HOME PAGE PRESENTS A ROUTING ERROR.

building_a_rails_app/user_group_8/app/views/layouts/application.html.erb

```
<li id="nav_home">
  <%= link_to "Home", :controller => "homepage" %>
</li>
<li id="nav_meetings">
  <%= link_to "Meetings", :controller => "meetings" %>
</li>
```

Hitting Refresh on our home page again will result in the screen shown in Figure 9.2, on the facing page.

This is likely to be the first page most users hit and reminds us that this will indeed be a public site. We need to start thinking about securing the administrative parts of our application.

9.2 Securing Our Actions

Currently anyone and everyone can add, edit, and delete our data. We'd like to restrict the access to these types of operations to administrators in our application.

Our first step is to identify the access level of the user visiting the site. We'll start by adding a new methods to determine whether a user is an administrator. Since we'll be using this method in all controllers, ApplicationController seems to be a good place for it.

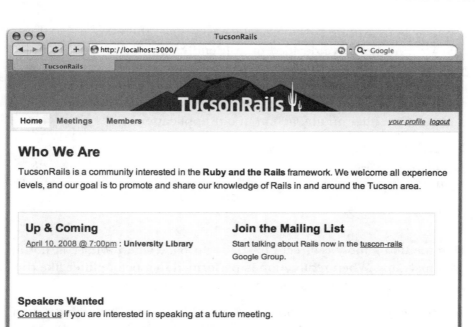

Figure 9.2: THE FINISHED HOME PAGE

building_a_rails_app/user_group_8/app/controllers/application.rb

```ruby
# make these available as ActionView helper methods.
helper_method :logged_in?, :admin?

protected

# Check if the user is already logged in
def logged_in?
  @current_user.is_a?(User)
end

def admin?
  logged_in? && @current_user.admin?
end
```

The admin? method checks whether the current user is both logged in and flagged as an admin. Just like the logged_in? method, we've added this method to helper_method to make it available in our views.

If a user is unauthorized to view a certain page, there are a few things that we can do. We've decided on a friendly approach of just redirecting the user over to the login page. To handle the redirection, we'll add another method to ApplicationController. We'll name this method admin_required, and by putting it in this controller, we'll be able to use it as a before filter on any action in our application.

Ruby | building_a_rails_app/user_group_7/app/controllers/application.rb

```ruby
def admin_required
  unless admin?
    redirect_to :controller => 'sessions', :action => 'new'
  end
end
```

This method simply redirects to the login page when a user is not an administrator. When redirection is performed in a before filter like this, Rails will know to not process the action any further.

We can now go into our controllers to add a before_filter using admin_required for any actions that require administrator access. Both our MeetingsController and PresentationsController are pretty straightforward. If the user is not an administrator, they should have only read access. Since our application displays presentations in the context of MeetingsController#show, every method in our PresentationController should be restricted to admin access.

Ruby | building_a_rails_app/user_group_8/app/controllers/presentations_controller.rb

```ruby
class PresentationsController < ApplicationController
  before_filter :admin_required
```

We do, however, want to be able to list and display specific meetings to the public. We'll add the same before filter to meetings, except that this time we'll add the :except option to allow public access to the index and show actions.

Ruby | building_a_rails_app/user_group_8/app/controllers/meetings_controller.rb

```ruby
class MeetingsController < ApplicationController
  before_filter :admin_required, :except => [:index, :show]
```

The last resource we need to worry about is our users. Since users can create (register) and edit their own records, we don't want to restrict access to those actions. We do, however, want to require the user to be logged into the application to edit their profile.

Let's return to our ApplicationController and add a separate method that requires a user to be logged in to perform an action. Once again, we want to redirect to the login page if the user is not logged in. Since we're duplicating our effort in admin_required, this is a good time to refactor this code a little bit by adding a redirect_to_login method.

Ruby | building_a_rails_app/user_group_8/app/controllers/application.rb

```ruby
def admin_required
  redirect_to_login unless admin?
end

def login_required
  redirect_to_login unless logged_in?
end

def redirect_to_login
  redirect_to(:controller => 'sessions', :action => 'new')
end
```

Now we can restrict the editing of records to logged-in users and the deletion of users to administrators.

Ruby | building_a_rails_app/user_group_8/app/controllers/users_controller.rb

```ruby
class UsersController < ApplicationController
  before_filter :admin_required, :only => [:destroy]
  before_filter :login_required, :only => [:edit, :update]
```

Joe reminds us that giving access for any logged-in user to edit and update user records isn't such a great idea. What we really want to do is give them access to edit their own user record. Once a user is logged in, we have their information stored in the @current_user instance variable. What we need to do is compare the id for this user with that of the record being edited. If this doesn't match, we'll simply redirect the user to edit their own record. Let's add a new method named confirm_user_owns_record at the bottom of UsersController.

Ruby | building_a_rails_app/user_group_8/app/controllers/users_controller.rb

```ruby
def find_user
  @user = User.find(params[:id])
end

# if the user is not an admin, make sure they can't edit other users
def confirm_user_owns_record
  return if admin?
  if @user.id != @current_user.id
    redirect_to :action => "edit", :id => @current_user.id
  end
end
```

For this method to work, we need to add it as a before filter to the edit
and update actions in this controller. We'll add this directly below our
before_filter for find_user.

Ruby | building_a_rails_app/user_group_8/app/controllers/users_controller.rb

```ruby
before_filter :find_user, :except => [:index, :new, :create]
before_filter :confirm_user_owns_record, :only => [:edit, :update]
```

The last step to this process will be to hide all of the add, edit, and
destroy links we made to our resources for anyone who is not an administrator. This should be easy to accomplish with some simple conditional statements using our custom admin? helper. We will start on
meetings in the index view, wherein we will hide the link to create
new meetings.

Ruby | building_a_rails_app/user_group_8/app/views/meetings/index.html.erb

```ruby
<% if admin? %>
<p class="add"><%= link_to "add meeting", new_meeting_path %></p>
<% end %>
```

Now in our users' show view, we need to hide the links to edit and
delete meetings. Since presentations are also edited from here, we need
to conceal the links to create and modify presentations as well.

Ruby | building_a_rails_app/user_group_8/app/views/meetings/show.html.erb

```ruby
<%=h presentation.title %> 
<% if admin? %>
<span class="modify">
(<%= link_to "edit", :controller => "presentations",
                     :action     => "edit",
                     :meeting_id => presentation.meeting.id,
                     :id         => presentation.id %> |

<%= link_to "destroy", { :controller => "presentations",
                         :action     => "destroy",
                         :meeting_id => presentation.meeting.id,
                         :id         => presentation.id },
                         :confirm => 'Are you sure?',
                         :method  => :delete %>)
</span>
<% end %>
```

Ruby | building_a_rails_app/user_group_8/app/views/meetings/show.html.erb

```ruby
<% if admin? %>
<p class="add">
  <%= link_to "add presentation", :controller => "presentations",
                                  :action     => "new",
                                  :meeting_id => @meeting.id  %>
</p>
```

```
<p class="modify">
  <%= link_to "edit", :action => "edit", :id => @meeting.id %>  |
  <%= link_to "destroy", { :action => "destroy", :id => @meeting.id },
                          :confirm => 'Are you sure?',
                          :method  => :delete %>
</p>
<% end %>
```

This will finish up both our meetings and presentations, so now we'll move on to the user pages. Editing users is a little trickier because we want users to be able to edit their own records. We need to add a little extra logic to determine whether they're able to edit the user. Let's open the user's profile page by taking a look at app/views/users/show.html.erb.

Ruby   building_a_rails_app/user_group_7/app/views/users/show.html.erb

```
<% # admin can edit everyone %>
<% if admin? %>
<div class="modify admin">
  <%= link_to "edit", :action => "edit", :id => @user.id %>  |
  <%= link_to "destroy", { :action => "destroy", :id => @user.id },
                          :confirm => 'Are you sure?',
                          :method  => :delete %>
</div>

<% # user can edit himself %>
<% elsif logged_in? && @user.id == @current_user.id %>
<div class="modify user">
  <%= link_to "edit your profile", :action => "edit",
                                   :id      => @user.id %>
</div>
<% end %>
```

Here we've added a simple conditional to check their authentication status. Administrators will have links to edit and delete the user. Meanwhile, users should be able to change their own profile while logged in. Taking a step back to look, we realize we're getting a little too much logic in the view, and it's starting to get a little cryptic. To clean this up a little, we'll replace some of our logic with a custom helper named user_owns_record?.

Ruby   building_a_rails_app/user_group_8/app/views/users/show.html.erb

```
<% elsif user_owns_record? %>
<div class="modify user">
  <%= link_to "edit your profile", :action => "edit",
                                   :id      => @user.id %>
</div>
<% end %>
```

This makes it much clearer what the conditional is doing. We can extract this logic over to app/helpers/users_helper.rb, which is a more appropriate place for it.

`Ruby` `building_a_rails_app/user_group_8/app/helpers/users_helper.rb`

```ruby
def user_owns_record?
  logged_in? && @user.id == @current_user.id
end
```

Finally, when a member is editing their profile, we obviously don't want them to have the ability to change their own admin status. This would negate all the work we've done hiding the links from them. To start, we'll hide the radio button for this attribute in our form.

`Ruby` `building_a_rails_app/user_group_8/app/views/users/edit.html.erb`

```erb
<% if admin? %>
<div>
  Administrator:
  <%= form.radio_button :admin, true, :class => "radio" %>
  <label for="user_admin_true">Yes</label>
  <%= form.radio_button :admin, false, :class => "radio" %>
  <label for="user_admin_false">No</label>
</div>
<% end %>
```

Hiding this field should make it so that only Joe can grant administration access, but this approach is not as secure as it may seem.

9.3 Protecting from Mass Assignment

As much as it seems secure on the surface to just hide the admin field, if we take a look at the update action in UsersController, we blindly assign the hash of user attributes to our User model. The hash is based on the request parameters, so it could contain the admin attribute even if the current user isn't an admin.

Although bulk assignment is more convenient than assigning each value individually, it leaves us little control over the attributes assigned during this operation. Even if we hide the admin attribute, a savvy user could send a request using a web tool that allows them to craft requests manually and include admin=1 in the request. Our application doesn't know any better and would blindly obey. Security by obscurity is not a good approach here.

`Ruby` building_a_rails_app/user_group_7/app/controllers/users_controller.rb

```ruby
def update
  if @user.update_attributes(params[:user])
    flash[:notice] = 'User successfully updated.'
    redirect_to :action => "show", :id => @user.id
  else
    render :action => "edit"
  end
end
```

The start of the solution for this problem is the attr_protected method. We can use this to assign a list of attributes that we never want to be updated through bulk update operations such as new, create, and update_attributes. Let's open our User model to add this.

`Ruby` building_a_rails_app/user_group_8/app/models/user.rb

```ruby
class User < ActiveRecord::Base
  # unencrypted password
  attr_accessor :password

  # Protect method from mass-update
  attr_protected :admin
```

Adding this will force us to manually update the specific attributes of our model that are sensitive and should be given more attention. In this case, we'll add logic to our update action to update this particular attribute only if the current user is an administrator.

`Ruby` building_a_rails_app/user_group_8/app/controllers/users_controller.rb

```ruby
def update
  @user.admin = params[:user][:admin] if admin?
  if @user.update_attributes(params[:user])
    flash[:notice] = 'User successfully updated.'
    redirect_to :action => "show", :id => @user.id
  else
    render :action => "edit"
  end
end
```

Now if an admin attribute is posted, the application would assign the attribute only if the logged-in user is in fact an administrator. Now that we've secured all our actions, we bring Joe over to show him the application. He is excited that his administrative privileges actually mean something now. As he's browsing, he asks whether there is any way to speed things up in the application. We assure him that Rails performs optimizations to make the application run much quicker in production. We can, however, do some optimizations that will help it go even faster.

9.4 Caching the Pages

Caching is one of the most important things you can do with your Rails application to increase performance. Each time a visitor hits an action in our application, the application goes to work by evaluating the request, querying the database, creating objects, and rendering views back to the user. This is quite a bit of work to return the page each time and is a lot of wasted computation when you consider that the action is essentially producing the same result for each user.

If you've used a PHP caching library such as the Cache_Lite in PEAR, you know that caching saves us this wasted computation. When a page is evaluated, we store the result as a temporary file on the server. The next time the same page is requested, we'll return the cached page instead of recomputing everything.

Rails has three different forms of caching, which are from the fastest to slowest.

Page Caching
: Caches pages as static HTML files to bypass Rails completely on future requests.

Action Caching
: Caches rendered actions templates but still loads up Rails so that we can authenticate pages.

Fragment Caching
: Caches page fragments to speed up expensive areas of the page, while keeping other areas dynamic.

We'll briefly explore each technique to find out what is best for our application. Caching is disabled by default in the development environment. During development we want to immediately view changes in the browser without having to purge the cache files. We can, however, test caching in development by changing a configuration setting. To do this, update the configuration file at config/environments/development.rb to set config.action_controller.perform_caching to true. Remember that we need to restart the web server for this setting to take effect.

Page Caching

This is the fastest form of caching in Rails but is the most limiting. We can use this form of caching only on actions that

- are displayed identically to all users,

- do not require authentication, and

- do not display conditional content such as flash messages.

This type of caching is so fast because Rails uses page caching to save our page as static HTML files in our public/ directory. The next time the page is requested, we won't even need to load the Rails framework. The server will instead directly serve the static HTML file from the public/ directory. We specify that an action is page cached using the caches_page method. Let's take a look at an example.

Ruby | building_a_rails_app/ruby/caching/caches_page.rb

```ruby
class SportsController < ApplicationController
  caches_page :index

  def index
    @sports = Sport.find(:all)
  end
end
```

When the index action is requested the first time, Rails will generate the cached page and save it to public/sports/index.html. Any subsequent request to this page will read this HTML file instead of going through Rails. We can expire the cache when data changes by using the expire_page method. We'll usually want to expire the cache when we create or edit records displayed on the cached pages.

Ruby | building_a_rails_app/ruby/caching/expire_page.rb

```ruby
class SportsController < ApplicationController
  # ...
  def create
    @sport = Sport.new(params[:sport])

    if @sport.save
      expire_page :controller => "sports", :action => "index"
      redirect_to :action => "index"
    end
  end
  # ...
end
```

This type of caching is blazingly fast, and you should use it on any action that fits the criteria. Applications that make good use of page caching require less computational resources on average and can serve a greater number of requests. Unfortunately for us, page caching will not work with our application. We fail to meet the conditions noted earlier for every action in our application. We authenticate users in this application, and most areas of our application display differently depending on the user's authentication status.

Action Caching

Action caching is the next fastest caching strategy behind page caching and is similar in many respects. The biggest difference is that action caching will always load the Rails framework for the request. Because of this, we can use before filters for the request prior to the page cache being loaded.

Ruby | building_a_rails_app/ruby/caching/caches_action.rb

```ruby
class ArticlesController < ApplicationController
  before_filter :login_required
  caches_action :show

  def show
    @article = Article.find(params[:id])
  end
end
```

Unlike page caching, if we place our login_required filter before the caches_action call, the application will be able to process authentication for this action. Action caching saves cache files to a different location than page caching. When we visit the URL http://localhost:3000/articles/show/1 for this example, Rails will generate a cached file at tmp/cache/localhost.3000/articles/show/1.cache. Just like page caching, it will then load this cache file on request instead of proceeding to process the action.

Also like page caching, we'll use a method to expire the cache. Since the cache is stored in a different location, we need to use the expire_action method this time.

Ruby | building_a_rails_app/ruby/caching/expire_action.rb

```ruby
class ArticlesController < ApplicationController
  # ...
  def update
    @article = Article.find(params[:id])

    if @article.update_attributes(params[:article])
      expire_action :controller => "articles", :action => "show"
      redirect_to :action => "show"
    end
  end
  # ...
end
```

Although this type of caching is a little more flexible than page caching, we still have some problems that will prevent us from using this for our application. Our biggest problem is that on every page we display a login link to unauthenticated users and a logout link to users who are logged in. Both action caching and page caching require that the page is the same for all users regardless of their state.

Fragment Caching

The final and most flexible caching strategy is fragment caching. This type of caching is not as speedy as the other two, but it makes up for that in versatility. We can use fragment caching to cache individual sections or fragments of a page. This finally gives us a solution to get past the problem of having the page change depending on the context or status of the user.

We add fragment caching to our views by passing a block to the built-in cache helper method. The contents of the block are what we want to cache in the view. We'll add some fragment caching to the listing of members for our application. The trick is to cache as much of the page that we can without caching anything that is dependent on the status of the user. It is important that the flash message is not included in the cached area, since it will change depending on the request. However, all the rest of the data on our user page will remain the same until a user is created, edited, or deleted.

`Ruby`   building_a_rails_app/user_group_9/app/views/users/index.html.erb

```
<% cache do %>
<div class="user_list">
<ul>
  <% for user in @users %>
  <li class="<%= cycle('shade', '') %>">
    <%= link_to h(user.name), :action => "show", :id => user.id %>
    <%= image_for_admin_status(user) %> <br />
    <span class="email"><%= h(user.email) %></span>
  </li>
  <% end %>
</ul>
</div>
<% end %>
```

If we take a look at our log as we request this page, we can see when the cache is writing and reading correctly. In the initial request we'll see something like this.

```
Cached fragment: localhost:3000/users (0.00036)
```

On the next request, when the view reaches the cache block, it will instead read the cache file.

```
Fragment read: localhost:3000/users (0.00010)
```

In this example, it writes the cache to a file named tmp/cache/localhost: 3000/users.cache. We are not finished, though. While our cache is working, the controller is still querying for the list of users. The biggest benefit to caching is to eliminate these queries to the database. We really want to query for users only when the cache hasn't been built yet. We can check this using the read_fragment method in our controller methods.

Ruby | building_a_rails_app/user_group_9/app/controllers/users_controller.rb

```ruby
def index
  unless read_fragment({})
    @users = User.find(:all, :order => "name")
  end
end
```

Our final step is to expire the cache when our list of users changes. Whenever a record is successfully created, updated, or destroyed, we'll have to call the expire_fragment method in a similar way that was presented with page and action caching.

Ruby | building_a_rails_app/user_group_9/app/controllers/users_controller.rb

```ruby
def destroy
  @user.destroy
  expire_fragment :controller => "users", :action => "index"
  flash[:notice] = 'User successfully destroyed.'
  redirect_to :action => "index"
end
```

The first argument to the cache helper method is a name. This name will default to the URL options for the current page, but we can build this name any way we want to make it unique from other cache fragments on the same page. As an example, we'll add a fragment cache to our meetings index page.

We would like to cache the list of upcoming meetings, but it turns out to be a little trickier than we thought. The "add meeting" link should display only for administrators. What we need to do is store two different versions of the cache based on the user's administration status. We can add the :admin option to the name of the cache to differentiate between the two.

`Ruby` `building_a_rails_app/user_group_9/app/views/meetings/index.html.erb`

```ruby
<% cache(:admin => admin?) do %>
<div class="meeting_list">
  <h2>Upcoming Meetings</h2>
  <ul>
    <%= render :partial => @upcoming_meetings %>
    <%= no_meetings(@upcoming_meetings) %>
  </ul>
  <% if admin? %>
  <p class="add"><%= link_to "add meeting", new_meeting_path %></p>
  <% end %>
</div>
<% end %>
```

This will now store two different versions of the cache: one as meetings.cache and one as meetings.admin=true.cache. It will also read the correct cache back depending on the admin status of the user viewing the page. Once we've done this, we also need to update our controller to check for the cache before querying for meetings. Notice that when we read the fragment now, we make sure to specify the same name parameters so that we check for the right cache file.

`Ruby` `building_a_rails_app/user_group_9/app/controllers/meetings_controller.rb`

```ruby
unless read_fragment(:admin => admin?)
  @upcoming_meetings = Meeting.upcoming_meetings
end
```

Finally, we will want to expire both these cache files when a meeting is created, updated, or deleted. This starts to present a problem since manually expiring two different cache files is a bit of a pain. The expire_fragment method will handle this for us by accepting a regular expression pattern for the cache file paths that we want to expire. In this case, we want to expire all of the meeting cache.

`Ruby` `building_a_rails_app/user_group_9/app/controllers/meetings_controller.rb`

```ruby
def destroy
  @meeting.destroy
  expire_fragment(/\/meetings./)
  flash[:notice] = 'Meeting successfully destroyed.'
  redirect_to :action => "index"
end
```

There are many other places that could be fragment cached in our application, but this gives us a good start to caching views. The end goal is to reduce the view parsing and number of database queries as much as possible.

232 PREPARING TO LAUNCH

A good strategy for this is to simply turn on caching in development and watch the log to find stray queries that could be cached.

9.5 Chapter Review

Congratulations! We've learned a lot about Rails by building a full application. Joe is really grateful for our help with the application and is excited to start building a community around Rails. After the experience of building this application, you're well on the way to building your own applications. You should also have some interesting ideas to bring back to your PHP applications.

Just for fun, let's take a look at some statistics on what we've just done. Rails includes a Rake task that will show us exactly how much code we've written for this application.

```
user_group> rake stats
(in /Users/derek/work/user_group)
+------------------+-------+------+---------+---------+-----+------+
| Name             | Lines | LOC  | Classes | Methods | M/C | LOC/M |
+------------------+-------+------+---------+---------+-----+------+
| Controllers      |  252  | 195  |    6    |   35    |  5  |   3  |
| Helpers          |   29  |  28  |    0    |    4    |  0  |   5  |
| Models           |   92  |  63  |    3    |    9    |  3  |   5  |
| Libraries        |    0  |   0  |    0    |    0    |  0  |   0  |
| Integration tests|    0  |   0  |    0    |    0    |  0  |   0  |
| Functional tests |   90  |  65  |   10    |   15    |  1  |   2  |
| Unit tests       |  222  | 159  |    3    |   24    |  8  |   4  |
+------------------+-------+------+---------+---------+-----+------+
| Total            |  685  | 510  |   22    |   87    |  3  |   3  |
+------------------+-------+------+---------+---------+-----+------+
  Code LOC: 286    Test LOC: 224    Code to Test Ratio: 1:0.8
```

Your stats will be different depending on the tests you wrote, of course, and the additional exercises you may have done. It's always neat to see how little code goes into building an application like this. This is also a great place to find out whether your code-to-test ratio is up to snuff.

9.6 Exercises

If you want to play around more with this application, there are plenty more places it can be taken:

- Try caching more of the application's pages with fragment caching. Try using more than one fragment cache block in a single view by naming the fragments something different.

- Try adding a link to download a PDF of each presentation's slides. You can place your PDF documents in a subdirectory of public/ named documents/.

- Allow members to upload a picture for their profile. If you have questions about figuring out file uploads, be sure to check out the reference in Section 13.3, *$_FILES*, on page 369.

- Add a page to view group photographs pulled down from the Flickr website using Flickr.rb.[1] This can be installed as a RubyGem, which is discussed in Section 12.6, *External Libraries and Packages*, on page 352.

---

1. http://redgreenblu.com/flickr/

Chapter 10

Deploying the Application

Now that we've completed our application, the next step is to make it live for the world to see. In PHP, we rarely even talk about deployment because it is often dead simple. PHP is easily served using Apache with mod_php, and hosting is ubiquitous. We know that PHP can be served on cheap shared hosting plans or more expensive virtual private servers and dedicated hosting.

There are many more choices to be made when deploying a Rails application. All of the choices could, and do, fill an entire book worth of material. For detailed instructions on deploying Rails applications from a variety of approaches, you may want to check out *Deploying Rails Applications* [ZT08] by Ezra Zygmuntowicz.

There was a time long ago when most people were running PHP as a CGI. Running PHP back then was much slower and more complicated than it is now. Due to these issues, years of effort were spent perfecting PHP and its integration with various web servers. Today, deploying PHP applications is perhaps easier than any other platform as a result.

Rails is a relatively new technology and has room for growth when it comes to deployment. It has, however, been making great strides in the past couple years. There are quite a few smart developers who are working hard on simplifying deployment.

A good example of this is the Mongrel server. Although most early Rails deployment solutions were based on a faster variation of the common gateway interface (FCGI), Mongrel is now the preferred way of serving Ruby code.

Another emerging project that looks promising for deployment is JRuby, which is a Ruby interpreter written in Java.[1] This promises to allow Rails applications to be managed by Java application servers.

In this chapter, we'll provide a basic overview of the issues that differentiate Rails from PHP in a typical deployment scenario. We'll start by discussing one of the most difficult decisions when deploying a Rails application—where to host it.

10.1 Choosing a Host

We have a few choices when it comes to the type of hosting that we'll use to deploy our application. The biggest choice is whether we want a shared host or whether we need to pay a little more to have full access of a virtual private server or a dedicated server.

From a PHP perspective, Rails' biggest strength is its maintainability and development speed. You'll have to weigh your choice of using PHP or Rails depending on the application. If you want just a cheap shared host to run a simple blog, Rails may not be the best solution. However, when you are actively developing an application that you are responsible for maintaining, you may find that it is worth using Rails at the expense of a virtual private server.

The bottleneck on hosting Rails applications tends to be memory. An important architectural aspect of PHP is that it completely tears down your application's environment at the end of every request. PHP applications can and do create large demands for memory, but the demands on the server are only temporary while the application is under load. This is one of the reasons that many PHP applications can coexist successfully on a shared host as long as they are not heavily loaded.

Rails applications running under Mongrel are persistent application processes. Unlike PHP, the memory consumed by a Rails application is not released back to the system if there are no requests. Rails applications can require quite a bit of dedicated memory. When you put MySQL into the mix, you are often looking at a baseline of 128MB–192MB to get a single application running. You will probably grow quickly to more than this depending on your traffic. With this in mind, you can see why you can grow out of a shared hosting plan fairly quickly.

---

1. http://jruby.codehaus.org/

Hosting in a Shared Environment

Some developers have had success with Rails applications in a shared environment, but it is not really recommended for anything that cannot be heavily cached.

If you do choose to go the shared hosting route, you'll want to find a host that supports Secure Shell (SSH) access. SSH will be crucial if you want to set up any automated deployment system for your application. You'll also want to get a host that supports Mongrel if at all possible. It is faster and more reliable than FCGI-based solutions and is one of our best weapons for Rails deployment. FCGI-based solutions can leak memory, causing sysadmins to kill your application if it encroaches on the resources of everyone else on the box.

After copying your code to the production server, you'll create your production database using the options provided by your host. Each host does this a little differently, so you'll need to examine the control panel to figure out how your particular host implements this. You'll next need to update the production section of your config/database.yml to work with your production database credentials.

All applications will be served with the public/ directory of your application as the document root. You'll need to set the document root to the /path/to/application/public directory through your host's control panel.

Remember that shared hosting is tough but possible for Rails applications. Support is usually not good on some of these really inexpensive hosting plans, and getting your Rails application working could take some patience. If your host advertises that it supports Rails applications, then it should have some online documentation on getting everything running (and possibly a support forum where you can get help from other Rails developers). These are some things you may look for as you search for a host. Pay close attention to feedback you are hearing from other developers about the service provided. The hosting landscape changes quickly, and a recommendation from another developer is one of the best ways to find a reliable host.

Hosting on a Virtual Private Server or Dedicated Server

There is a good chance you'll grow out of shared hosting rather quickly. A virtual private server (VPS) is the preferred hosting option for most Rails developers. A VPS is a slice of a dedicated server but operates in an isolated environment.

This means you will receive a chunk of resources and will not have to share this with other developers. Each VPS has its own filesystem, so no one else has access to your files. Since you are on a dedicated slice with your own resources, you'll also not have to worry about a sysadmin killing off processes to protect other customers.

Hosting on a VPS is a little more expensive than shared hosting, but you get a lot more. You'll have root access to your box and will have much more freedom with what you can install and configure. Most VPS solutions make it easy to upgrade your hosting plan with a mere reboot. This means you can easily upgrade your resources as your application's demands grow.

You may need a dedicated server depending on the needs of your application. Dedicated servers are more expensive than a VPS but will essentially work in the same way. If you think you'll need a dedicated server, you may want to start out with a VPS and work your way up depending on the demands of your application.

The one caveat to having a VPS or dedicated server is that you will be doing much more sysadmin work. Everyone values their time and wants an easy solution. We've certainly been spoiled in PHP, where we can just drop an application on a shared host and forget about it. We hope one day Rails will be the same.

Since a VPS is the preferred choice for deploying Rails applications, the rest of this chapter will show how to get set up and deployed in this type of environment. Let's start by taking a look at some of the differences Rails makes when it runs in a production environment.

10.2 The Production Environment

We learned a little bit about Rails environments in Section 6.2, *Using Rails Environments*, on page 154. We kind of glossed over the production environment at the time, but this is where this environment becomes important. We'll be running our applications in the production environment when we deploy. When our application runs in this environment, it will perform a series of changes to make the code run faster and more efficiently.

In production, Rails stores your Ruby classes in memory. This prevents your application from performing the slow process of reloading the Ruby code on every request. This will make your application run quite a bit faster, but remember that any changes to the code will require a server restart to take effect.

Rails caches the database structure so that it doesn't need to examine the database to build our ActiveRecord model attributes. You might also notice that the logging level in production is more minimal than that in the development and test environments. Remember that to view the log, you will now want to view the log/production.log file.

Exceptions are no longer displayed to the client in production. We obviously want to see error information while we are developing the application but would rather not have end users see this. In PHP, it is considered a best practice to set the display_errors directive to 0 on a production application. Although this merely hides errors from the end user in a PHP application, Rails will actually stop execution of code and redirect to the public/500.html file in your application. You might want to customize this page to fit in with the rest of your application's design. Exceptions will be logged, but it is often tedious to review logs for errors. A better approach is to install the Exception Notification plug-in.[2] This plug-in will email exceptions to us so we can act quickly when errors occur. To view more information on installing plug-ins in Rails, see Section 13.13, *Rails Plug-Ins*, on page 392.

The different configuration settings that Rails uses for our application in production are set in config/environments/production.rb. You can view and change these settings, and later in this chapter we'll discuss some strategies for optimization. Let's not get ahead of ourselves, though. We need to get our application up and running before we start making additional optimizations that might not be warranted. Before we deploy, we'll need to make some preparations to our application.

10.3 Preparing Our Application

Preparing our application involves the process of reviewing security concerns, freezing our gems, and dumping our schema. We discussed security in the process of creating our application, but this is a good time to review.

---

2.   http://svn.rubyonrails.org/rails/plugins/exception_notification

Reviewing Security

Rails makes it easy to create secure applications, but we must be mindful of a few things each time we develop an application. Most of these items are the same issues we would be concerned about in a PHP application.

There are a few things that Rails gives us for free. The way our application's files are organized helps prevent our Ruby code from being executable or downloadable through the browser. Rails also protects against cross-site request forgery when we use the built-in Rails form helpers to create our web forms.

Every time we display variable output in our views, we should escape output. In our application, we did this by escaping entities with the h method. In PHP, we would have done this using the htmlentities function.

Anytime we use a variable in a SQL fragment, we should filter the input data to prevent SQL injection. Our application didn't perform any queries that needed variable interpolation, but it is likely that future applications will. This is the same concept as using mysql_real_escape_string in PHP to filter input given to the database. More information and examples of doing this in Rails can be found in Section 13.8, *Filter Input*, on page 378.

All sensitive data should be protected from bulk-assignment operations. In our application, we did this using the attr_protected method on our user's admin attribute. We should also always secure actions that we don't want the public to have access to. Our application uses a before_filter to perform authentication on administrative actions.

This is a brief overview of some best Rails security practices, and many of these should not be new to you as a web developer. You can find more information on best security practices in Section 13.8, *Security*, on page 377. Now that we've double-checked that our application is secure, we need to make sure our code environment is stable for our application.

Freezing Gems

When we installed Rails using the gem command, it was installed to a systemwide directory on our computer. This is a directory such as /usr/local/lib/ruby/gems/1.8/gems/, where the code is shared between all the Ruby applications on our machine. This is similar to the way PEAR manages libraries in PHP. When we deploy our application, it is quite possible that server will need to have a different version of Rails than we used on our development machine. It is also possible that the gem version of Rails on the server could change with unintended consequences on our application.

An important part of preparing our application for deployment is to include a local copy of Rails within the application. This is called *freezing* Rails. Freezing Rails will unpack the entire Rails source code into the vendor/rails directory of our application. When the Rails source code is present in this directory, our application will use this version of Rails instead of the systemwide Rails gem code. We'll initiate this process using a Rake task. Navigate to the root directory of your application, and run the following.

```
user_group> rake rails:freeze:gems
(in /Users/derek/work/user_group)
Freezing to the gems for Rails 2.0.2
Unpacked gem: ...
```

Doing this removes some surprises that we might encounter when we deploy our application. Now that our application is ready, it's time to look at the database.

Dumping the Schema

When we deploy our application to production, we'll need to rebuild the database in our production environment. Although we could do this by running all of our migrations from scratch, the preferred way of rebuilding the database from scratch in Rails is to dump the entire schema to a file named db/schema.rb.

Rails provides a Rake task to do just this. The db:schema:dump task creates a single file that describes our entire database structure in Ruby.

```
current> rake db:schema:dump
(in /Users/derek/work/user_group)
```

If you look at the db/schema.rb file this task generated, you'll see that this uses Ruby just like our migration files. We'll use this file later to build our database on our production server.

10.4 Preparing Our Deployment Server

We're going to assume you're deploying the application on a Unix-like server. Deploying on the Windows operating system is certainly possible but is beyond the scope of this book.

In this section we'll go over the steps involved in deploying an application. The basic checklist is as follows.

1. Copy application source code to the server.
2. Install the necessary tools on the server.
3. Set the server environment.
4. Launch the application.

You have no doubt copied source code to a server when deploying PHP applications, and you probably have a favorite tool for doing this already. Some developers favor using a desktop application that supports the SSH File Transfer Protocol (SFTP), while others use Subversion. Many Rails developers like to use a deployment tool called Capistrano.[3] With Capistrano, we can deploy to multiple servers at once and easily roll back to a previous version if something goes wrong. Capistrano is written in Ruby but is not exclusive to Rails. Developers have successfully used it to deploy PHP applications as well.

Installing Tools on Your Server

You will find that deploying a Rails application takes a little more knowledge about sysadmin than you may be used to in PHP. Many Rails developers set up their own deployment environments on a virtual private server and customize the environment to meet the needs of their application. Some hosting companies that support Rails provide a Rails stack that comes preinstalled with most of the tools needed to deploy your application. If you are not comfortable with sysadmin tasks, we recommend starting with something like this if possible. This way, you can get your feet wet without having to compile and install everything yourself. There are a few tools that we need when serving a Rails application.

Ruby

>We'll need Ruby installed on your server. We highly recommend at least version 1.8.6 to be compatible with the Mongrel Cluster gem that we'll demonstrate. Installation instructions for Ruby can be found on the Ruby website.[4]

RubyGems

>We'll use the RubyGems packaging system to install both Rails and Mongrel on our server. We'll want to install at least version

---

3. http://www.capify.org/
4. http://www.ruby-lang.org/en/downloads/

1.0.1 of RubyGems. Instructions for installation can be found on the RubyGems website.[5]

Rails

We'll use RubyGems to install Rails in the same method discussed in Section 1.5, *Installing Ruby and Rails*, on page 9. We'll want to install at least version 2.0.2.

Mongrel

We'll use RubyGems to install Mongrel. Mongrel is a lightweight web server written by Zed Shaw.[6] This server is written specifically to serve Ruby applications and came out of a need for a good alternative to FCGI-based hosting solutions. We need to install the Daemons, Mongrel, and Mongrel Cluster gems. We should install the latest stable version of Mongrel, which at the time of this writing is version 1.1.1.

```
work> sudo gem install daemons mongrel mongrel_cluster
Successfully installed daemons-1.0.9
Building native extensions.  This could take a while...
Successfully installed mongrel-1.1.1
Successfully installed mongrel_cluster-1.0.5
3 gems installed
...
```

Apache

To get a performance boost, we can use Apache to serve static content such as our images, JavaScript, and CSS. Apache is much better suited for this than Mongrel. Apache also gives us the mod_deflate and mod_proxy_balancer modules, which we can use for further performance tuning. We'll need Apache 2.2 for this configuration. Apache is by far the most popular server for PHP applications, and there is a good chance you already have Apache installed on your host. If not, you can use your favorite package manager to install it, or you can compile from source.[7] Your Apache installation will require the following modules.

- mod_proxy, mod_proxy-html, and mod_proxy_balancer
- mod_rewrite
- mod_deflate
- mod_headers

5. http://www.rubygems.org/read/chapter/3
6. http://mongrel.rubyforge.org/
7. http://httpd.apache.org/download.cgi

There is a mod_ruby module that embeds the Ruby interpreter into the Apache web server. Using this extension is discouraged for serving Rails applications since multiple Rails applications in the same Apache environment will share framework classes. This makes it unsafe to run more than one Rails application on the server at a time.

MySQL

Our last component is the database, and we recommend MySQL version 5.0. As a PHP developer, you may be already familiar with installing MySQL on a server. Installation varies by platforms, so please reference the instructions on the MySQL website as needed.[8]

Once you've installed all these software packages, you're much closer to getting the application up and running. Our next step is to set up our Rails environment.

Setting the Environment

Before we start up anything on production, we need to make sure the database is set up correctly. Let's take a look at the production section of config/database.yml.

```
building_a_rails_app/user_group_8/config/database.yml
production:
  adapter: mysql
  encoding: utf8
  database: user_group_production
  username: root
  password:
  socket: /tmp/mysql.sock
```

If you choose to put your application on shared hosting, you might need to change this to a database name provided by your host. The biggest thing to pay attention to here is you'll need to change the username and password used to connect to your production database. You should always have proper authentication in place in your production environment.

The generated database.yml file assumes you're running your database and application on the same host and does not include a specification for the host or port. We'll need to add the host option if the MySQL server

---

8. http://dev.mysql.com/doc/refman/5.0/en/installing.html

is not running on the same server as the application. We also may need to specify the port option if the MySQL server is configured differently than the default 3306.

Rails will create the correct socket for whatever machine we initially run the rails command on, but it is common to deploy on a different platform than we develop on. For example, OS X typically uses /tmp/mysql.sock, but deployment on a Ubuntu server will need to update this to /var/run/mysqld/mysqld.sock. Once we have this set up, we can use a Rake task to create our database.

```
current> rake db:create RAILS_ENV=production
(in /var/www/tucsonrails.org/current)
```

Notice that we added an argument when we executed this task to set our environment. Adding RAILS_ENV=production will execute any Rake task in the production environment instead of the default development environment. The next step is to build our production database. Earlier when preparing our application, we dumped our database schema using the db:schema:dump task. We'll now use the db:schema:load task to load our entire structure into the production environment.

```
current> rake db:schema:load RAILS_ENV=production
(in /var/www/tucsonrails.org/current)
```

We can also launch the console using production environment. This is slightly different from the option we use with Rake tasks.

```
current> ruby script/console production
Loading production environment
>>
```

Remembering to add the environment each time is a pain. A better strategy is to simply set our application to be in production mode at all times when we're on our production machine. This way we'll never accidentally migrate the development database or deploy the site in development mode. We can do this in a few different ways.

The best option is to set an environment variable for your user on the production machine. This is typically done by editing your user's .bash_profile or equivalent file to add the following snippet.

```
export RAILS_ENV="production"
```

Rails will use this variable to assign the environment for our application as it starts. An alternative option is to edit your application's config/environment.rb file to use the production environment.

> Ruby   building_a_rails_app/user_group_9/config/environment.rb

```ruby
ENV['RAILS_ENV'] ||= 'production'
```

Here we've simply uncommented the line that assigns our application's environment. However, this is not an ideal solution since it requires us to change the source code of our application.

Once we have our application, database, and environment ready to go, all we have left is to launch the application.

10.5 Launching the Application

The server configuration we'll use to deploy uses both Apache and Mongrel. The most basic usage is to deploy a single Mongrel server instance. Starting up Mongrel to serve your application is simple and is done with the mongrel_rails command. Switch to the root directory of your application, and run the following.

```
current> mongrel_rails start -d -p 8000 -e production
```

This starts Mongrel as a daemon listening on port 8000. The -e production option starts our application using the production environment. With Mongrel running, we should now be able to access the site on port 8000. If we have a problem getting Mongrel started, we can troubleshoot the server by viewing the mongrel log file located at log/mongrel.log.

Although Mongrel is pretty quick, mixing Apache in will give us more options for speeding things up. Apache 2 makes it easy to organize our configuration files into separate .conf files. We typically put them in a directory within the main Apache install and include them from our main httpd.conf file using Include.

> deploying_the_application/apache_include.txt

```
# Load config files from the config directory "conf.d".
Include conf.d/*.conf
```

The simplest configuration is to forward all requests to Apache over to Mongrel on port 8000. We can do this by adding a simple virtual host entry to Apache.

We'll be referring to this application as tucsonrails.org, but you'll obviously replace this with your own application's name when the time comes.

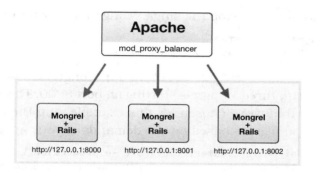

Figure 10.1: BALANCING REQUESTS

deploying_the_application/single/tucsonrails.org.conf

```
<VirtualHost *:80>
  ServerName tucsonrails.org

  ProxyPass / http://tucsonrails.org:8000/
  ProxyPassReverse / http://tucsonrails.org:8000
  ProxyPreserveHost on
</VirtualHost>
```

current> **sudo apachectl restart**

This gets us up and running, but there is a chance you'll need to run additional Mongrel servers for your application as it grows. Rails code is not thread safe, and high-traffic websites usually need more concurrency than is allowed by a single Mongrel. Since Mongrel uses one thread per request, more traffic means we need to increase the number of Mongrel servers that respond to our requests.

A great way to do this is using Apache's mod_proxy_balancer module as a software load balancer. With this load balancer, we can start up multiple Mongrel instances to handle requests. We'll then use Apache to evenly distribute the requests between Mongrels, as shown in Figure 10.1. Apache can also help us out by serving static content such as images, CSS, and JavaScript.

We know how to start up a single Mongrel, and we can manually start up multiple Mongrels by simply specifying different port numbers for each server. This is somewhat of a pain, and we thankfully have a better way of doing this using the Mongrel Cluster gem.

Before we do this, let's stop the single Mongrel server that we started.

```
current> mongrel_rails stop
Sending TERM to Mongrel at PID 11240...Done.
```

Next we'll use cluster::configure to set up our Mongrel cluster. We'll configure this to run three Mongrels starting on port 8000. Three is an arbitrary number that we've chosen for this example, and the real number of Mongrels you need is based on the demands of your application.

```
current> mongrel_rails cluster::configure -e production \
  -p 8000 -a 127.0.0.1 -N 3 -c /var/www/tucsonrails.org/current
Writing configuration file to config/mongrel_cluster.yml.
```

As you can see, this operation spits out a configuration file that it will use to start and stop the Mongrels. With this configuration, we can start all of our Mongrels using cluster::start.

```
current> mongrel_rails cluster::start
starting port 8000
starting port 8001
starting port 8002
```

Now that we're using multiple Mongrels, Apache's proxy balancer needs a special configuration file to know where requests should be passed. We'll do this by adding a proxy_cluster.conf file in our Apache configuration directory. This configuration is simply a list of where the balancer will send requests.

deploying_the_application/cluster/tucsonrails.org.proxy_cluster.conf

```
<Proxy balancer://mongrel_cluster>
  BalancerMember http://127.0.0.1:8000
  BalancerMember http://127.0.0.1:8001
  BalancerMember http://127.0.0.1:8002
</Proxy>
```

We'll also to update to a more robust virtual host configuration to use the balancer and take advantage of Apache to serve our static content.

deploying_the_application/cluster/tucsonrails.org.conf

```
<VirtualHost *:80>
  ServerName tucsonrails.org

  DocumentRoot /var/www/tucsonrails.org/public

  <Directory "/var/www/tucsonrails.org/public">
    Options FollowSymLinks
    AllowOverride None
    Order allow,deny
    Allow from all
  </Directory>
```

```
RewriteEngine On

# Rewrite index to check for static
RewriteRule ^/$ /index.html [QSA]

# Rewrite to check for Rails cached page
RewriteRule ^([^.]+)$ $1.html [QSA]

# Redirect all non-static requests to cluster
RewriteCond %{DOCUMENT_ROOT}/%{REQUEST_FILENAME} !-f
RewriteRule ^/(.*)$ balancer://mongrel_cluster%{REQUEST_URI} [P,QSA,L]

ErrorLog logs/tucsonrails.org_errors_log
CustomLog logs/tucsonrails.org_log combined
</VirtualHost>
```

With these in place, we can restart Apache to see our application deployed in all its Mongrel clustered glory. The next step is to check out how our application performs.

Learning proper benchmarking tools is essential in locating bottlenecks in our application. The Railsbench library is a good place to start for measuring application performance. This library is available for free on the RubyForge site.[9] Geoffrey Grosenbach and Zed Shaw (the author of Mongrel) have also created a useful screencast that details using the httperf command-line tool, along with the statistics you should be familiar with to compare benchmarks. This screencast is for sale on the Peepcode website.[10]

When we start finding slow areas of our application, it's time to make some performance enhancements to make things snappier.

10.6 Enhancing Performance

There are many ways to increase the performance of our Rails application. It is always good to remember Hoare's Dictum, which states that "premature optimization is the root of all evil." In this section, we won't cover micro-enhancements such as using single vs. double quotes. We'll instead focus on some broader performance enhancements that make some differences in the real or perceived responsiveness of our application.

One performance tip that we mentioned Section 8.6, *Reducing Queries*, on page 211, is eager loading. It is a useful practice to view our

---

9. http://railsbench.rubyforge.org/
10. http://peepcode.com/products/benchmarking-with-httperf

development.log as we sweep through our application a final time before deployment. By paying attention to the number of queries run on each page, there is a good chance that we may find additional opportunities to eager load data.

We also discussed caching earlier in Section 9.4, *Caching the Pages*, on page 226, and it is good to remember how important a caching strategy is. The first step to increasing performance is to aggressively cache your pages. Caching helps both reduce the database queries that your application performs and reduces the processing that Rails has to do when evaluating Ruby within views.

Compress Content

One of the easiest ways to increase performance with minimal effort is to send our content compressed. Sending content using a gzip or deflate compression will save bandwidth and speed up content delivery to our users.

When we use Apache, the easiest solution is to use the mod_deflate module. We can update Apache configuration to deflate the response by content type. Add this snippet to your application's VirtualHost entry.

`deploying_the_application/deflate.txt`

```
# Deflate static data
AddOutputFilterByType DEFLATE text/html
AddOutputFilterByType DEFLATE text/plain
AddOutputFilterByType DEFLATE text/xml
AddOutputFilterByType DEFLATE text/css
AddOutputFilterByType DEFLATE application/x-javascript
AddOutputFilterByType DEFLATE application/xml
AddOutputFilterByType DEFLATE application/xhtml+xml

BrowserMatch ^Mozilla/4 gzip-only-text/html
BrowserMatch ^Mozilla/4.0[678] no-gzip
BrowserMatch \bMSIE !no-gzip !gzip-only-text/html
```

Another alternative is to install the Output Compression plug-in.[11] In PHP there are a few popular solutions for gzipping content by using the gzcompress or gzdeflate function along with output buffering. This plug-in uses a similar approach by using Ruby to send the output compressed. This is better than no compression but does not compress JavaScript and CSS files like the Apache solution.

---

11. http://craz8.com/svn/trunk/plugins/output_compression/

Reduce HTTP Requests

In modern web applications, we usually place our JavaScript and CSS in externally referenced files. We also tend to further split these into separate files for organizational purposes. This is especially true if you are including external JavaScript libraries. When we are serving many CSS and JavaScript files, each file results in another HTTP request to the server, causing a noticeable lag for the user. We can solve much of this by combining all external JavaScript and CSS to a single file for each.

When we included the style sheet for our application, we used the stylesheet_link_tag helper. In our case, we had only a single external CSS file and linked to it explicitly by name as "screen." To play devil's advocate, let's say that we now want to include an additional style sheet named more_styles.css. Adding this file would require our application to serve up two style sheets for each request. We could explicitly add this new style sheet in the stylesheet_link_tag tag, but Rails gives us a better option. When we pass :all as the first parameter to this helper, Rails will include every file within the public/stylesheets/ directory. We can then use the :cache => true option for Rails to combine these two style sheets into a single file named public/stylesheets/all.css.

`Ruby` building_a_rails_app/user_group_9/app/views/layouts/application.html.erb

```
<%= stylesheet_link_tag "screen", "more_stles",
                        :cache => "all" %>
```

By default, Rails will combine and cache these files only when in the production environment. This helps keeps the code easy to debug in development but zippy when we're live. We set this option in our respective environment configuration files with the config.action_controller. perform_caching option. We can see that in development this is set to false.

`Ruby` building_a_rails_app/user_group_9/config/environments/development.rb

```
config.action_controller.perform_caching = false
```

We probably need this asset packaging feature more for our JavaScript files than CSS. There are a lot of useful JavaScript libraries, and even Rails includes the Prototype and Scriptaculous libraries with every application. The downside is that each time we add another JavaScript file, we get another HTTP request. We can use this same cache technique with the built-in javascript_include_tag helper.

Ruby | building_a_rails_app/user_group_9/app/views/layouts/application.html.erb

```
<%= javascript_include_tag "prototype", "application",
                          :cache => "all" %>
```

This works the same way as stylesheet_link_tag and includes every Java-Script file within the public/javascripts/ directory. When combined, it produces a public/javascripts/all.js file.

Serving Assets

The previous technique works wonderfully for reducing the number of requests for CSS and JavaScript files, but we can do even better. Although we can't reduce the number of requests further, we can speed up the process of pulling down resources from the server.

Most popular browsers limit the number of simultaneous connections that we can open to a specific host. Our application is measurably slower when we use lots of external resources, since they are not being pulled down concurrently. This can be a real drag when we serving up a lot of images, CSS, and JavaScript files. We can use asset hosting in Rails to increase the number of hosts from which we are pulling these resources. We do this by adding a simple configuration option to our application's config/environments/production.rb file.

Ruby | building_a_rails_app/user_group_9/config/environments/production.rb

```
config.action_controller.asset_host = "http://assets%d.tucsonrails.org"
```

Rails will use this configuration to create four different asset hosts for us at asset0.tucsonrails.org, asset1.tucsonrails.org, asset2.tucsonrails.org, and asset3.tucsonrails.org. When we deploy our application to production, Rails will alternate between these different domains when serving up the images, CSS, and JavaScript files. The good news is that browsers will download our resources quicker by treating each of these as a different host.

The last step is to add DNS aliases for each of these so that they point to your original domain. If your server slows down from a traffic spike, you can easily change the asset host to serve your images from a different location. Some developers use this to host their application's static resources on Amazon's S3 Service.[12] This can help alleviate load on the application server in a crunch.

---

12. http://www.amazon.com/gp/browse.html?node=16427261

There is a certain point where it is more economically beneficial to scale out the website than it is to continue spending time doing small performance enhancements. Although performance is the speed at which our system responds to a given request, scalability is our system's capacity to serve a growing number of concurrent requests gracefully.

10.7 Scaling Your Application

Despite Rails applications using persistent application processes in the most common deployment configurations, most other aspects of Rails embrace the same shared nothing philosophy as PHP. Like PHP, Rails tends to always push responsibilities away from itself and onto other parts of the system. This is usually the database.

Generally, well-written Rails applications will scale horizontally in the same way that their PHP counterparts do. If you have ever scaled a PHP application to handle a high volume of requests, you'll find that scaling a Rails application will present the same challenges. Often, the same solutions will apply as well.

Scaling horizontally is essentially distributing our traffic to multiple machines. Scaling MySQL will work the same as we've done with PHP, and one of the first things we'll do when scaling out is to put the database on a dedicated machine. Connecting to multiple databases at once can be done with the help of the Magic Multi-Connections plug-in by Nic Williams.[13]

Scaling out application servers should be fairly easy if you've configured your Apache server to use the proxy balancer. The great thing about our load balancer is that we can easily configure it to work across multiple machines. The proxy cluster configuration file we used pointed to three Mongrels. We can add many more Mongrels to this, and any of these can be spread across multiple servers.

`deploying_the_application/scale_cluster/tucsonrails.org.proxy_cluster.conf`

```
<Proxy balancer://mongrel_cluster>
  # cluster 1
  BalancerMember http://192.168.0.1:8000
  BalancerMember http://192.168.0.1:8001
  BalancerMember http://192.168.0.1:8002
```

---

13. http://magicmodels.rubyforge.org/magic_multi_connections/

```
# cluster 2
BalancerMember http://192.168.0.2:8000
BalancerMember http://192.168.0.2:8001
BalancerMember http://192.168.0.2:8002

# cluster 3
BalancerMember http://192.168.0.3:8000
BalancerMember http://192.168.0.3:8001
BalancerMember http://192.168.0.3:8002
</Proxy>
```

This cluster configuration is spread over nine Mongrels on three different machines, as shown in Figure 10.2, on the next page. One decision we must be careful of when scaling out across many servers like this is the type of session storage that we choose to use. We must make sure the session data is not saved to a specific box where it won't be available to a subsequent request on a different server. The default cookie-based session storage works fine for scaling this way, as does ActiveRecord storage discussed in Section 13.6, *Sessions*, on page 374.

Manual deployment across multiple servers is not a good idea. We mentioned Capistrano as a deployment tool earlier, and this is where it really shines. Capistrano makes deployment across multiple servers as easy as typing cap deploy.

10.8 Chapter Review

We've learned a basic overview of how to get our application out into the wild. Now all we need to do is start spreading the word so that we can get some traffic!

Let's review the highlights of what we've learned in this chapter:

- We figured out how to prepare our application for the deployment phase. We reviewed security concerns and learned how Rails behaves differently when in production mode.
- We covered the fundamentals of deploying a Rails application to a load-balanced Mongrel cluster under Apache.
- We learned strategies for improving performance in our application and how to load balance the application to scale it out.

To learn more and keep track of all of the current deployment strategies, you might want to join the Rails deployment mailing list.[14] If you're

---

14. http://groups.google.com/group/rubyonrails-deployment/topics?start=270\&sa=N

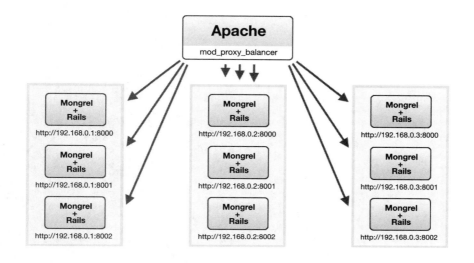

Figure 10.2: SCALING TO MULTIPLE SERVERS

partial to Mongrel (and aren't we all?), you might want to keep up-to-date on the Mongrel mailing list.[15]

10.9 Exercises

Here are some exercises for you to try:

- View the logs for our application to see whether there is anywhere else you might add eager loading to reduce the load on the database.
- Install and set up the Exception Notification plug-in to receive email notifications of errors. Go ahead and raise an exception on your production application to see whether it is working.
- Try to configure your application to run on five Mongrel instances instead of three.
- Deploy a Rails application from your development platform to a production server. You get extra points if the two platforms run different operating systems.

---

15. http://rubyforge.org/mailman/listinfo/mongrel-users

Part III

PHP to Ruby at a Glance

## Chapter 11

PHP to Ruby Basics Reference

The reference part of this book is meant to serve as a guide when you need to translate your PHP skills to what might be the equivalent code in Ruby or Rails. Although most PHP translates fairly directly to Ruby, web-specific programming is more appropriate to show in the context of the Rails framework. These examples are covered in Chapter 13, *PHP to Rails Reference*, on page 367. In some examples, a more direct translation is available, but we avoid it because it violates a higher concept or philosophy of Ruby.

In this chapter, we'll cover the difference and similarities between basic PHP and Ruby data and operations. You'll notice that many of the basic ideas between the languages are shared.

11.1 Basic Syntax

We'll start with the fundamentals of writing code in any language. This will give us a good start for testing the rest of the examples in this chapter.

Output a String

One of the most common operations you'll perform in any language is sending output to the screen or terminal. Ruby's equivalent to PHP's print construct is a method by the same name. Ruby's print method will automatically convert nonstring objects to their equivalent string by implicitly using their to_s method. Ruby also provides the puts method, which will add a trailing newline to the string.

> PHP `php_to_ruby_language/php/basic_syntax/output_string.php`

```php
print "Hello World";
print 1;
print "This string will output with a trailing newline\n";
```

> Ruby `php_to_ruby_language/ruby/basic_syntax/output_string.rb`

```ruby
print "Hello World"
print 1
puts "This string will output with a trailing newline"
```

Instruction Separation

Like many languages such as C and Java, PHP requires that instructions are terminated by semicolons. In most PHP programs, there is one instruction per line, and the line ends with a semicolon.

Ruby allows instructions to be delimited by semicolons but does not require them. Ruby will automatically recognize separate instructions when they are placed on new lines. Most Ruby programs do not use semicolons to delimit instructions, and it is discouraged to do so.

Occasionally, it is possible to write an instruction that spans multiple lines and causes some ambiguity to the Ruby interpreter. When this happens, you can use the backslash character to hint to Ruby that the instruction continues on the next line. This is not usually required, but it helps to be aware of the issue.

> PHP `php_to_ruby_language/php/basic_syntax/instruction_separation.php`

```php
print "An instruction";
print "Multiple instructions"; print "Another instruction";
print 1 + 2
    + 3;
```

> Ruby `php_to_ruby_language/ruby/basic_syntax/instruction_separation.rb`

```ruby
print "An instruction"
print "Multiple instructions"; print "Another instruction"
print 1 + 2 \
      + 3
```

Comments

A single-line comment in PHP can either start with the hash character (#) or start with two forward slashes (//). In Ruby, you can use only the hash character.

Comments spanning multiple lines in PHP are most commonly formed with /* */, and it is considered poor practice to use the other syntaxes for multiline comments. In Ruby, using the hash character (#) for multiline comments is the most common practice and is encouraged.

Ruby also supports a syntax where you can form multiple-line comments using =begin and =end markers. This style of comments cannot be indented. It is usually reserved for embedded documentation and even as such is uncommon in the Rails community.

`PHP`   `php_to_ruby_language/php/basic_syntax/comments.php`

```
# single-line comment
// another single-line comment

/* comment multiple
lines of text */
```

`Ruby`   `php_to_ruby_language/ruby/basic_syntax/comments.rb`

```
# single-line comment

=begin
comment multiple
lines of text
=end
```

Good PHP programs are usually heavily commented with PHPDoc, a system of embedding tags inside comments for documentation tools to process. Ruby programs are not typically commented by anything that looks like Javadoc. Most Ruby programs, including Ruby on Rails, are documented with RDoc. This is a lightweight markup system with its own unique syntax. An in-depth comparison of PHPDoc and Rdoc is provided in Section 12.7, *Documenting Code*, on page 354.

You'll find in general that Ruby programs are written to be readable as English and that many classes of short, concise methods are encouraged. As a result, most Ruby programs have substantially less commenting than their PHP counterparts but remain understandable.

11.2 Basic Data Types

While remembering that Ruby types are in fact objects compared to PHP's primitive types, we can still make a fair comparison of how similar types of data play a role in the two different languages.

Booleans

Like PHP, booleans are one of the most basic types and are either true or false.

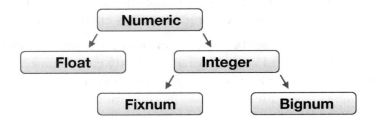

Figure 11.1: NUMERIC HIERARCHY

Unlike PHP where booleans are case-insensitive, booleans in Ruby should be all lowercase.

PHP | php_to_ruby_language/php/types/booleans.php

```php
$foo = true;
var_export($foo); // => true

$bar = True;
var_export($bar); // => true
```

Ruby | php_to_ruby_language/ruby/types/booleans.rb

```ruby
foo = true
p foo       # => true

bar = True # => NameError: uninitialized constant True
```

Integers

Integers in both PHP and Ruby are represented by an optional sign (- or +), optional base indicator, and one or more digits. Ruby will ignore any underscores added to the string of digits. This convention is often used to increase the readability of large numbers. Both languages represent hexadecimal and octal numbers (preceding 0x and 0, respectively) using the same notation.

The size of an integer in both PHP and Ruby is platform dependent. In PHP when a number exceeds the bounds of the integer type, it will be interpreted as a floating-point number. Ruby will automatically convert numbers to either Fixnum and Bignum object types where appropriate.

Numbers in Ruby fall into an object hierarchy described in Figure 11.1, on the preceding page.

PHP

`php_to_ruby_language/php/types/integers.php`

```php
$positive    = 4;
$negative    = -4;
$hexidecimal = 0x4;
$octal       = 04;
$large       = 123234345456;
```

Ruby

`php_to_ruby_language/ruby/types/integers.rb`

```ruby
positive    = 4
negative    = -4
hexidecimal = 0x4
octal       = 04

# the same as 123234345456
large       = 123_234_345_456
```

Floating-Point Numbers

Floating-point numbers are defined by a number that contains a decimal point or exponent. Unlike PHP, Ruby requires a number placed before the decimal point because the decimal point is part of the Ruby syntax used to call methods. This means that floating-point numbers less than zero require a leading zero.

PHP

`php_to_ruby_language/php/types/floating_point.php`

```php
$a =  2.3;
$b =   .5;
$c = 2e-5;
```

Ruby

`php_to_ruby_language/ruby/types/floating_point.rb`

```ruby
a =  2.3
b =  0.5
c = 2e-5
```

Strings

Ruby and PHP both use a 256-value set of single-byte characters and have multiple ways to represent a string literal. Ruby contains some additional quoting syntax not available in PHP. Strings in both languages will contain newline characters when they span multiple lines.

Single-quote syntax is similar in the two languages. Both languages perform minimal substitution when using single quotes. You can escape a single quote character using a backslash (\') and escape a single backslash character using an additional backslash (\\).

	PHP	Ruby
linefeed	\n	\n
carriage return	\r	\r
horizontal tab	\t	\t
backslash	\\	\\
dollar sign	\$	$
double quote	\"	\"
variable interpolation	$var	#{var}

Figure 11.2: STRING SUBSTITUTION

PHP · php_to_ruby_language/php/types/strings.php

```php
$a = 'hello world';                 // hello world
$b = 'escaping string\'s quote';    // escaping the string's quote
$c = 'escaping a backslash (\\)';   // and escaping a backslash (\)
```

Ruby · php_to_ruby_language/ruby/types/strings.rb

```ruby
a = 'hello world'                   # hello world
b = 'escaping string\'s quote'      # escaping the string's quote
c = 'escaping a backslash (\\)'     # and escaping a backslash (\)

# additional syntax specific to ruby
d = %q{no escape needed 'within'}   # no escape needed 'within'
e = %q/using a different delimiter/ # using a different delimiter
```

Although the first example of the additional syntax uses a standard convention of curly braces, we can use any other character as the delimiter. This includes characters such as the backslash (/) shown.

Double-quoted strings will perform more substitution of characters than single quotes when interpreted. Both languages share the most common substitutions. The list of substitutions is displayed in Figure 11.2. The most notable difference is how the languages handle variable substitution. Although PHP will evaluate simple variables within a string, Ruby can also evaluate full expressions within the string.

PHP

php_to_ruby_language/php/types/variable_interpolation.php

```
$name = ucfirst('joe');
$myString = "hello $name!";
```

Ruby

php_to_ruby_language/ruby/types/variable_interpolation.rb

```
my_string = "hello #{'joe'.capitalize}!"
```

Heredoc syntax is available in both languages in a similar fashion. The heredoc syntax in PHP is <<< followed by an identifier, a string of characters, and the closing identifier. Ruby begins with << and follows the same rules. The closing identifier must begin at the first character on the final line of the string and must not be indented.

PHP

php_to_ruby_language/php/types/heredoc.php

```
$lines = 3;
$myString = <<<EOT
This string can span $lines
lines, and contain variables and
"quotes" without the need to escape.
EOT;
```

Ruby

php_to_ruby_language/ruby/types/heredoc.rb

```
lines = 3
my_string = <<EOT
This string can span #{lines}
lines, and contain variables and
"quotes" without the need to escape.
EOT
```

Ruby provides some additional syntax that adds the ability to specify whether the heredoc should evaluate the string using single or double quotes. We do this by enclosing the opening identifier in the desired quote structure. Additionally, a minus sign can prefix the identifier to remove the restriction of the final identifier being the first character on the line.

We can indent the final identifier for better readability when this prefix is attached.

Ruby

php_to_ruby_language/ruby/types/heredoc.rb

```
my_string = <<'EOT'
This string will be evaluated
as a single quoted string because
the identifier is enclosed in single
quotes.
EOT
```

```
my_string = <<"EOT"
This string will be evaluated
as a double quoted string because
the identifier is enclosed in double
quotes.
EOT

my_string = <<-'EOT'
  Adding the minus sign will allow
  the ending identifier to be indented.
  EOT
```

Symbols

Symbols are constructs that are unavailable in PHP. They are constructed using a leading colon followed by a string of characters. They look similar to strings but are likely used in a different way. Symbols are immutable and cannot be modified like a string. You can think of them as a memory-efficient way of creating a name or identifier for something. They are often used as the keys of items in a hash (similar to an associative array in PHP).

`Ruby` `php_to_ruby_language/ruby/types/symbols.rb`

```
# the key is a name/identifier for the data
list = { :style  => "stone-washed", :color  => "blue" }

# spaces can be used by using quotes
example = :"hey mom"
```

While multiple instances of the same string are actually completely different objects, there will only ever be a single symbol by the same name. We can demonstrate this by viewing the object_id for these objects.

`Ruby` `php_to_ruby_language/ruby/types/symbol_ids.rb`

```
"magazine".object_id # => 1740770
"magazine".object_id # => 1729310

:magazine.object_id  # => 158498
:magazine.object_id  # => 158498
```

Numerically Indexed Arrays

PHP uses the versatile *array* data type to handle both numerically ordered collections and associative key/value pair collections. Ruby collections work a little differently in that the functionality found in PHP arrays is split into two different objects. Ruby uses arrays for lists, but this type of object does not allow for an associative-style declaration of key/value pairs. For this Ruby uses hashes. If a PHP function is meant to be used with an associative array, the Ruby code will most likely use a hash to solve the problem. This section will explain more about arrays in Ruby, while Section 11.2, *Associative Arrays and Hashes*, on page 273, covers hashes.

Arrays in Ruby do not use a numbered index in the same way as PHP. Arrays in Ruby are a simple stack of elements, and the index of an element is determined by the position of the element in the stack. You'll notice that as a result, there is never a need to rebuild or renumber arrays when removing elements.

`PHP`   php_to_ruby_language/php/array/array_index.php

```php
$fruit = array('banana', 'apple', 'orange');
unset($fruit[1]);

// notice how key #1 is skipped
var_export($fruit);
// => array (0 => 'banana', 2 => 'orange')
```

`Ruby`   php_to_ruby_language/ruby/array/array_index.rb

```ruby
fruit = ['banana', 'apple', 'orange']
fruit.delete_at(1)

p fruit
# => ["banana", "orange"]
```

Another notable difference is that Ruby holds no internal pointer to the current array element. Since Ruby has no equivalent of this type of array traversal, there is no translation to the related PHP functions such as current, next, prev, end, and reset.

Creating Arrays

Arrays in PHP are created using the array function. Various influential community leaders in PHP have opposed adding additional syntax for creating arrays in an effort to prevent PHP moving down a slippery slope that leads to multiple ways to perform every operation. Ruby has quite a few different ways of creating arrays, but you'll find that there are only a couple that are used regularly.

`PHP`   php_to_ruby_language/php/array/array_creation.php

```php
$colors = array('blue', 'red', 'yellow');
$empty  = array();
```

`Ruby` php_to_ruby_language/ruby/array/array_creation.rb

```ruby
# the most common syntax
colors = ['blue', 'red', 'yellow']
empty  = []

# creating an array from a list of words
colors = %w{ blue red yellow }

# creating an array with a defined size
empty = Array.new(2)
# [nil, nil]
```

In the three different Ruby approaches shown, you will most often run into the bracket syntax. This style contains a series of comma-separated objects and is by far the most common method of creating arrays. The other two methods are used less frequently but are convenient in some situations. We can use the %w{} construct to define a list of words as an array, and the Array.new syntax will enable us to specify an initial size for an array during creation.

Adding Elements

In Ruby, the << method will replace PHP's empty square-bracket syntax for appending elements to an array. We can assign a value to a specific numerical index using square brackets just as we would in PHP. The result is a little different than you might expect in PHP because of how Ruby stores array elements. To store an element at index 5, Ruby will need to fill any gaps before that position with nil elements. In this case, the same operation would yield a three-element array in PHP but a six-element array in Ruby.

`PHP` php_to_ruby_language/php/array/array_add_elements.php

```php
$fruit = array('apple');
$fruit[] = 'pear';
$fruit[5] = 'grape';

// array(0 => 'apple', 1 => 'pear', 5 => 'grape');
```

`Ruby` php_to_ruby_language/ruby/array/array_add_elements.rb

```ruby
fruit = ['apple']
fruit << 'pear'
fruit[5] = 'grape'

# ["apple", "pear", nil, nil, nil, "grape"]
```

Retrieving Elements

Accessing elements of an array is nearly identically in Ruby and PHP and is done by specifying a numeric index in square brackets.

PHP
`php_to_ruby_language/php/array/array_retrieve_elements.php`

```php
$colors = array('blue', 'red', 'yellow');
print $colors[0];
// => blue
```

Ruby
`php_to_ruby_language/ruby/array/array_retrieve_elements.rb`

```ruby
colors = ['blue', 'red', 'yellow']
puts colors[0]
# => blue
```

The most important distinction is that Ruby requires the key to be an integer. While PHP considers 0 and '0' to be the same value, Ruby will throw an error if the key is enclosed in quotes.

PHP
`php_to_ruby_language/php/array/array_retrieve_elements_integer.php`

```php
$colors = array('blue', 'red', 'yellow');
print $colors['0'];
// => blue
```

Ruby
`php_to_ruby_language/ruby/array/array_retrieve_elements_integer.rb`

```ruby
colors = ['blue', 'red', 'yellow']
puts colors['0']
# => can't convert String into Integer (TypeError)
```

Another important difference is that while PHP throws a notice when you access a nonexistent key, Ruby expects this type of behavior and returns nil.

PHP
`php_to_ruby_language/php/array/array_retrieve_elements_nonexistent.php`

```php
$colors = array('blue', 'red', 'yellow');
var_export($colors[5]);
// PHP Notice:  Undefined offset:  5
// => NULL
```

Ruby
`php_to_ruby_language/ruby/array/array_retrieve_elements_nonexistent.rb`

```ruby
colors = ['blue', 'red', 'yellow']
puts colors[5]
# => nil
```

Modifying Elements

Just as in PHP, we can modify elements of an array by simply redefining them by their specific numerical index.

PHP
`php_to_ruby_language/php/array/array_modify_elements.php`

```php
$colors = array('blue', 'red', 'yellow');
$colors[1] = 'orange';

// array(0 => 'blue', 1 => 'orange', 2 => 'yellow')
```

Ruby
`php_to_ruby_language/ruby/array/array_modify_elements.rb`

```ruby
colors = ['blue', 'red', 'yellow']
colors[1] = 'orange'

# ["blue", "orange", "yellow"]
```

Removing Elements

Ruby's equivalent of using unset to remove an element from an array is the delete_at method. This method will remove the element at the given index.

PHP
`php_to_ruby_language/php/array/array_removing_elements.php`

```php
$colors = array('blue', 'red', 'yellow');
unset($colors[1]);

// array(0 => 'blue', 2 => 'yellow')
```

Ruby
`php_to_ruby_language/ruby/array/array_removing_elements.rb`

```ruby
colors = ['blue', 'red', 'yellow']
colors.delete_at(1)

# ["blue", "yellow"]
```

Simple Array Iteration

The most common way of iterating over an array in PHP is the foreach control structure. To do the same thing in Ruby, we can use the each method on our array. Each uses a Ruby block to iterate through the values. Ruby blocks are discussed further in Section 12.1, *Blocks*, on page 311.

PHP
`php_to_ruby_language/php/array/array_simple_iteration.php`

```php
$colors = array('blue', 'red', 'yellow');

foreach ($colors as $color) {
  print "$color\n";
}
// => blue
//    red
//    yellow
```

Ruby

`php_to_ruby_language/ruby/array/array_simple_iteration.rb`

```ruby
colors = ['blue', 'red', 'yellow']

colors.each {|color| puts color }
# => blue
#    red
#    yellow
```

Multidimensional Array Iteration

Array's each method shines when dealing with iterating through a multidimensional array. Here we can use three separate elements in the argument list of the block to automatically split out each array's components.

PHP

`php_to_ruby_language/php/array/array_multidimensional_iteration.php`

```php
$people = array(array('Joe',  'W', 'Smith'),
                array('Jane', 'M', 'Doe'));

foreach ($people as $person) {
  list($first, $middle, $last) = $person;
  print "$first $middle. $last\n";
}
```

Ruby

`php_to_ruby_language/ruby/array/array_multidimensional_iteration.rb`

```ruby
people = [['Joe', 'W', 'Smith'], ['Jane', 'M', 'Doe']]

people.each do |first, middle, last|
  puts "#{first} #{middle}. #{last}"
end
```

Converting to an Array

While in PHP we cast a data type to an array using type casting, we convert basic types to an array in Ruby by enclosing an object within the square brackets with a leading splat (*) operator.

The splat operator will make sure that if the value is already an array, it won't be enclosed in an additional outer array.

PHP

`php_to_ruby_language/php/array/array_conversion.php`

```php
$stringValue = 'apple';
$converted = (array) $stringValue; // array(0 => 'apple')

$arrayValue = array('apple', 'kiwi');
$converted = (array) $arrayValue; // array(0 => 'apple', 1 => 'kiwi')
```

Ruby   php_to_ruby_language/ruby/array/array_conversion.rb

```ruby
string_value = "apple"
converted = [*string_value] # ["apple"]

array_value = ['apple', 'kiwi']
converted = [*array_value] # ["apple", "kiwi"]
```

Type casting objects to an array in PHP works differently than basic types. It instead returns an associative array of the object's attributes, with special annotation for the names of protected and private attributes. Ruby has no direct equivalent of this, and the best solution is to probably implement a custom to_hash method on your object.

PHP   php_to_ruby_language/php/array/array_conversion_objects.php

```php
class User {
  public    $name;
  protected $admin;
  private   $age;

  public function __construct($name, $admin, $age) {
    $this->name  = $name;
    $this->admin = $admin;
    $this->age   = $age;
  }
}

$joe = (array) new User('Joe', true, 32);
var_export($joe);
// => array ('name' => 'Joe', '*admin' => true, 'Userage' => 32)
```

Ruby   php_to_ruby_language/ruby/array/array_conversion_objects.rb

```ruby
class User
  attr_reader :name

  def initialize(name, admin, age)
    @name, @admin, @age = name, admin, age
  end

  def to_hash
    {:name => @name, :admin => @admin, :age => @age}
  end
end

joe = User.new('Joe', true, 32).to_hash
p joe
# {:admin=>true, :age=>32, :name=>"Joe"}
```

Associative Arrays and Hashes

A hash in Ruby is the closest we get to an associative array in PHP. The most important difference to remember is that hashes in Ruby are unordered collections. Ruby will store items in the most efficient manner to prepare for quicker retrieval of elements.

`PHP` php_to_ruby_language/php/hash/hash_ordering.php

```php
$person = array("name" => "joe", "age" => 35);
// array("name" => "joe", "age" => 35)
```

`Ruby` php_to_ruby_language/ruby/hash/hash_ordering.rb

```ruby
person = { :name => "joe", :age => 35 }
# => { :age=>35, :name=>"joe" }
```

While PHP uses a string for the key name in associative arrays, Ruby can use any object for the key. The most common object used for keys are Ruby symbols because they provide a lighter-weight alternative to a full Ruby string object.

Creating Hashes

We can create a new hash by creating a new instance of the Hash class, but the far more common approach is to create hashes using the {} syntax.

`PHP` php_to_ruby_language/php/hash/hash_creation.php

```php
$person = array('age' => 25, 'name' => 'Joe', 'eyes' => 'blue');
$empty  = array();
```

`Ruby` php_to_ruby_language/ruby/hash/hash_creation.rb

```ruby
person = { :age => 25, :name => 'Joe', :eyes => 'blue' }
empty  = {}
```

We've used the same comma-separated key/value pair idiom seen in PHP associative arrays. A string could certainly be used as the key value of hash items, but keys are usually just a name or label we use to refer to the values in that hash. In this case, it makes more sense to use more memory-efficient symbols for our keys.

Adding Elements

The most common method of adding elements to an associative array works identically to PHP by using a square-bracket syntax to assign an element by key.

PHP
`php_to_ruby_language/php/hash/hash_add_elements.php`

```php
$person = array('age' => 25);

$person['name'] = 'Joe';
var_export($person);
// => array('age' => 25, 'name' => 'Joe')
```

Ruby
`php_to_ruby_language/ruby/hash/hash_add_elements.rb`

```ruby
person = { :age => 25 }

person[:name] = 'Joe'
p person
# => { :age => 25, :name => "Joe" }
```

We can use the hash's update method as an equivalent of PHP's +=
syntax for adding multiple keys at once.

PHP
`php_to_ruby_language/php/hash/hash_add_elements_multiple.php`

```php
$person = array('age' => 25);

$person += array('name' => 'Joe', 'eyes' => 'blue');
var_export($person);
// => array('age' => 25, 'name' => 'Joe', 'eyes' => 'blue')
```

Ruby
`php_to_ruby_language/ruby/hash/hash_add_elements_multiple.rb`

```ruby
person = { :age => 25 }

person.update(:name => 'Joe', :eyes => 'blue')
p person
# => { :age => 25, :eyes => "blue", :name => "Joe" }
```

Retrieving Elements

Accessing elements of an associative array and hash work similarly
in Ruby and PHP. You can use the square-bracket syntax to access
the element by its key name/object. PHP throws a notice when you
attempt to access a key that doesn't exist, while Ruby expects this type
of behavior.

PHP
`php_to_ruby_language/php/hash/hash_retrieve_elements.php`

```php
$person = array('age' => 25, 'name' => 'Joe');
print $person['age'];
// => 25

var_export($person['hair']);
// PHP Notice:  Undefined index:  hair
// => NULL
```

`php_to_ruby_language/ruby/hash/hash_retrieve_elements.rb`

```ruby
person = { :age => 25, :name => 'Joe' }
puts person[:age]
# => 25

puts person[:hair]
# => nil
```

Modifying Elements

Just as in PHP, we can modify elements of an array by simply redefining them by their specific index key.

`php_to_ruby_language/php/hash/hash_modify_elements.php`

```php
$person = array('age' => 25, 'name' => 'Joe');
$person['age'] = 26;

// => array('age' => 26, 'name' => 'Joe')
```

`php_to_ruby_language/ruby/hash/hash_modify_elements.rb`

```ruby
person = { :age => 25, :name => 'Joe' }
person[:age] = 26

# => { :name => "Joe", :age => 26 }
```

Removing Elements

Usually we'll want to remove an element of a hash by either its key or its value, and Ruby makes it easy to do both. The replacement for PHP's unset function to remove an element by key is the hash's delete method. This takes a single argument with the key name and returns the element removed.

`php_to_ruby_language/php/hash/hash_remove_elements.php`

```php
$person = array('name' => 'Joe', 'eyes' => 'blue');

unset($person['name']);
var_export($person);
// => array('eyes' => 'blue');
```

`php_to_ruby_language/ruby/hash/hash_remove_elements.rb`

```ruby
person = { :name => 'Joe', :eyes => 'blue' }

person.delete(:name)
p person
# => { :eyes => "blue" }
```

Removing an element by value in PHP requires an iteration of the array to find the element. Ruby creates a shortcut for this type of operation using the delete_if method. This method uses a block and deletes all elements in the hash where the block expression evaluates to true.

PHP

`php_to_ruby_language/php/hash/hash_remove_elements_by_value.php`

```php
$person = array('name' => 'Joe', 'eyes' => 'blue');

foreach ($person as $key => $value) {
    if ($value == "Joe") {
        unset($person[$key]);
    }
}
var_export($person);
// => array('eyes' => 'blue');
```

Ruby

`php_to_ruby_language/ruby/hash/hash_remove_elements_by_value.rb`

```ruby
person = { :name => 'Joe', :eyes => 'blue' }

person.delete_if {|key, value| value == "Joe" }
p person
# => { :eyes => "blue" }
```

Simple Hash Iteration

Iterating over an associative array in PHP uses foreach just like a numeric array, but with a key => value given to identify both parts of the hash element. Ruby takes a similar approach using the each method. It passes two arguments to the block to give us both the key and value for each element. Ruby blocks are discussed further in Section 12.1, *Blocks*, on page 311.

PHP

`php_to_ruby_language/php/hash/hash_simple_iteration.php`

```php
$person = array('age' => 25, 'name' => 'Joe', 'eyes' => 'blue');

foreach ($person as $key => $value) {
    print "$key = $value\n";
}
// => age = 25
//    name = Joe
//    eyes = blue
```

Ruby

`php_to_ruby_language/ruby/hash/hash_simple_iteration.rb`

```ruby
person = { :age => 25, :name => 'Joe', :eyes => 'blue' }

person.each {|key, value| puts "#{key} = #{value}" }
# => age = 25
#    name = Joe
#    eyes = blue
```

Using Objects as Hash Keys

In PHP we can use either an integer or a string as a key for an array. Ruby, on the other hand, can use any object as a key.

It is important to remember that these keys are references to the original object. When we change the original objects, the key name in the hash will change as well.

Ruby | php_to_ruby_language/ruby/hash/hash_objects_as_keys.rb

```ruby
class User; end
fruit = ['apple', 'orange']

# use objects/arrays as keys
hash = { User.new => 'Joe', fruit => 'yummy' }
p hash
# => { #<User:0x1eb2c0> => "Joe", ["apple", "orange"] => "yummy" }

# access values using them as the key
puts hash[['apple', 'orange']]
# => "yummy"

# changing the fruit array also changes the key.
fruit << 'kiwi'
puts hash[['apple', 'orange']]
# => nil
```

Evaluation Expressions as Keys

Just as in PHP, it is perfectly valid to add any Ruby expression as a key in a hash when using the square-bracket syntax.

PHP | php_to_ruby_language/php/hash/hash_expressions_as_keys.php

```php
function myfunc($a) {
  return strtoupper($a);
}

$fruit = array();
$fruit[myfunc('apple')] = 'red';
$fruit[myfunc('pear')]  = 'green';

var_export($fruit);
// array('APPLE' => 'red', 'PEAR' => 'green')
```

Ruby | php_to_ruby_language/ruby/hash/hash_expressions_as_keys.rb

```ruby
def myfunc(a)
  a.upcase
end
```

```
fruit = {}
fruit[myfunc('apple')] = 'red'
fruit[myfunc('pear')]  = 'green'

p fruit
# => { "APPLE" => "red", "PEAR" => "green" }
```

NULL (Nil)

PHP's NULL constant is similar to Ruby's nil constant in that they both represent a lack of value for a variable. Nil in Ruby is a little more interesting because it is actually an object just like everything else; it's just an object that represents "no value."

PHP php_to_ruby_language/php/types/null_nil.php

```php
$car = 'red';
var_export(is_null($car));
// => false

unset($car);
var_export(is_null($car));
// PHP Notice:  Undefined variable: car
// => true

// in PHP, we check the data type
if (is_string($car)) {
    print strtoupper($car)."\n";
}
```

Ruby php_to_ruby_language/ruby/types/null_nil.rb

```ruby
car = 'red'
p car.nil?
# => false

# variables are 'unset' by assigning nil
car = nil
p car.nil?
# => true

# car is nil, but can still let us know what methods it responds to
puts car.upcase if car.respond_to?(:upcase)
```

Although this may seem strange that nil is an object, it actually falls right in line with how Ruby uses duck typing. We can ask a nil object whether it responds to a message just like any other object. In the previous PHP example, we checked whether the variable was a string before printing an uppercase version of it. Instead of checking the variable type, Ruby uses duck typing to ask the object whether it can perform the upcase method. In this case, the nil object returns false to responds_to(:upcase) and thus never prints the result. More information on the idea of duck typing can be found in Section 3.4, *Duck Typing*, on page 67.

Type Juggling

Ruby does not automatically convert data types in the way PHP does. To interpret a string as an integer or float, we need to first convert it to that data type.

`PHP` | php_to_ruby_language/php/types/juggling.php

```php
print 1.4 + 4;
// => 5.4

print 1.1 + "2";
// => 3.1

print "3" + 5;
// => 8
```

`Ruby` | php_to_ruby_language/ruby/types/juggling.rb

```ruby
puts 1.4 + 4
# => 5.4

puts 1.1 + "2"
# => String can't be coerced into Float (TypeError)
puts 1.1 + "2".to_f
# => 3.1

puts "3" + 5
# => can't convert Fixnum into String (TypeError)
puts "3".to_i + 5
# => 8
```

Although PHP implements type casting to convert our variables to different data types, Ruby takes a different approach. Ruby objects implement conversion methods such as to_s to convert to different types. The equivalent of common type casts in PHP are shown in Figure 11.3, on the next page.

11.3 Variables

Variables in Ruby come in a variety of styles. Like PHP, we can choose to use a local, global, static, or instance variable depending on the context.

	PHP	Ruby
convert to integer	`(int) "3";`	`"3".to_i`
convert to boolean	`(bool) "";`	`!"".blank?`
convert to float	`(float) "1.2";`	`"1.2".to_f`
convert to string	`(string) 1;`	`1.to_s`
convert to array	`(array) "test";`	`[*"test"]`

Figure 11.3: Type conversion

Local Variables

Local variables in Ruby start with an underscore or lowercase letter followed by name characters. While PHP uses the dollar ($) sign to define local variables, the dollar sign is reserved for global variables in Ruby.

It is important to remember that since invoking a method does not require the use of parentheses, variable and method names in Ruby can conflict. There are various ways to work around this, of which the best is probably to simply rename your local variable to something that does not conflict. An additional approach is to use parentheses when invoking a method that conflicts with a variable name.

`PHP` `php_to_ruby_language/php/variables/variables_local.php`

```php
$name = "Joe";

// function names never conflict with variables
function name()
{
    return "Jane";
}

print $name."\n";
// => "Joe"

print name()."\n";
// => "Jane"
```

`php_to_ruby_language/ruby/variables/variables_local.rb`

```ruby
name = "Joe"

# methods can have the same name as a variable
def name
  "Jane"
end

puts name
# => "Joe"

# we have to use the parentheses to explicitly call the method
# so that it doesn't conflict with the variable
puts name()
# => "Jane"
```

Instance Variables

Instance variables names start with an "at" sign (@) and are shared between all methods of a single object instance. Instance variables are discussed in depth in Section 12.3, *The Basics (class/new/extends)*, on page 321.

Class Variables

Class variables in Ruby start with a double "at" sign (@@) and most closely resemble static class members in PHP. These variables are shared between all instances of the class. Class variables are explored more in depth in Section 12.3, *Static Keyword*, on page 330.

Global Variables

Global variables in Ruby start with a leading dollar sign ($) followed by name characters. It is important to recognize that the leading dollar sign in Ruby is very different from PHP in this respect.

Any Ruby variable using a dollar sign will be the equivalent of a super-global in PHP and is available anywhere and everywhere. PHP makes no distinction in variable syntax between local and global scope, and the global keyword is needed to declare global variables within a function or method. Ruby global variables are similar to a PHP superglobal in that they are available in all scopes.

`PHP` php_to_ruby_language/php/variables/variables_global.php

```php
$name = 'Joe';

function foo()
{
    global $name;
    print $name;
}

foo();
// => Joe
```

`Ruby` php_to_ruby_language/ruby/variables/variables_global.rb

```ruby
$name = 'Joe'

def foo
  print $name
end

foo
# => Joe
```

The previous example demonstrates the scope of the variable type but is an example of horrible programming practices. In reality, you should rarely if ever define global variables if you want your code to be maintainable.

Predefined Variables

Ruby is a general-purpose language that is not natively built for the Web the way PHP is. Because of this, the equivalent of PHP's super-globals such as $_GET, $_POST, $_COOKIE, and $_SESSION are all part of the Rails framework and are discussed in Chapter 13, *PHP to Rails Reference*, on page 367.

Scope

You'll find that the basic scoping of variables in Ruby is almost identical to that in PHP. Top-level scoped variables are available within control structures, but not functions or methods.

`PHP` php_to_ruby_language/php/variables/scope.php

```php
// local to the top-level
$a = 1;
```

```php
// also top-level scope
if (true) {
    $a = 2;
    print $a; // => 2
}
print $a; // => 2
```

Ruby `php_to_ruby_language/ruby/variables/scope.rb`

```ruby
# local to the top level scope
a = 1

# also top-level scope
if true
  a = 2
  puts a # => 2
end
puts a # => 2
```

Functions and methods contain their own local scope in both PHP and Ruby.

PHP `php_to_ruby_language/php/variables/scope_functions.php`

```php
$a = 2

// local to the function
function myFunction()
{
    $a = 3;
    print $a; // => 3
}
print $a; // => 2
```

Ruby `php_to_ruby_language/ruby/variables/scope_functions.rb`

```ruby
a = 2

# local to the function
def my_function
  a = 3
  puts a # => 3
end
puts a # => 2
```

While in PHP we use various control structures to perform loops, Ruby often uses a block to do the same thing. Blocks behave a little differently than you may expect in regard to scope.

Ruby   php_to_ruby_language/ruby/variables/scope_blocks.rb

```ruby
foo = "initial value"

[true].each do |var|
  foo = "changed value"
  bar = "local to block scope"
end

puts foo # => changed value
puts bar # => undefined local variable or method `bar'
```

Local variables defined before the block is executed are available within the context of that block but will remain local in scope. Variables defined in the block that were not previously defined will remain local to that block. This is demonstrated in the earlier example. The foo variable is defined before the block is executed and remains in the top-level scope even when it is modified within the block context. The bar variable comes into existence only within the block and therefore remains local to the block only.

Another notable difference in variable definition and scope is that we can set local variables or execute methods within a Ruby class definition. PHP has no way for us to do such a thing, and it may seem strange performing an operation in the scope of a class like this. This is useful when you need to execute operations as a class is defined at runtime. Rails uses this to do things such as defining model associations and validations.

Ruby   php_to_ruby_language/ruby/variables/scope_class.rb

```ruby
class MyClass
  a = 2
  puts a # => 2

  def my_method
    a = 3
    puts a # => 3
  end
end
```

Variable Variables

Ruby does not implement variable variables. Although PHP does support variable variables, their use is discouraged. Using this type of variable in PHP inevitably leads to confusion for anyone coming back to read the code at a later date.

isset/empty

We'll often use the isset function in PHP to check whether a variable has been assigned. You need to do this type of check less often when programming in Ruby. Since Ruby is object oriented, local variables are often passed in as an argument to a method and are guaranteed to have a value. Just like in PHP, it is a best practice to define local variables before using them. Accessing an undefined local variable in Ruby will result in a NameError.

`PHP`   `php_to_ruby_language/php/variables/isset.php`

```php
if (!isset($var1)) {
    print "var1 not set\n";
}
// => var1 not set

$var2 = null;
if (!isset($var2)) {
    print "var2 not set\n";
}
// => var2 not set
```

`Ruby`   `php_to_ruby_language/ruby/variables/isset.rb`

```ruby
puts "var1 not set" unless var1
# => NameError: undefined local variable or method `var1'

var2 = nil
puts "var2 not set" unless var2
# => var2 not set
```

We can, however, access instance variables in Ruby that have not been defined yet. In this case, Ruby will simply return nil if the variable has not been assigned a value. More details on instance variables can be found in Section 12.3, *The Basics (class/new/extends)*, on page 321.

`Ruby`   `php_to_ruby_language/ruby/variables/isset_instance.rb`

```ruby
puts "var3 not set" unless @var3
# => var3 not set
```

Ruby has a construct named defined? that is similar to PHP's isset function. This construct checks whether a variable has been defined and returns the type of variable stored. Using this construct is usually not necessary when you are defining your variables properly. Because of this, you won't find this construct used often in typical Ruby applications.

PHP Expression	empty($x)	is_null($x)	if ($x)	isset($x)	
$x = "";	TRUE	FALSE	FALSE	TRUE	
$x = null;	TRUE	TRUE	FALSE	FALSE	
$x = array();	TRUE	FALSE	FALSE	TRUE	
$x = false;	TRUE	FALSE	FALSE	TRUE	
$x = 0;	TRUE	FALSE	FALSE	TRUE	
$x = "0";	TRUE	FALSE	FALSE	TRUE	

Ruby Expression	x.empty?	x.nil?	if (x)		x.zero?	x.blank?**
x = ""	TRUE	FALSE	TRUE		u/m*	TRUE
x = nil	u/m*	TRUE	FALSE		u/m*	TRUE
x = []	TRUE	FALSE	TRUE		u/m*	TRUE
x = {}	TRUE	FALSE	TRUE		u/m*	TRUE
x = false	u/m*	FALSE	FALSE		u/m*	TRUE
x = 0	u/m*	FALSE	TRUE		TRUE	FALSE
x = "0"	FALSE	FALSE	TRUE		FALSE	FALSE
	* NoMethodError: undefined method			** Only Available in Rails		

Figure 11.4: EMPTY VARIABLES AND BOOLEAN HANDLING

Ruby php_to_ruby_language/ruby/variables/defined.rb

```
puts defined? var1
# => nil

var1 = "orange"
puts defined? var1
# => local-variable
```

PHP and Ruby behave quite differently while evaluating empty variables and determining what is considered false in a conditional. The diagram in Figure 11.4 illustrates some of these important differences. While PHP uses the empty function to check whether any variable type is empty, Ruby does not implement an empty? method on every data type. Thankfully, Rails comes to the rescue with the addition of the blank? method. This makes a consistent interface for checking whether strings, numbers, arrays, hashes, nil, or boolean objects are blank. Take note that the blank? method still doesn't consider any form of zero as blank, so you'll have to continue to pay attention to the type of data you're passing around. This method is available only from within your Rails project and is not a core Ruby method.

Another important distinction is that Ruby will evaluate anything other than nil and false only as true in a conditional. This is quite different from PHP, and if you want to check whether a value is blank or zero, be sure to use the blank? or zero? methods, respectively.

11.4 Constants

While only scalar data can be contained in PHP constants, we can store any data we want in Ruby constants. This gives us the flexibility to use them in many situations where they would be inappropriate in PHP.

Basic Syntax

Ruby considers any name starting with a capital letter a constant. While PHP community standards and conventions usually instruct you to use all caps for constant names, it is not required by the language syntax as it is in Ruby.

Ruby takes an unconventional approach to constants, allowing them to be redefined at runtime. Both PHP and Ruby throw a warning when you try to redefine a constant, but the value of the constant will indeed change in Ruby. We can do many things in Ruby that aren't great general programming practices but are useful in certain situations. Watch out for these types of warnings in your program because they usually indicate problems with your code. As with PHP, Ruby also implements class constants, which are discussed in Section 12.3, *Class Constants*, on page 332.

PHP

php_to_ruby_language/php/constants/constants.php

```php
define("MY_CONSTANT", "a");
print MY_CONSTANT; // => a

define("MY_CONSTANT", "b");
// PHP Notice:  Constant MY_CONSTANT already defined
print MY_CONSTANT; // => a
```

Ruby

php_to_ruby_language/ruby/constants/constants.rb

```ruby
MY_CONSTANT = "a"
puts MY_CONSTANT # => a

MY_CONSTANT = "b"
# warning: already initialized constant MY_CONSTANT
puts MY_CONSTANT # => b
```

Magic Constants

PHP uses five magic constants, which are constants that change depending on where they are used. These constants do things such as obtain the current line, file, function, class, and method. Both the __LINE__ and __FILE__ constants are also in Ruby, although __FILE__ behaves slightly differently in Ruby, giving the relative path of the file. We can retrieve the entire path by using Ruby's File#expand_path method.

PHP
`php_to_ruby_language/php/constants/constants_magic.php`

```php
print __LINE__;
// => 2

print __FILE__;
// => /Users/derek/code/php_to_ruby_language/php/constants_magic.php
```

Ruby
`php_to_ruby_language/ruby/constants/constants_magic.rb`

```ruby
puts __LINE__
# => 2

puts __FILE__
# => constants_magic.rb

puts File.expand_path(__FILE__)
# => /Users/derek/code/php_to_ruby_language/ruby/constants_magic.rb
```

Ruby has no equivalent of PHP's __FUNCTION__, __METHOD__, or __CLASS__ constants, but we can access the same information using a different approach. We can retrieve the class of any object using that object's class method. We must always explicitly call self.class when calling this method since class is a reserved word in Ruby.

PHP
`php_to_ruby_language/php/constants/constants_class.php`

```php
class MyClass {
    public function myMethod() {
        print __CLASS__;
        // => MyClass
    }
}
```

Ruby
`php_to_ruby_language/ruby/constants/constants_class.rb`

```ruby
class MyClass
  def my_method
    puts self.class
    # => MyClass
  end
end
```

Retrieving the method name from inside an object is slightly more complex and requires adding a custom method to help us.

`PHP` `php_to_ruby_language/php/constants/constants_method.php`

```php
function myFunction() {
    print __FUNCTION__;
    // => myFunction
}

class MyClass {
    public function myMethod() {
        print __METHOD__;
        // => MyClass::myMethod
    }
}
```

`Ruby` `php_to_ruby_language/ruby/constants/constants_method.rb`

```ruby
# we first extend all objects to have a 'method_name' method
class Object
  def method_name
    "#{self.class}##{$1}" if /`(.*)'/.match(caller.first)
  end
end

def top_level_method
  puts method_name
  # => Object#top_level_method
end

class MyClass
  def my_method
    puts method_name
    # => MyClass#my_method
  end
end
```

The previous example code reopens the Object class to add the method_name method. Since every object in Ruby extends from the Object class, we can call this method from within any object's method to retrieve the name of the method.

11.5 Expressions

Expressions in Ruby work pretty similarly to those in PHP with a few exceptions. Control structures in Ruby evaluate as an expression and return a value. This can be quite useful in cutting down repeated code.

`PHP` `php_to_ruby_language/php/expressions/expressions_control_structures.php`

```php
// in php, we must make an assignment for each condition
if ($day == 'saturday' || $day == 'sunday') {
    $type = 'weekend';
} else {
    $type = 'weekday';
}
```

`Ruby` `php_to_ruby_language/ruby/expressions/expressions_control_structures.rb`

```ruby
# if/else statements return the value of the last expression
# we can use this to make a single assignment for 'type'
type = if day == 'saturday' || day == 'sunday'
  'weekend'
else
  'weekday'
end
```

Switch statements in Ruby evaluate and return a value as well.

`PHP` `php_to_ruby_language/php/expressions/expressions_control_structures_switch.php`

```php
// switch statements also require us to make multiple assignments
switch ($sound) {
case 'meow':
    $animal = 'cat';
    break;
case 'bark':
    $animal = 'dog';
    break;
default:
    $animal = 'unidentified';
}
```

`Ruby` `php_to_ruby_language/ruby/expressions/expressions_control_structures_switch.rb`

```ruby
# case statements also return the value of the last expression
animal = case sound
         when 'meow': 'cat'
         when 'bark': 'dog'
         else 'unidentified'
         end
```

Even class and method definitions evaluate as an expression in Ruby, returning nil.

`Ruby` `php_to_ruby_language/ruby/expressions/expressions_class_definition.rb`

```ruby
# class and method declarations evaluate to nil
class MyClass; end # => nil
def my_method; end # => nil
```

11.6 Operators

Operators in Ruby are unique in that most of them are actually method calls on an object. Ruby provides a convenient syntax for these method calls to make them appear to work like they do in most other languages.

PHP

`php_to_ruby_language/php/operators/operators.php`

```php
print 1 + 2;
// => 3
print 'Hello, '.'World!';
// => Hello, World!
```

Ruby

`php_to_ruby_language/ruby/operators/operators.rb`

```ruby
puts 1.+(2)
# => 3
puts 'Hello, '.+('World!')
# => Hello, World!
```

In the Ruby examples, we have substituted the usual operators with their method equivalents to display what happens behind the scenes during their use. Details about overriding operators in Ruby can be found in Section 3.7, *Overriding Operators*, on page 78.

Assignment, Arithmetic, and Bitwise

In Figure 11.5, on the next page, we can see that basic arithmetic, assignment, and bitwise operators are used nearly identically in both PHP and Ruby. Ruby provides an additional operator for exponention (**) that provides the equivalent of PHP's pow() function.

In Ruby we can use parallel variable assignment to assign multiple variables on a single line. This is similar to using the list function in combination with the array function in PHP.

PHP

`php_to_ruby_language/php/operators/operators_parallel_assignment.php`

```php
list($a, $b, $c) = array(1, 2, 3);
print $a; # => 1
print $b; # => 2
print $c; # => 3
```

Ruby

`php_to_ruby_language/ruby/operators/operators_parallel_assignment.rb`

```ruby
a, b, c = 1, 2, 3
puts a # => 1
puts b # => 2
puts c # => 3
```

Ruby has additional assignment operators as shorthand for assigning variables depending on their current value.

	PHP	Ruby
Assignment	$a = 2;	a = 2;
Arithmetic	-2; 2 + 1; 2 - 1; 2 * 3; 8 / 2; 4 % 3; pow(2, 3);	-2 2 + 1 2 - 1 2 * 3 8 / 2 4 % 3 2 ** 3
Arithmetic Assignment	$a += 1; $a -= 1; $a *= 2; $a /= 2;	a += 1 a -= 1 a *= 2 a /= 2
Bitwise	2 & 1; 2 | 1; 1 ^ 1; ~2; 2 << 1; 2 >> 1;	2 & 1 2 | 1 1 ^ 1 ~2 2 << 1 2 >> 1

Figure 11.5: OPERATORS

This is similar to using a ternary operator in PHP to assign a value depending on a variable's existing value. The first allows us to conditionally assign a value if the variable evaluates to false.

PHP

php_to_ruby_language/php/operators/operators_conditional_assignment.php

```php
$result = isset($result) ? $result : 'foo';
print $result; // => 'foo'

// will not assign since $result already has a value
$result = isset($result) ? $result : 'bar';
print $result; // => 'foo'
```

Ruby

php_to_ruby_language/ruby/operators/operators_conditional_assignment.rb

```ruby
result ||= 'foo'
print result # => 'foo'

# will not assign since result already has a value
result ||= 'bar'
print result # => 'foo'
```

This is a popular idiom in Ruby, and you'll likely see it used as a convenient replacement for either the ternary operator or short-circuit assignment logic. We can also do the opposite of the previous code and assign a value only if the variable contains a value.

	PHP	**Ruby**
Comparison	`$foo == $bar;`	`foo == bar`
	`$foo != $bar;`	`foo != bar`
	`$foo < $bar;`	`foo <  bar`
	`$foo > $bar;`	`foo >  bar`
	`$foo <= $bar;`	`foo <= bar`
	`$foo >= $bar;`	`foo >= bar`

Figure 11.6: COMPARISON OPERATORS

Comparison

As shown in Figure 11.6, most comparison operators for basic types are the same between PHP and Ruby. Ruby does not, however, implement the <> operator, which is simply a synonym for != in PHP. Ruby also does not include greater-than (>) or less-than (<) operators for arrays.

The concept of "equal" and "identical" values in Ruby is quite different from that in PHP since Ruby is strongly typed and PHP is loosely typed. When using an equal operator, PHP ignores variable types in value comparisons and thus considers values such as 1, '1', and true all equal. In Ruby these values are not considered equal. Ruby does, however, consider the value of 1 and 1.0 as equal and can convert most values to a string for comparison using the to_s method.

PHP

php_to_ruby_language/php/operators/operators_equals.php

```php
// same value
var_export(1 == 1);     // => true
var_export(1 == 1.0);   // => true
var_export(1 == '1');   // => true
var_export(1 == true);  // => true

# casting an integer into a string
var_export((string)1 == '1'); // => true
```

Ruby

php_to_ruby_language/ruby/operators/operators_equals.rb

```ruby
# same value
puts 1 == 1     # => true
puts 1 == 1.0   # => true
puts 1 == '1'   # => false
puts 1 == true  # => false

# we can cast an integer to compare it with a string
puts 1.to_s == '1' # => true
```

To perform the equivalent of PHP's identical operator (===), Ruby implements the eql? method on every object to compare both the type and the value of the object. The triple-equals (===) operator in Ruby is reserved for case statement comparisons.

PHP   php_to_ruby_language/php/operators/operators_identical.php

```
// same type and value
var_export(1 === 1);    // => true
var_export(1 === 1.0);  // => false
var_export(1 === '1');  // => false
var_export(1 === true); // => false
```

Ruby   php_to_ruby_language/ruby/operators/operators_identical.rb

```
# same type and value
puts 1.eql?(1)      # => true
puts 1.eql?(1.0)    # => false
puts 1.eql?('1')    # => false
puts 1.eql?(true)   # => false
```

Every time we create a new object, Ruby stores a reference to that object using an ID. We can also use an additional comparison method in Ruby named equal?. This method checks whether two objects have the same object_id. Different strings composed of the same characters may have an equal value, but they actually are full objects that are stored as a separate ID.

Ruby symbols, on the other hand, will always use a single reference ID for the same string of characters. This is one of the reasons why we prefer to use symbols over strings where appropriate.

Ruby   php_to_ruby_language/ruby/operators/operators_equals_string.rb

```
# same object_id
puts "a".equal?("a") # => false
puts :a.equal?(:a)   # => true
```

Error Control

The closest we can get to the error silencing operator (@) in Ruby is changing the $VERBOSE level to nil to suppress warnings. Rails even introduces a silence_warnings method to make this a little nicer to read. Most of the time in Ruby, however, we will not want to ignore errors but handle them with proper rescue statements. A detailed explanation on differences in error handling can be found in Section 2.8, *Handling Errors*, on page 45.

`PHP`

```
php_to_ruby_language/php/operators/operators_error_control.php
```

```php
define('MY_CONSTANT', 'a');

@define('MY_CONSTANT', 'b');
```

`Ruby`

```
php_to_ruby_language/ruby/operators/operators_error_control.rb
```

```ruby
MY_CONSTANT = 'a'

# using Ruby, we can change the verbosity level to
# suppress warnings
$VERBOSE = nil
MY_CONSTANT = 'b'
$VERBOSE = true

# Rails provides a convenient method that uses a block to do the same
silence_warnings do
  MY_CONSTANT = 'c'
end
```

Execution

Both Ruby and PHP will interpret a string within backticks (`) as a shell command. Ruby also gives the %x{} syntax to perform the same operation.

`PHP`

```
php_to_ruby_language/php/operators/operators_execution.php
```

```php
print `pwd`;  // => /Users/derek/code/php_to_ruby_language/php
```

`Ruby`

```
php_to_ruby_language/ruby/operators/operators_execution.rb
```

```ruby
puts `pwd`    # => /Users/derek/code/php_to_ruby_language/ruby
puts %x{pwd}  # => /Users/derek/code/php_to_ruby_language/ruby
```

Incrementing/Decrementing

Ruby does not implement pre- or post-increment and decrement operators as used in PHP. We instead use the modified assignment operator to increment or decrement a value.

`PHP`

```
php_to_ruby_language/php/operators/operators_inc_dec.php
```

```php
$a = 1;

print ++$a; // => 2
print $a++; // => 2
print $a;   // => 3

print --$a; // => 2
print $a--; // => 2
print $a;   // -> 1
```

> Ruby | `php_to_ruby_language/ruby/operators/operators_inc_dec.rb`

```ruby
a = 1

puts a += 1 # => 2
puts a += 1 # => 3
puts a      # => 3

puts a -= 1 # => 2
puts a -= 1 # => 1
puts a      # -> 1
```

Logical

Ruby implements almost all the same logical operators as PHP. Ruby does not implement PHP's xor operator, but it adds the not operator.

> PHP | `php_to_ruby_language/php/operators/operators_logical.php`

```php
$result = !true; // $result == false

# "&&" and "||" have higher precedence than "="
$result = 'test' && false; // $result == false
$result = 'test' || false; // $result == true

# "and" and "or" have lower precedence than "="
$result = 'test' and false;   // $result == "test"
$result = 'test' or  false;   // $result == "test"
$result = ('test' and false); // $result == false
$result = ('test' or  false); // $result == true
```

> Ruby | `php_to_ruby_language/ruby/operators/operators_logical.rb`

```ruby
# "!" has a higher precedence than "not"
result = !true     # result == false
result = (not true) # result == false

# "&&" and "||" have higher precedence than "="
result = 'test' && false # result == false
result = 'test' || false # result == "test"

# "and" and "or" have lower precedence than "="
result = 'test' and false   # result == "test"
result = 'test' or  false   # result == "test"
result = ('test' and false) # result == false
result = ('test' or  false) # result == true
```

The most important change to note is that Ruby's && and || operators return the last value evaluated, wherein PHP they return a boolean value. This becomes helpful when evaluating short-circuit logical operations where we want a return value.

PHP `php_to_ruby_language/php/operators/operators_short_circuit.php`

```php
$myVar = "test";
$myVar = $myVar || null;

var_export($myVar); // => true
```

Ruby `php_to_ruby_language/ruby/operators/operators_short_circuit.rb`

```ruby
my_var = "test"
my_var = my_var || nil

puts my_var # => "test"
```

String

Operators for strings in Ruby work similar to PHP, except Ruby uses the plus sign (+) instead of a dot (.) for concatenation.

PHP `php_to_ruby_language/php/operators/operators_string.php`

```php
// concatenation
$a = "Chunky";
$b = $a . " Bacon!";
print $b; // => Chunky Bacon!

// concatenation assignment
$a = "Chunky";
$a .= " Bacon!";
print $a; // => Chunky Bacon!
```

Ruby `php_to_ruby_language/ruby/operators/operators_string.rb`

```ruby
# concatenation
a = "Chunky"
b = a + " Bacon!"
puts b # => Chunky Bacon!

# concatenation assignment
a = "Chunky"
a += " Bacon!"
puts a # => Chunky Bacon!
```

Array

The union operator for Ruby arrays works quite differently than in PHP. Since Ruby arrays don't have keys, there are never key conflicts, and the values are always joined. The union operator is not defined for Ruby hashes but can be easily added if we were to reopen the Hash class to add a + method. We can make + an alias to Hash#update.

PHP php_to_ruby_language/php/operators/operators_array_union.php

```php
// union
$fruit = array('apple') + array('kiwi', 'orange');
var_export($fruit); // => array(0 => 'apple', 1 => 'orange')

// union with associative keys
$result = array('a' => 1, 'b' => 2) + array('c' => 3);
var_export($result); // => array('a' => 1, 'b' => 2, 'c' => 3)
```

Ruby php_to_ruby_language/ruby/operators/operators_array_union.rb

```ruby
# array union (+ doesn't work for hashes)
fruit = [:apple] + [:kiwi, :orange]
p fruit # => [:apple, :kiwi, :orange]

# add + operator to hash
class Hash; alias + update; end
result = { :a => 1, :b => 2 } + { :c => 3 }
p result # => { :b => 2, :c => 3, :a => 1 }
```

Array comparison works pretty similar to PHP with the PHP's identity operator (===) being replaced by Ruby's eql? method.

PHP php_to_ruby_language/php/operators/operators_array.php

```php
// equality
$result = array('a' => 1, 'b' => 2) == array('b' => 2, 'a' => 1);
var_export($result); // => true

// identity also checks order
$result = array('a' => 1, 'b' => 2) === array('b' => 2, 'a' => 1);
var_export($result); // => false
```

Ruby php_to_ruby_language/ruby/operators/operators_array.rb

```ruby
# equality
result = { :a => 1, :b => 2 } == { :b => 2, :a => 1 }
puts result # => true

# identity
result = { :a => 1, :b => 2 }.eql?({ :b => 2, :a => 1 })
puts result # => false
```

Type

Object-oriented PHP has drawn inspiration from Java and uses interfaces, type hints, and the instanceof operator to check object types before operating on them. Ruby takes quite a different approach to this by embracing the idea of duck typing.

PHP

`php_to_ruby_language/php/operators/operators_type.php`

```php
class MyClass
{
    public function myMethod()
    {
        return 'true';
    }
}
class OtherClass {}

$a = new MyClass;
$b = new OtherClass;

if ($a instanceof MyClass) {
    print $a->myMethod(); // => 'true'
}

// this won't evaluate
if ($b instanceof MyClass) {
    print $b->myMethod();
}
```

Ruby

`php_to_ruby_language/ruby/operators/operators_type.rb`

```ruby
class MyClass
  def my_method
    'true'
  end
end
class OtherClass; end

a = MyClass.new
b = OtherClass.new

# In ruby we check the interface, not the class
if a.respond_to? :my_method
  puts a.my_method # => true
end

# this won't evaluate
if b.respond_to? :my_method
  b.my_method
end
```

If we truly wanted to check an object type, Ruby objects all have an is_a? method, and we could call a.is_a? MyClass. However, the more appropriate approach in Ruby is to check whether the object responds to the my_method message it wants to send instead of trying to check the object type. If the object does indeed implement the needed method, Ruby knows it can continue into the block. More details on typing in Ruby are described in Section 3.4, *Understanding Typing*, on page 66.

11.7 Control Structures

Many of PHP's native control structures for looping operations are replaced by a special iterator methods that use blocks. Ruby also adds statement modifiers, which are great tools for making your code succinct and expressive.

if

Ruby uses an if/end syntax to define the opening and closing of conditional statements, and parentheses around the evaluated expression are optional.

PHP | php_to_ruby_language/php/control/control_if.php

```php
$value = 10;

// mutiple line if
if ($value > 5) {
    print "value is \n";
    print "greater than 5\n";
}
```

Ruby | php_to_ruby_language/ruby/control/control_if.rb

```ruby
value = 10

# mutiple line if
if value > 5
  puts 'value is '
  puts 'greater than 5'
end
```

We can also write single-line conditionals using the if and unless statement modifiers.

PHP | php_to_ruby_language/php/control/control_if_modifiers.php

```php
$value = 10;

// single line if
if ($value > 5)
    print "value is greater than 5\n";

// negated if
if (! $value > 5)
    print "value is NOT greater than 5\n";
```

Ruby | php_to_ruby_language/ruby/control/control_if_modifiers.rb

```ruby
value = 10

# single line if
puts 'value is greater than 5' if value > 5
```

```
# negated if in ruby uses unless
puts 'value is NOT greater than 5' unless value > 5
```

else

Using else in Ruby is similar to that in PHP, and the ternary operator works the same in both languages.

php_to_ruby_language/php/control/control_else.php

```php
$value = 10;

if ($value > 5) {
    print 'value is greater than 5';
} else {
    print 'value is NOT greater than 5';
}

// ternary operator
$color = $value == 1 ? 'red' : 'blue';
```

php_to_ruby_language/ruby/control/control_else.rb

```ruby
value = 10

if value > 5
  puts 'value is greater than 5'
else
  puts 'value is NOT greater than 5'
end

# ternary operator
color = value == 1 ? 'red' : 'blue'
```

elseif/elsif

PHP's elseif keyword loses the middle *e* to become elsif in Ruby. If we want to put our statements on the same line as the conditional expression in Ruby, we can use either a colon (:) or the then keyword.

php_to_ruby_language/php/control/control_ifelse.php

```php
$value = 7;

if ($value > 8) {
    print 'value is greater than 8';
} elseif ($value > 5) {
    print 'value is greater than 5'
} else {
    print 'value is NOT greater than 5';
}
```

Ruby `php_to_ruby_language/ruby/control/control_ifelse.rb`

```ruby
value = 7

if value > 8
  puts 'value is greater than 8'
elsif value > 5
  puts 'value is greater than 5'
else
  puts 'value is NOT greater than 5'
end

# variation using ":"
if value > 8:    puts 'value is greater than 8'
elsif value > 5: puts 'value is greater than 5'
else            puts 'value is NOT greater than 5'
end

# variation using "then"
if value > 8    then puts 'value is greater than 8'
elsif value > 5 then puts 'value is greater than 5'
else                 puts 'value is NOT greater than 5'
end
```

while

Ruby uses a while/end style syntax to define the opening and closing of while loops.

PHP `php_to_ruby_language/php/control/control_while.php`

```php
// multiple line while
$page = 1;
while ($page < 5) {
    print "$page\n";
    $page++;
}
```

Ruby `php_to_ruby_language/ruby/control/control_while.rb`

```ruby
# multiple line while
page = 1
while page < 5
  puts page
  page += 1
end
```

Ruby adds the while and until statement modifiers so that we can write simple while statements in a single line of code.

`PHP` php_to_ruby_language/php/control/control_while_modifiers.php

```php
// single line while
$page = 1;
while ($page < 5)
    $page++;

// negated while
$page = 1;
while (! $page >= 5)
    $page++;
```

`Ruby` php_to_ruby_language/ruby/control/control_while_modifiers.rb

```ruby
# single line while
page = 1
page += 1 while page < 5

# negated while
page = 1
page += 1 until page >= 5
```

do while

Ruby has no support for do/while but has an equivalent syntax that uses a while or until statement modifier on a begin/end block expression.

`PHP` php_to_ruby_language/php/control/control_dowhile.php

```php
$page = 1;
do {
    print "$page\n";
    $page++;
} while ($page < 10);
```

`Ruby` php_to_ruby_language/ruby/control/control_dowhile.rb

```ruby
page = 1
begin
  puts page
  page += 1
end while < 10
```

for

Ruby takes a little bit of a different approach than PHP when it comes to loops. It does this in an effort to cut down on pesky "fence-post" or "one-off" errors. There is no for construct in Ruby, and most approaches to loops take advantage of iterators methods on an integer object. We can write a loop with an incrementor using either the times or upto method.

PHP   php_to_ruby_language/php/control/control_for.php

```php
// incremented by 1
for ($i = 0; $i < 5; $i++) {
    print "$i ";
}
// => 0 1 2 3 4
```

Ruby   php_to_ruby_language/ruby/control/control_for.rb

```ruby
# incremented by 1
5.times do |i|
  print "#{i} "
end
# => 0 1 2 3 4

# incremented by 1
0.upto(4) do |i|
  print "#{i} "
end
# => 0 1 2 3 4
```

Likewise, we can create a loop with a decrementor by using the downto method.

PHP   php_to_ruby_language/php/control/control_for_decrement.php

```php
// decremented by 1
for ($i = 4; $i >= 0; $i--) {
    print "$i ";
}
// => 4 3 2 1 0
```

Ruby   php_to_ruby_language/ruby/control/control_for_decrement.rb

```ruby
# decremented
4.downto(0) do |i|
  print "#{i} "
end
# => 4 3 2 1 0
```

To create an interval other than 1 when incrementing or decrementing, we can use Ruby's step method to perform a loop. The first argument to this method is the final value we're counting up to, and the second argument is the interval.

PHP   php_to_ruby_language/php/control/control_for_interval.php

```php
// by an interval
for ($i = 0; $i < 5; $i += 2) {
    print "$i ";
}
// => 0 2 4
```

Ruby | php_to_ruby_language/ruby/control/control_for_interval.rb

```ruby
# by an interval
0.step(5, 2) do |i|
  print "#{i} "
end
# => 0 2 4
```

foreach

The foreach construct on arrays can be done with one of two iterator methods in Ruby. We'll use each only when we need to loop through the value in an array.

PHP | php_to_ruby_language/php/control/control_foreach.php

```php
# array
$colors = array('blue', 'orange', 'red');
foreach ($colors as $color) {
    print "$color ";
}
// => blue orange red
```

Ruby | php_to_ruby_language/ruby/control/control_foreach.rb

```ruby
# array
colors = ['blue', 'orange', 'red']
colors.each do |color|
  print "#{color} "
end
# => blue orange red
```

When we also need the numeric index of an array, we can iterate over the results using the each_with_index method, which will pass us two block arguments.

PHP | php_to_ruby_language/php/control/control_foreach_index.php

```php
# array with index
foreach ($colors as $key => $color) {
    print "$key=$color ";
}
// => 0=blue 1=orange 2=red
```

Ruby | php_to_ruby_language/ruby/control/control_foreach_index.rb

```ruby
# array with index
colors.each_with_index do |color, i|
  print "#{i}=#{color} "
end
# => 0=blue 1=orange 2=red
```

When we use the each method on a hash, it will pass both the key and value of the current element to the block.

PHP   php_to_ruby_language/php/control/control_foreach_assoc.php

```php
// associative array
$person = array('name' => 'Joe', 'eyes' => 'blue');
foreach ($person as $key => $value) {
    print "$key=$value ";
}
// => name=Joe eyes=blue
```

Ruby   php_to_ruby_language/ruby/control/control_foreach_assoc.rb

```ruby
# hash
person = {:name => 'Joe', :eyes => 'blue'}
person.each do |key, value|
  print "#{key}=#{value} "
end
# => eyes=blue name=Joe
```

break

Stopping the execution in both PHP and Ruby is done using the break statement, but the argument to break works differently in the two languages.

While PHP uses the argument to determine how many enclosing statements to break out of, Ruby treats this as a return value for the statement.

PHP   php_to_ruby_language/php/control/control_break.php

```php
$i = 0;
while (true) {
    if ($i == 5) break;
    print "$i ";
    $i++;
}
// => 0 1 2 3 4

// argument determines how many levels to break
$i = 1;
while ($i < 100) {
    while ($i < 10) {
        if ($i == 5) break 2; // skip out of both while loops
        $i++;
    }
    $i++;
}
print $i;
```

Ruby   php_to_ruby_language/ruby/control/control_break.rb

```ruby
i = 0
while true
  break if i == 5
  puts "#{i} "
  i += 1
end
# => 0 1 2 3 4

# argument to break is a return value
i = 1
result = while i < 100
  break "test" if i == 5
  i += 1
end
puts result # => test
```

continue/next

PHP's continue keyword is replaced by next in Ruby. Unlike PHP, Ruby does not allow an additional argument to specify how many loops to skip.

PHP   php_to_ruby_language/php/control/control_continue.php

```php
// only print even numbers
$i = 0;
while ($i <= 10) {
    $i++;
    if ($i%2 == 1) continue;
    print "$i ";
}
// => 2 4 6 8 10
```

Ruby   php_to_ruby_language/ruby/control/control_continue.rb

```ruby
# only print even numbers
i = 0
while i <= 10
  i += 1
  next if i%2 == 1
  puts "#{i} "
end
# => 2 4 6 8 10
```

switch

Ruby implements a case expression as a replacement for PHP's switch. Although case achieves the same goal, it works quite differently. The expression will not continue to evaluate statements once it finds a matching value, and thus it doesn't need a break statement to stop execution.

PHP php_to_ruby_language/php/control/control_switch.php

```php
// without a break, PHP keeps evaluating
switch (1) {
case 0:
    print "equals 0\n";
case 1:
    print "equals 1\n";
case 2:
    print "equals 2\n";
}
// => equals 1
//    equals 2
```

Ruby php_to_ruby_language/ruby/control/control_switch.rb

```ruby
# there is no need for a break
case 1
when 0: puts "equals 0"
when 1: puts "equals 1"
when 2: puts "equals 2"
end
# => equals 1
```

We can check multiple values for a statement by using comma-separated values, and we can take advantage of a case's return value to shorten our code.

PHP php_to_ruby_language/php/control/control_switch_multiple.php

```php
// multiple values are on additional lines
$color = 'blue';
switch ($color) {
case 'red':
case 'yellow':
    $type = "Warm";
    break;
case 'blue':
case 'green':
    $type = "Cool";
    break;
default:
    $type = "Invalid";
}
print "$type color\n";
// => Cool color
```

```
php_to_ruby_language/ruby/control/control_switch_multiple.rb
# multiple values are comma separated
color = 'blue'
case color
when 'red', 'yellow':
  type = "Warm"
when 'blue', 'green':
  type = "Cool"
else
  type = "Invalid"
end
puts "#{type} color"

# We can use case's return value to shorten the statement
type = case color
       when 'red', 'yellow': "Warm"
       when 'blue', 'green': "Cool"
       else                  "Invalid"
       end
puts "#{type} color"
```

return

The return statement in both PHP and Ruby will interrupt the normal flow of code to return a value from a block of code. Return values are discussed further in Section 12.2, *Return Values*, on page 318.

Require and Include

The require method in Ruby loads an external file a single time in the same form as PHP's require_once construct. The .rb extension on the filename is optional in Ruby and is often left off.

We can load the same external file more than once using Ruby's load method. This is just like PHP's require construct. This method differs from the Ruby's require method in that it does require the file extension of the loaded file.

Ruby does not implement the equivalent of PHP's include and include_ once, because they are simply a difference in error handling to Ruby. If we don't want the program execution to stop when a file cannot be loaded, we can simply enclose Ruby's require or load method calls within a rescue block to catch the raised exception.

PHP

```php
require_once 'lib/sample_file.php';
// => in the sample file
require_once 'lib/sample_file.php';


require 'lib/sample_file.php';
// => in the sample file
require 'lib/sample_file.php';
// => in the sample file
```

Ruby

```ruby
require 'lib/sample_file'
# => in the sample file
require 'lib/sample_file'


load 'lib/sample_file.rb'
# => in the sample file
load 'lib/sample_file.rb'
# => in the sample file
```

## Chapter 12

PHP to Ruby Advanced Reference

In this chapter, we'll go over some of the more complex language constructs, and we'll start to see some more radical differences in PHP and Ruby. Ruby has a different approach to using objects than PHP. Since the Ruby world consists nearly entirely of objects and methods, Ruby puts more focus on making them easier to create and use.

12.1 Blocks

Quite a few control structures from PHP are implemented using blocks in Ruby. Blocks are a feature in Ruby that are not available in PHP and serve as a method of passing an enclosure of code into a method. We can pass a block two different ways: using either curly braces ({}) or a do/end-style syntax. Rubyists generally agree on using the curly brace syntax when the block is on a single line and using the do/end-style block when the code spans multiple lines.

Ruby | php_to_ruby_language/ruby/blocks/basics.rb

```ruby
# single line block
['a', 'b', 'c'].each {|letter| puts letter }

# multiple line block
['a', 'b', 'c'].each do |letter|
  puts letter
  puts letter.upcase
end
```

It's obvious why we would pass values as arguments to a method, but you are probably wondering why we would need to pass in a block of code. The answer is that the method can then execute that block of code an arbitrary amount of times and can also pass arguments to the block of code to use just as we would with a method call.

One practical use of blocks is performing transactional operations. Using a block enables us to ensure that certain code always gets executed before and after an operation. We use the yield keyword to execute the block that was passed in.

Ruby php_to_ruby_language/ruby/blocks/transactions.rb

```ruby
def dinner
  puts "prepare meal"
  yield
  puts "wash dishes"
end

dinner { puts "eat lasagna" }
# => prepare meal
#    eat lasagna
#    wash dishes
```

In this case, we've made the dinner method accept a block. When we use this method, we'll make sure we always "prepare meal" before we eat and "wash dishes" afterward. We'll use this same concept in Ruby when we perform operations such as reading files. We can use this style of transaction to open the file before we read it and later close the file when we're finished.

We can also pass arguments to the yield keyword, which will be passed into the block for use. Let's create a method that will yield three variations on the word given. Each time we execute the block with yield, we will pass in the name and value of the variation. In the block we accept these arguments in a comma-separated list enclosed with pipe (|) characters.

Ruby php_to_ruby_language/ruby/blocks/arguments.rb

```ruby
def variations(name)
  yield("upcase",     name.upcase)
  yield("downcase",   name.downcase)
  yield("capitalize", name.capitalize)
end

variations('joe') {|name, value| puts "#{name} = #{value}" }
# => upcase = JOE
#    downcase = joe
#    capitalize = Joe
```

We can check whether a block was passed into a method by calling block_given?.

`Ruby`

```
php_to_ruby_language/ruby/blocks/block_given.rb
```

```ruby
def my_method
  if block_given?
    puts "block passed in"
  else
    puts "no block"
  end
end

my_method
# => no block

my_method {}
# => block passed in
```

It's also possible to pass the code block into the method and execute it directly in our method using call. When we add a final parameter to a method definition that is prefixed with an ampersand (&), Ruby will store the block of code in that variable.

`Ruby`

```
php_to_ruby_language/ruby/blocks/as_proc.rb
```

```ruby
# the block code is stored in arg2
def my_method(arg1, &arg2)
  arg2.call('block argument')
end

my_method('test') {|arg1| puts "Some data with #{arg1}" }
# => Some data with block argument
```

12.2 Functions

There are actually no functions in Ruby in the way we think of them in PHP. In Ruby every function is actually a method defined on a class or object. Any methods defined in the global scope are actually methods of the Object class. Since every Ruby object inherits from Object, methods defined in this scope are available everywhere unless overridden in a subclass.

`Ruby`

```
php_to_ruby_language/ruby/functions/functions_global.rb
```

```ruby
# this gets added to the Object class
def my_global_method
  puts "I'm available everywhere!"
end
o = Object.new
o.my_global_method
# => I'm available everywhere!
```

```ruby
# every new object inherits from object
class Car; end
c = Car.new
c.my_global_method
# => I'm available everywhere!
```

Defining and invoking methods in Ruby don't require us to use parentheses, and they are often left off when there are no arguments to the method.

A good rule of thumb is to use parentheses when calling a method with multiple arguments or when you need to chain additional methods calls to the result.

Ruby | php_to_ruby_language/ruby/functions/functions_invocation.rb

```ruby
# parentheses left out of method definition
def drink_water
  puts "Gulp, Gulp"
end
# stylisticly, parentheses would often be left off here as well
drink_water


# we need parentheses when we have arguments to pass in
def drink_beverage(type, size)
  puts "Gulping down #{size} of #{type}"
end
# we can invoke like this
drink_beverage "Gatorade", "gallon jug"

# but it is more stylisticly appropriate to use parentheses
drink_beverage("Gatorade", "gallon jug")
```

User-Defined

Methods are defined using a def/end syntax instead of PHP's curly braces. Unlike PHP, method names in Ruby are case sensitive.

PHP | php_to_ruby_language/php/functions/functions_user_defined.php

```php
// user defined function
function myFunction($arg1, $arg2, $arg3) {
    return "return value \n";
}
print myFunction('a', 'b', 'c');
// => return value

print mYfunCtion('a', 'b', 'c');
// => return value
```

php_to_ruby_language/ruby/functions/functions_user_defined.rb

```ruby
# user defined function
def my_function(arg1, arg2, arg3)
  "return value"
end
puts my_function('a', 'b', 'c')
# => return value

puts mY_funCtion('a', 'b', 'c')
# => undefined method `mY_funCtion' for main:Object
```

Ruby names can optionally end with a question mark (?), exclamation mark (!), or equals sign (=). The question mark is typically used on methods that return a boolean, as if we're asking a question. The equals sign is reserved for methods that act as a left-hand attribute assignment method.

php_to_ruby_language/ruby/functions/functions_naming.rb

```ruby
class User
  def admin=(admin)
    @admin = admin
  end

  def admin?
    @admin || false
  end
end
joe = User.new
joe.admin = true

puts joe.admin?
# => true
```

The exclamation point is often used to symbolize that the method performs an operation that is destructive or changes the receiving object. You'll probably notice that many built-in Ruby methods have a corresponding method that ends in an exclamation point.

php_to_ruby_language/ruby/functions/functions_bang.rb

```ruby
foo = [2, 1, 3]
# "sort" returns the sorted result, but "foo" remains the same
p foo.sort
# => [1, 2, 3]
p foo
# => [2, 1, 3]

# "sort!" actually changes the value of "foo"
p foo.sort!
# => [1, 2, 3]
p foo
# => [1, 2, 3]
```

Ruby allows nested methods. Just as with nested functions in PHP, they are not callable until the outer method has executed.

PHP   php_to_ruby_language/php/functions/functions_nested.php

```php
// nested functions
function myFunction() {
    function myInnerFunction() {
        print "inner value\n";
    }
}
myFunction();
myInnerFunction();
// => inner value
```

Ruby   php_to_ruby_language/ruby/functions/functions_nested.rb

```ruby
# nested functions
def my_function
  def my_inner_function
    print "inner value"
  end
end
my_function
my_inner_function
# => inner value
```

Arguments

Like in PHP, we can use default values to arguments by assigning values to the method parameters in the definition. While PHP cannot assign a new object as a default value, Ruby can assign any data type as a default value.

PHP   php_to_ruby_language/php/functions/functions_arguments.php

```php
// passing default values
function myFunction($arg1='default', $arg2=array('a', 'b')) {
    print "$arg1 $arg2[0]\n";
}

myFunction();
// => default a
```

Ruby   php_to_ruby_language/ruby/functions/functions_arguments.rb

```ruby
# passing default values
def my_function(arg1='default', arg2=['a', 'b'], arg3=Object.new)
  puts "#{arg1} #{arg2[0]}"
end
my_function
# => default a
```

Hashes can be passed into a method without the enclosed curly braces, which allows for a syntax that simulates named arguments. This idiom is used quite often in Rails to make the code more readable when there are many options to pass into a method.

php_to_ruby_language/ruby/functions/functions_arguments_hash.rb

```ruby
def format(text, options = {})
  text.reverse! if options[:reverse]
  text.upcase!  if options[:upcase]
  text
end

puts format('Live not on evil.', :reverse => true, :upcase => true)
# => .LIVE NO TON EVIL
```

We can pass an optional block to a method using either a single-line curly brace block or a multiline do/end-style block. We can reference the block with a final parameter in the method definition that is prefixed with an ampersand (&).

When we call this method, Ruby will convert the block to a Proc object and assign it to this argument.

php_to_ruby_language/ruby/functions/functions_arguments_blocks.rb

```ruby
# when we use a block, it's passed in as an argument
def checker(value, &block)
  value << block.call if block
  value
end

# not passing a block
puts checker('test')
# => 'test'

# passing in a single-line block
puts checker('test') { " with a block" }
# => "test with a block"
```

Ruby has a nice way of dealing with variable arguments. Instead of using a function to get the arguments as in PHP, we can add an array argument to the end of our argument list by prepending the name of the argument with an asterisk (*).

This is called the *splat* operator and will collect all remaining elements into this argument as an array.

PHP `php_to_ruby_language/php/functions/functions_variable_args.php`

```php
function myFunction() {
    $argNum = func_num_args();
    $args   = func_get_args();
    $first  = array_shift($args);
    $second = array_shift($args);

    print "($argNum) total, first: $first\n";
}
myFunction('red', 'green', 'blue');
// => (2) total, first: red
```

Ruby `php_to_ruby_language/ruby/functions/functions_variable_args.rb`

```ruby
def my_function(*args)
  arg_num = args.size
  first   = args.shift
  second  = args.shift

  puts "(#{arg_num}) total, first: #{first}"
end
my_function('red', 'green', 'blue')
# => (3) total, first: red
```

We can also require a specified number of requirements and collect the rest using the splat operator on the last argument.

PHP `php_to_ruby_language/php/functions/functions_variable_args_req.php`

```php
function anotherFunction($first, $second) {
    $args  = func_get_args();
    $third = $args[2];
    print "first: $first, third: $third\n";
}
anotherFunction('red', 'green', 'blue');
// => first: red, third: blue
```

Ruby `php_to_ruby_language/ruby/functions/functions_variable_args_req.rb`

```ruby
# we can require some args, and collect all the rest
def another_function(first, second, *more)
  third = more.first
  puts "first: #{first}, third: #{third}"
end
another_function('red', 'green', 'blue')
# => first: red, third: blue
```

Return Values

Like PHP, Ruby uses the return keyword to return a value from a method. However, unlike PHP, Ruby will implicitly return the last expression evaluated in any method. Although it may take some getting used to, it is a common Ruby convention to not use the return keyword when not needed.

PHP

`php_to_ruby_language/php/functions/functions_return_values.php`

```php
// single value
function sayHi($name) {
    return "hello, $name\n";
}
print sayHi('Joe');
// => hello, Joe
```

Ruby

`php_to_ruby_language/ruby/functions/functions_return_values.rb`

```ruby
# single value
def say_hi(name)
  "hello, #{name}"
end
puts say_hi('Joe')
# => hello, Joe
```

As in PHP, we can return any value from a method, and it is normal to return an array that is then split into multiple variables. Ruby does not require the use of a function such as list to assign the variables and can simply use a comma-separated list of names.

PHP

`php_to_ruby_language/php/functions/functions_return_values_array.php`

```php
// array of values
function myColors() {
    return array('red', 'green', 'blue');
}
list($color1, $color2, $color3) = myColors();
print "$color1\n";
// => red
```

Ruby

`php_to_ruby_language/ruby/functions/functions_return_values_array.rb`

```ruby
# array of values
def my_colors
  %w{red green blue}
end
color1, color2, color3 = my_colors
puts color1
# => red
```

Variable Functions

Variables storing a method name can be used to invoke that method just as in PHP. In Ruby we pass the name of the method and an array of arguments to the send method to invoke it.

PHP
`php_to_ruby_language/php/functions/functions_variable_functions.php`

```php
function myFunction($arg1) {
    print "$arg1 in my function!\n";
}

$a = 'myFunction';
$a('value');
// => value in my function!
```

Ruby
`php_to_ruby_language/ruby/functions/functions_variable_functions.rb`

```ruby
def my_method(arg1)
  puts "#{arg1} in my method!"
end

a = "my_method"
send(a, ["value"])
# => "value in my method!"
```

Internal (Built-In) Functions

Although PHP has a wide selection of built-in functions that all exist within the global scope, Ruby takes quite a different approach. Ruby methods are built around the objects that they modify. This means that each data type we're dealing with has its methods. To reverse an array in PHP, we would pass it to the array_reverse function. In Ruby, we instead send a message to the array to reverse itself with the reverse method.

PHP
`php_to_ruby_language/php/functions/functions_array_reverse.php`

```php
$colors = array('blue', 'red');
$reversed = array_reverse($colors);
var_export($reversed); // => array(0 => 'red', 1 => 'blue');
```

Ruby
`php_to_ruby_language/ruby/functions/functions_array_reverse.rb`

```ruby
colors = [:blue, :red]
reversed = colors.reverse
p reversed # => [:red, :blue]
```

This difference is important because it allows us to logically separate the functionality out of the global namespace. This makes remembering functions much easier, since there is no need to have arbitrary prefixes grouping related functions. PHP uses array_reverse to reverse an array and strrev to reverse a string. Ruby method names don't conflict since they're not in the global namespace. This means we can use the reverse method name to reverse both array and string objects.

PHP

php_to_ruby_language/php/functions/functions_reverse.php

```php
$reversed = array_reverse(array('car', 'truck'));
$reversed = strrev('van');
```

Ruby

php_to_ruby_language/ruby/functions/functions_reverse.rb

```ruby
reversed = [:car, :truck].reverse
reversed = 'van'.reverse
```

Another advantage to this is that we can perform reflection on an object to ask the object what methods it implements. This is a nice way of quickly referencing available methods that we might want to use. We do this using the methods method on our object. To make this list easier to parse through, we'll often sort the results of that output with the sort method.

Ruby

php_to_ruby_language/ruby/functions/functions_reflection.rb

```ruby
'water'.methods
# => ["%", "select", "[]=", "inspect", "<<", "each_byte", "clone",
#      ...
#      "max", "chop!", "is_a?", "capitalize!", "scan", "[]"]

'water'.methods.sort
# => ["%", "*", "+", "<", "<<", "<=", "<=>", "==", "===", "=~", ">"
#      ...
#      "type", "unpack", "untaint", "upcase", "upcase!", "upto", "zip"]
```

12.3 Classes and Objects

The difference between classes and objects in PHP and Ruby is a complex topic. Some of the important differences in object philosophy are explained in Section 3.1, *Thinking in Objects*, on page 59.

The Basics (class/new/extends)

In Ruby, we declare basic class definitions using the class keyword just as in PHP. Ruby once again rejects curly braces in favor of the end keyword to signify the end of our class. We define each method in our class as discussed in Section 12.2, *Functions*, on page 313.

Ruby does not declare data members in the class definition. It instead shares data using instance variables. Instance variable names start with an "at" (@) sign and are shared between all methods of a single object instance. While PHP has the idea of private, public, and protected members, Ruby approaches this quite differently. All instance variables in a Ruby class are assigned at runtime and are available only within the object. There is no way to access these outside of the object without getter and setter methods.

`PHP` php_to_ruby_language/php/variables/variables_instance.php

```php
class Car
{
    // we declare instance variables first in PHP
    public  $color;
    private $doors;

    public function __construct($color, $doors)
    {
        $this->color = $color;
        $this->doors = $doors;
    }

    public function getDoors()
    {
        return $this->doors;
    }
}

$car = new Car('blue', 4);
print $car->color."\n";
// => blue

print $car->getDoors()."\n";
// => 4
```

`Ruby` php_to_ruby_language/ruby/variables/variables_instance.rb

```ruby
class Car
  # we can make this attribute public using attr_accessor
  attr_accessor :color

  def initialize(color, doors)
    @color = color
    @doors = doors
  end

  def doors
    @doors
  end
end

car = Car.new('blue', 4)
puts car.color
# => blue

puts car.doors
# => 4
```

In the PHP example we declared the color and doors members to our class, which we can access within our class using $this->. Although we can directly access the color from outside of the class because of its public declaration, we had to define a getter method to access the data stored in the protected doors attribute. Our corresponding Ruby code has used attr_accessor for our color instance variable. This dynamically adds getter and setter methods for this attribute to essentially make it public.

Ruby uses self. as a comparable syntax to PHP's $this-> to access the current instance of the object. The main difference is that self. is implied in Ruby and can usually be left out. It is generally used only to disambiguate code that may be interpreted otherwise.

PHP `php_to_ruby_language/php/objects/class.php`

```php
class User {
    // members
    public $name;

    // methods
    public function info() {
        return "Name: $this->name\n";
    }

    public function printer() {
        print $this->info();
    }
}

$u = new User;
$u->name = "Joe";
$u->printer();
// => Name: Joe
```

Ruby `php_to_ruby_language/ruby/objects/class.rb`

```ruby
class User
  def name
    @name
  end

  def name=(name)
    @name = name
  end

  # methods
  def info
    "Name: #{@name}"
  end
```

```ruby
  def printer
    # "self." is implied, and would generally be left out here
    puts self.info
  end
end

u = User.new
u.name = "Joe"
u.printer
# => Name: Joe
```

Since we don't declare data members in the class definition, Ruby must assign any default values for the instance variables within the constructor method named initialize. A good strategy for doing this is to assign the default values to class constants. We can then assign incoming parameters to these values in the constructor.

PHP

php_to_ruby_language/php/objects/member_defaults.php

```php
class Document {
    public $orientation = 'portrait';

    public function info() {
        print "Orientation: $this->orientation\n";
    }
}

$d = new Document;
$d->info();
```

Ruby

php_to_ruby_language/ruby/objects/member_defaults.rb

```ruby
class Document
  DEFAULT_ORIENTATION = 'portrait'

  def initialize(orientation = DEFAULT_ORIENTATION)
    @orientation = orientation
  end

  def info
    puts "Orientation: #{@orientation}"
  end
end

d = Document.new
d.info
```

Creating an instance of an object in Ruby flips PHP's new User syntax to read as User.new. The new keyword is now a method definition on our User class instead of a language construct.

PHP

`php_to_ruby_language/php/objects/new.php`

```php
class User {}

$user = new User;
```

Ruby

`php_to_ruby_language/ruby/objects/new.rb`

```ruby
def User; end

user = User.new
```

Ruby uses the less-than (<) character to denote inheritance and as an equivalent of the extends keyword in PHP. We can call the parent method within a method by using the super keyword instead of PHP's parent:: syntax. Calling super without any parameters or parentheses will automatically pass all parameters from the child method call. We can optionally pass a specific set of parameters to the parent method such as super(arg1, arg2).

PHP

`php_to_ruby_language/php/objects/extends.php`

```php
class Media {
    public function title() {
        return "Media";
    }
}

class Book extends Media {
    public function title() {
        $parentTitle = parent::title();
        return "$parentTitle: Book Title";
    }
}

$book = new Book;
print $book->title()."\n";
```

Ruby

`php_to_ruby_language/ruby/objects/extends.rb`

```ruby
class Media
  def title
    "Media"
  end
end

class Book < Media
  def title
    parent_title = super
    "#{parent_title}: Book Title"
  end
end
```

```
book = Book.new
puts book.title
```

Autoloading Objects

There is no magic method in Ruby that is the equivalent of PHP's
__autoload function. It is, however, easy enough to use Ruby's const_
missing class method to accomplish the same thing.

Notice that we've gone through an extra step to convert the class name
to an underscore version. It is generally accepted in the Ruby/Rails
community that we name all source files using an underscore format.

Rails has its own autoloading implementation, which makes this something you can mostly ignore when working within the context of the
Rails framework.

PHP

php_to_ruby_language/php/objects/autoloading.php

```php
function __autoload($name) {
    require_once "lib/$name.php";
}

// load up SampleClass.php
$sample = new SampleClass;
print "loaded: ".get_class($sample)."\n";
```

Ruby

php_to_ruby_language/ruby/objects/autoloading.rb

```ruby
def Object.const_missing(name)
  # convert camel name to underscore
  require "lib/#{name.to_s.gsub(/([a-z])([A-Z])/,'\1_\2').downcase}"
  return const_get(name)
end

# load up lib/sample_class.rb
sample = SampleClass.new
puts "loaded: #{sample.class}"
```

Constructors/Destructors

Ruby's constructor is named initialize and is called during the creation
of any new object instance just as in PHP. We can call the constructor
of a parent class by using the super method.

`php_to_ruby_language/php/objects/construct.php`

```php
class Media {
    public $title;

    public function __construct($title) {
        $this->title = $title;
    }
}

class Book extends Media {
    public $author;

    public function __construct($title, $author) {
        parent::__construct($title);
        $this->author = $author;
    }
}

$book = new Book('Dracula', 'Bram Stoker');
print "$book->title by $book->author\n";
```

`php_to_ruby_language/ruby/objects/construct.rb`

```ruby
class Media
  def initialize(title)
    @title = title
  end

  def title
    @title
  end
end

class Book < Media
  def initialize(title, author)
    super(title)
    @author = author
  end

  def author
    @author
  end
end

book = Book.new('Dracula', 'Bram Stoker')
puts "#{book.title} by #{book.author}"
```

There are no destructors in Ruby that are equivalent to those in PHP. Ruby's best alternative is to encapsulate your object usage within a block. Doing this gives us the option of performing some destruction or teardown code before we finish with the object.

PHP   php_to_ruby_language/php/objects/destruct.php

```php
class MyClass {
    public $name;

    public function __construct($name) {
        $this->name = $name;
        print "constructing\n";
    }

    public function __destruct() {
        print "destructing\n";
    }
}

$obj = new MyClass('test class');
// => constructing

print $obj->name."\n";
// => test class

unset($obj);
// => destructing
```

Ruby   php_to_ruby_language/ruby/objects/destruct.rb

```ruby
class MyClass
  attr_accessor :name

  def initialize(name)
    @name = name
    puts "constructing"
    yield self
    puts "destructing"
  end
end

MyClass.new('test class') do |obj|
  # => constructing

  puts obj.name
  # => test class

end
# => destructing
```

Visibility

PHP uses public, private, or protected data members to share data of an object instance. Ruby instead uses special instance variables to share data. Instance variables all have the same visibility, which is that they are completely encapsulated within the object. They cannot be directly accessed from outside the class without a public method. Since instance variables are inherited in subclasses, they most closely resemble data members with a protected visibility in PHP.

Although we have no option to set the visibility of data members, we can set visibility for Ruby methods as public, private, or protected. Like in PHP, all Ruby methods are public unless otherwise stated. We define visibility for multiple methods at once with a single keyword. All methods below that keyword will be assigned that visibility until either another visibility is defined or the class ends.

`PHP` php_to_ruby_language/php/objects/method_visibility.php

```php
class MyClass {
    public function myPublicMethod() {}

    protected function myProtectedMethod() {}

    protected function anotherProtectedMethod() {}

    private function myPrivateMethod() {}

    public function mySecondPublicMethod() {}
}
```

`Ruby` php_to_ruby_language/ruby/objects/method_visibility.rb

```ruby
class MyClass
  # default is public
  def my_public_method
  end

  protected
  def my_protected_method
  end

  def another_protected_method
  end

  private
  def my_private_method
  end

  public
  def my_second_public_method
  end
end
```

More subtle differences in visibility and object attributes can be found in Section 3.2, *Understanding Attributes*, on page 62.

Static Keyword

The closest we get to PHP's static data members in Ruby are class variables. These variables are accessed and assigned within the object or class by using the double "at" symbol variable name convention. Just like instance variables, there is no way to make these public, and we must define a class method to provide access to the data.

`PHP` `php_to_ruby_language/php/objects/static_members.php`

```php
class MyClass {
    public static $myStaticVar = 'static value';

    public function myMethod() {
        return self::$myStaticVar;
    }
}

print MyClass::$myStaticVar."\n";
// => static value

$obj = new MyClass;
print $obj->myMethod();
// => static value
```

`Ruby` `php_to_ruby_language/ruby/objects/static_members.rb`

```ruby
class MyClass
  @@my_class_var = 'class value'

  def self.my_class_var
    @@my_class_var
  end

  def self.my_method
    self.my_class_var
  end
end

puts MyClass.my_class_var
# => class value

puts MyClass.my_method
# => class value
```

Ruby class methods are the closest construct we have to PHP's static methods for performing class-specific operations. The most common way of defining class methods is to prefix the method name with self.. While in PHP we call static methods using the double colon (::) syntax, Ruby invokes class methods with a dot (.) as used for any other Ruby method call. The reason for this is that classes in Ruby are actually full object instances in themselves with methods and properties.

PHP

php_to_ruby_language/php/objects/static_methods.php

```php
class MyClass {
    public static function staticMethod() {
        return 'a static method';
    }

    public function instanceMethod() {
        return $this->staticMethod();
    }
}

print MyClass::staticMethod()."\n";
// => a static method

$obj = new MyClass;
print $obj->instanceMethod()."\n";
// => a static method
```

Ruby

php_to_ruby_language/ruby/objects/static_methods.rb

```ruby
class MyClass
  def self.class_method
    'a class method'
  end

  def instance_method
    self.class.class_method
  end
end

puts MyClass.class_method
# => a class method

obj = MyClass.new
puts obj.instance_method
# => a class method
```

Although PHP can call a static method using $this-> while in the context of an object instance, Ruby cannot do this. Ruby must first reference the class of the current object before calling the method.

There are some addition variations on syntax for defining class methods. It is important to be able to recognize any of these styles when reading another developer's code.

Ruby

php_to_ruby_language/ruby/objects/static_variations.rb

```ruby
class MyClass
  def self.class_method
    'a class method'
  end
```

```ruby
  # this is the same as using def self.another_class_method,
  # but not as stylish in the Ruby community
  def MyClass.another_class_method
    'another class method'
  end

  # all methods defined within this block are class methods
  class << self
    def yet_another
      'yet another'
    end

    def and_another
      'and another'
    end
  end
end

puts MyClass.class_method            # => a class method
puts MyClass.another_class_method    # => another class method
puts MyClass.yet_another             # => yet another
puts MyClass.and_another             # => and another
```

Class Constants

Class constants are similar between Ruby and PHP, and both are declared within the class body. Ruby imposes no restrictions on the data type used for a constant and does not require any keyword to signify that we're declaring a constant. Any variable beginning with a capital letter is always assumed to be a constant in Ruby. While PHP uses self:: to scope the constant from within an object, Ruby needs no such prefix.

Both languages have a similar syntax when accessing the constant from outside of the class.

PHP   php_to_ruby_language/php/objects/constants.php

```php
class MyClass {
    const MY_CONSTANT = 'constant value';

    public function myMethod() {
        print self::MY_CONSTANT; // => constant value
    }
}

print MyClass::MY_CONSTANT; // => constant value
```

Ruby

`php_to_ruby_language/ruby/objects/constants.rb`

```ruby
class MyClass
  MY_CONSTANT = 'constant value'

  def my_method
    puts MY_CONSTANT # => constant value
  end
end

print MyClass::MY_CONSTANT # => constant value
```

Class Abstraction

Ruby does not implement abstract classes because of its inherent object philosophy of not enforcing types. It is possible to write a type of abstraction by declaring the new method of the parent as private and raise exceptions when specific methods are not implemented in the concrete subclass.

PHP

`php_to_ruby_language/php/objects/abstraction.php`

```php
abstract class MyAbstractClass {
    abstract public function getMyValue();
}

class MyConcreteClass extends MyAbstractClass {
    public function __construct($value) {
        $this->value = $value;
    }

    public function getMyValue() {
        return $this->value;
    }
}


$obj = new MyConcreteClass('test value');
print $obj->getMyValue()."\n";
// => test value

$obj = new MyAbstractClass;
// => Cannot instantiate abstract class MyAbstractClass
```

Ruby

`php_to_ruby_language/ruby/objects/abstraction.rb`

```ruby
class MyAbstractClass
  private_class_method :new

  def get_my_value
    raise "Cannot call abstract method"
  end
end
```

```ruby
class MyConcreteClass < MyAbstractClass
  public_class_method :new

  def initialize(value)
    @value = value
  end

  def get_my_value
    @value
  end
end

obj = MyConcreteClass.new('test value')
puts obj.get_my_value
# => test value

obj = MyAbstractClass.new
# => private method `new' called for MyAbstractClass:Class
```

In PHP we often use abstract classes to create an interface for an object that includes concrete methods implementations. In Ruby we can use an alternate strategy to achieve the same result.

We can mixin concrete method implementations using modules. More details on how this works are discussed in Section 3.5, *Implementing Interfaces with Mixins*, on page 71.

Object Interfaces

Interfaces are not implemented in Ruby because of a basic difference in object philosophy. Ruby instead uses mixins to add both interface and implementation to a class. Mixins are described in more detail in Section 3.5, *Implementing Interfaces with Mixins*, on page 71.

Overloading

Ruby replaces the functionality of PHP's __get, __set, and __call magic methods with a single method named method_missing. Since Ruby has no public attributes, we can handle all situations with a single method for catching any missing methods.

A common usage of overloading is to delegate method calls to a different object. In this example, any methods missing on a Boss get delegated to the Assistant instance.

PHP

```php
class Assistant {
    public $answeredCalls = 0;

    public function writeReport() {
        return 'assistant writing report...';
    }
}

class Boss {
    protected $assistant;

    // delegate undefined member/methods to assistant
    public function __construct($assistant) {
        $this->assistant = $assistant;
    }

    public function __set($name, $value) {
        $this->assistant->$name = $value;
    }

    public function __get($name) {
        return $this->assistant->$name;
    }

    public function __call($name, $args) {
        return call_user_func_array(
            array($this->assistant, $name), $args);
    }
}

$assistant = new Assistant;
$boss = new Boss($assistant);

$boss->answeredCalls = 5;
print $assistant->answeredCalls."\n";
// => 5

print $boss->writeReport()."\n";
// => assistant writing report...
```

Ruby

```ruby
class Assistant
  attr_accessor :answered_calls

  def initialize
    @answered_calls = 0
  end
```

```ruby
  def write_report
    'assistant writing report...'
  end
end

class Boss
  # proxy undefined member/methods to assistant
  def initialize(assistant)
    @assistant = assistant
  end

  def method_missing(name, *args)
    @assistant.send(name, *args)
  end
end

assistant = Assistant.new
boss = Boss.new(assistant)

boss.answered_calls = 5
puts assistant.answered_calls
# => 5

puts boss.write_report
# => assistant writing report
```

PHP's __isset can also be implemented by method_missing by returning nil for methods that are not set. The equivalent of PHP's __unset is best achieved by adding a custom delete method to the Ruby object.

PHP · php_to_ruby_language/php/objects/__isset.php

```php
class MyClass {
    protected $values = array('first'  => 'value one',
                              'second' => 'value two');

    public function __isset($name) {
        return isset($this->values[$name]);
    }

    public function __unset($name) {
        unset($this->values[$name]);
    }

    public function __get($name) {
        return $this->values[$name];
    }
}
```

```php
$obj = new MyClass;
if (isset($obj->first)) {
    print $obj->first."\n";
    // => value one

    unset($obj->first);
    var_export(isset($obj->first));
    // => false
}
```

Ruby

`php_to_ruby_language/ruby/objects/__isset.rb`

```ruby
class MyClass
  def initialize
    @values = { :first => 'value one', :second => 'value two' }
  end

  def delete(name)
    @values.delete(name)
  end

  def method_missing(name, *args)
    if name.to_s.include?('=')
      @values[name] = *args
    else
      @values[name]
    end
  end
end

obj = MyClass.new
if obj.first
  puts obj.first
  # => value one

  obj.delete(:first)
  puts obj.first
  # => nil
end
```

Object Iteration

Since there are no public attributes in Ruby, there is no native way to loop through the public attributes as we could in PHP. To do this, we would need to add a method that returns the list of attributes we want to loop through.

PHP · php_to_ruby_language/php/objects/iteration_simple.php

```php
class Book {
    public    $title;
    public    $author;
    protected $price;

    public function __construct($title, $author, $price) {
        $this->title  = $title;
        $this->author = $author;
        $this->price  = $price;
    }
}
$book = new Book('Dracula', 'Bram Stoker', 9.95);

foreach ($book as $key => $value) {
    print "$key : $value\n";
}
// => title : Dracula
//    author : Bram Stoker
```

Ruby · php_to_ruby_language/ruby/objects/iteration_simple.rb

```ruby
class Book
  attr_accessor :title, :author

  def initialize(title, author, price)
    @title, @author, @price = title, author, price
  end

  def publics
    [:title, :author]
  end
end
book = Book.new('Dracula', 'Bram Stoker', 9.95)

book.publics.each do |name|
  puts "#{name} : #{book.send(name)}"
end
# => title : Dracula
#    author : Bram Stoker
```

Oftentimes we want to iterate over a collection within an object using the language's native iteration syntax such as PHP's foreach. PHP provides a way for us to do this by implementing an interface such as IteratorAggregate on our class.

The native iteration in Ruby is typically done with a call to the each
method of that object, and thus customizing it entails redefining the
each method to do our bidding.

```
php_to_ruby_language/php/objects/iteration_iterator.php
```

```php
class Errors implements IteratorAggregate {
    protected $errors;

    public function __construct() {
        $this->errors = array();
    }

    public function add($name, $message) {
        $this->errors[$name][] = $message;
    }

    public function getIterator() {
        $errors = array();
        foreach ($this->errors as $name => $msgs) {
            foreach ($msgs as $msg) {
                $errors[] = ucfirst($name)." ".$msg;
            }
        }
        return new ArrayIterator($errors);
    }
}

$errors = new Errors;
$errors->add('title',  'has invalid characters');
$errors->add('title',  'is too short');
$errors->add('author', "can't be empty");

foreach ($errors as $error) {
    print "$error\n";
}
// => Title has invalid characters
//    Title is too short
//    Author can't be empty
```

```
php_to_ruby_language/ruby/objects/iteration_iterator.rb
```

```ruby
class Errors
  def initialize
    @errors = {}
  end

  def add(name, message)
    @errors[name] ||= []
    @errors[name] << message
  end
```

```ruby
  # each is the
  def each
    @errors.each do |name, msgs|
      msgs.each {|msg| yield name.capitalize + " " + msg }
    end
  end
end

errors = Errors.new
errors.add('title',  'has invalid characters')
errors.add('title',  'is too short')
errors.add('author', "can't be empty")

errors.each {|error| puts error }
# => Title has invalid characters
#    Title is too short
#    Author can't be empty
```

In these examples, we have a collection of errors that are added and stored in a nested data structure. The PHP example loops through each error and compiles a flat list of errors that we can pass into an ArrayIterator. The Ruby uses a similar approach but takes advantage of Ruby blocks to pass each error to the block as it builds them. The end result is the same, and we are able to iterate over our object's data structure as if it were a normal array.

Patterns

Ruby objects can implement design patterns just like PHP objects and are often even better suited to doing so because of Ruby's inherent object-oriented nature. The Singleton pattern in Ruby is quite simple and takes advantage of few unique Ruby idioms. We can use a class variable to store the instance of the object. Assigning this class variable in the get_instance method is simplified by using Ruby's conditional assignment operator (||=). We're able to make the original constructor private by using the private_class_method declaration for the :new method at the top of our class definition.

PHP · php_to_ruby_language/php/objects/singleton.php

```php
// implements the singleton pattern
class Log {
    private static $instance;

    private function __construct() {
        print "constructed\n";
    }
```

```php
    public static function getInstance() {
        if (!isset(self::$instance)) {
            $className = __CLASS__;
            self::$instance = new $className;
        }
        return self::$instance;
    }
}

$log1 = Log::getInstance();
// => constructed
$log2 = Log::getInstance();

var_export($log1 === $log2);
// => true
```

Ruby php_to_ruby_language/ruby/objects/singleton.rb

```ruby
# implements the singleton pattern
class Log
  private_class_method :new
  @@instance = nil

  def initialize
    puts "constructed"
  end

  def self.get_instance
    @@instance ||= new
  end
end

log1 = Log.get_instance
# => constructed
log2 = Log.get_instance

puts log1.equal?(log2)
# => true
```

Magic Methods

Ruby's equivalent of PHP's serialize and unserialize functions are the Marshal.dump and Marshal.load methods, respectively. Just as in PHP, we can perform custom operations before and after an object is serialized. Ruby's equivalent of __sleep is the _dump method, and the replacement for __wakeup is the _load class method.

`PHP` php_to_ruby_language/php/objects/__sleep.php

```php
class MyClass {
    protected $name;

    public function __construct($name) {
        $this->name = $name;
    }

    public function __sleep() {
        print "calling sleep\n";
        return array('name');
    }

    public function __wakeup() {
        print "calling wakeup\n";
    }
}

$obj = new MyClass('my_var');
$serialized = serialize($obj);
// => calling sleep

print $serialized."\n";
// => O:7:"MyClass":1:{s:7:"*name";s:6:"my_var";}

unserialize($serialized);
// => calling wakeup
```

`Ruby` php_to_ruby_language/ruby/objects/__sleep.rb

```ruby
class MyClass
  def initialize(name)
    @name = name
  end

  def _dump(depth)
    puts "calling sleep"
    @name
  end

  def MyClass._load(str)
    puts "calling wakeup"
    MyClass.new(str)
  end
end


obj = MyClass.new('my_var')
serialized = Marshal.dump(obj)
# => calling sleep
```

```
p serialized
# => "\004\bu:\fMyClass\vmy_var"

obj = Marshal.load(serialized)
# => calling wakeup
```

All objects in Ruby have a to_s method implementation, which is the equivalent of PHP's __toString magic method. Adding a custom implementation of a string conversion is as easy as redefining the to_s method for that class.

`PHP` php_to_ruby_language/php/objects/__to_string.php

```php
class User {
    protected $first;
    protected $last;

    public function __construct($first, $last) {
        $this->first = $first;
        $this->last  = $last;
    }

    public function __toString() {
        return "First: $this->first, Last: $this->last";
    }
}

$user = new User("Clark", "Kent");
print $user;
// => First: Clark, Last: Kent
```

`Ruby` php_to_ruby_language/ruby/objects/__to_string.rb

```ruby
class User
  def initialize(first, last)
    @first, @last = first, last
  end

  def to_s
    "First: #{@first}, Last: #{@last}"
  end
end

user = User.new("Clark", "Kent")
print user
# => First: Clark, Last: Kent
```

Final Keyword

Ruby does not implement any equivalent of PHP's final keyword for methods or classes. This is a general difference in programming philosophy between the two languages.

Ruby embraces the idea of keeping things open for modification while trusting the developer to not override something they shouldn't.

Object Cloning

When directly assigned to a new variable name, objects in both PHP and Ruby will perform a copy by reference. All Ruby objects have a dup method that returns a shallow copy of the object just like using the clone keyword in PHP. Ruby also provides the initialize_copy method as an equivalent of PHP's __clone magic method.

PHP `php_to_ruby_language/php/objects/cloning.php`

```php
class MyClass {
    public $name;

    public function __construct($name) {
        $this->name = $name;
    }

    public function __clone() {
        print "cloning object...\n";
    }
}
$obj1 = new MyClass("first name");

// perform copy by reference
$obj2 = $obj1;

// perform shallow copy
$obj3 = clone $obj1;
// => cloning object
```

Ruby `php_to_ruby_language/ruby/objects/cloning.rb`

```ruby
class MyClass
  attr_accessor :name

  def initialize(name)
    @name = name
  end

  def initialize_copy(other)
    puts "duping object..."
  end
end
obj1 = MyClass.new("first name")

# perform copy by reference
obj2 = obj1
```

```
# perform shallow copy
obj3 = obj1.dup
# => duping object
```

Comparing Objects

By default, Ruby will consider two objects equal using the equality operator (==) only if both objects are the same object instance. This isn't always useful, and we'll often want to redefine the equality operator method on our object.

php_to_ruby_language/php/objects/comparing.php

```php
class User {
    protected $first;
    protected $last;

    public function __construct($first, $last) {
        $this->first = $first;
        $this->last  = $last;
    }
}

var_export(new User('john', 'doe') == new User('john', 'doe'));
// => true

var_export(new User('john', 'doe') == new User('jane', 'doe'));
// => false

$user = new User('jean', 'dupont');
var_export($user === $user);
// => true
```

php_to_ruby_language/ruby/objects/comparing.rb

```ruby
class User
  attr_accessor :first, :last

  def initialize(first, last)
    @first, @last = first, last
  end

  # custom comparison method compares instance values
  def ==(other)
    [:first, :last].each do |attr|
      return false unless self.send(attr) == other.send(attr)
    end
    true
  end
end
```

```
puts User.new('john', 'doe') == User.new('john', 'doe')
# => true

puts User.new('john', 'doe') == User.new('jane', 'doe')
# => false

user = User.new('jean', 'dupont')
puts user.equal?(user)
# => true
```

In this example we have redefined the == method to make the equality operator behave more like PHP's. We consider the two objects equal if the attribute values match. The equal? method on our object will still check whether the objects are of the same instance and is similar to the identity operator (===) in PHP.

Reflection

Reflection of objects in Ruby is an integral part of the language and is built into each class and object instance. Instead of instantiating a reflection object, we can simply call the reflection-related methods on plain Ruby objects.

In PHP we can get a list of methods objects for a class and determine their visibility using a getter such as isPublic() or isPrivate(). Ruby's approach is different and instead filters each method into smaller subsets that can be accessed using methods such as public_instance_methods and private_instance_methods.

> PHP   `php_to_ruby_language/php/objects/reflection_class.php`

```php
class User {}

class Employee extends User {
    public        $first;
    protected     $last;
    public static $userCnt;

    public function __construct($first=null, $last=null) {
        $this->first = $first;
        $this->last  = $last;
        self::$userCnt++;
    }

    public function getFirst() {
        return $this->first;
    }
```

```php
    public function getLast() {
        return $this->last;
    }
}

$class = new ReflectionClass('Employee');

print $class->getName()." descends from ".
    $class->getParentClass()->getName()."\n";
// => Employee descends from User

foreach ($class->getMethods() as $method) {
    $methods[] = $method->getName();
}
print join(', ', $methods)."\n";
// => __construct, getFirst, getLast

foreach ($class->getProperties() as $property) {
    $properties[] = $property->getName();
}
print join(', ', $properties)."\n";
// => first, last, userCnt
```

Ruby   php_to_ruby_language/ruby/objects/reflection_class.rb

```ruby
class User; end
class Employee < User
  @@user_cnt = 0

  def initialize(first=nil, last=nil)
    @first, @last = first, last
    @@user_cnt += 1
  end

  def first
    @first
  end

  def last
    @last
  end
end

puts "#{Employee.name} descends from #{Employee.superclass}"
# => Employee descends from User

puts Employee.instance_methods(false).join(', ')
# => last, first

puts Employee.private_methods(false).join(', ')
# => initialize, initialize_copy, inherited
```

```
# we need to create an instance to reflect on instance variables
puts Employee.new.instance_variables.join(', ')
# => @last, @first

puts Employee.class_variables.join(', ')
# => @@user_cnt
```

You'll notice in our example that we passed false to many of the Ruby reflection methods. Leaving this parameter out would bring back all methods inherited from parent classes as well.

Type Hinting

PHP has adopted a lot of its object model from Java, including the idea of interfaces and type hinting. Ruby takes a different approach to this by using the idea of duck typing. Instead of enforcing a specific object type or interface, Ruby will continue execution as long as the object responds to the messages thrown at it.

PHP php_to_ruby_language/php/objects/type_hinting.php

```php
class Duck {
    public function waddle() {
        print "duck waddling...\n";
    }
}

class Goose {
    public function waddle() {
        print "goose waddling...\n";
    }
}

class Kangaroo {
    public function hop() {
        print "kangaroo hopping...\n";
    }
}

// only accept Duck
function go(Duck $duck)
{
    $duck->waddle();
}

go(new Duck);
// => duck waddling...

go(new Goose);
// => Argument 1 passed to go() must be an instance of Duck

go(new Kangaroo);
// => Argument 1 passed to go() must be an instance of Duck
```

`php_to_ruby_language/ruby/objects/type_hinting.rb`

```ruby
class Duck
  def waddle
    puts "duck waddling..."
  end
end

class Goose
  def waddle
    puts "goose waddling..."
  end
end

class Kangaroo
  def hop
    puts "kangaroo hopping..."
  end
end

def go(duck)
  duck.waddle
end
go Duck.new
# => duck waddling...
go Goose.new
# => goose waddling...
go Kangaroo.new
# => undefined method `waddle' for #<Kangaroo:0x1eaca8>
```

12.4 Exceptions

Ruby's error model is completely built on exceptions and is much more straightforward than the dual error model in PHP. Actual exception handling in Ruby is quite similar to how PHP handles exceptions aside from syntactical differences. When handling exceptions in Ruby, we start with a begin statement instead of PHP's try. In Ruby we define a rescue block instead of the catch block and raise errors instead of throwing them.

`php_to_ruby_language/php/exceptions/throwing.php`

```php
try {
    throw new Exception('Something bad happened');

    print "this should never print...";

} catch (Exception $e) {
    print "caught it! ".$e->getMessage()."\n";
    // => caught it! Something bad happened
}
```

```
// continue code
print "after exception\n";
// => after exception
```

`php_to_ruby_language/ruby/exceptions/throwing.rb`

```ruby
begin
  raise Exception, "Something bad happened"

  puts "this should never print..."

rescue Exception => e
  puts "caught it! #{e.message}"
  # => caught it! Something bad happened
end

# continue code
print "after exception"
# => after exception
```

Ruby provides additional syntax for cleaning up the state of our application after handling an exception. The else block will execute when no error is rescued, and the ensure block will execute regardless of whether an error has happened. PHP has no equivalent of these features.

`php_to_ruby_language/ruby/exceptions/additional.rb`

```ruby
begin
  raise "Something bad happened"
rescue
  puts "caught an error!"
else
  puts "no errors, yay!"
ensure
  puts "ensure this always gets run."
end
```

12.5 References

There is no Ruby equivalent to PHP's assign-by-reference equals-ampersand operator (&=). Since all data is stored as objects in Ruby, nearly all data is assigned by-reference. This includes strings, arrays, and hashes. The exception is with numbers, booleans, and nil, which are not stored by reference. Because these data types cannot be directly modified, there is not usually any visible effect of this during their use.

`php_to_ruby_language/php/references/assign_by_reference.php`

```php
$colors1 = array('red', 'blue');
$colors2 =& $colors1;
```

```php
// adding to $colors2 doesn't change $colors1
$colors2[] = 'green';

var_export($colors1);
// => array(0 => 'red', 1 => 'blue', 2 => 'green')

var_export($colors2);
// => array(0 => 'red', 1 => 'blue', 2 => 'green')
```

Ruby php_to_ruby_language/ruby/references/assign_by_reference.rb

```ruby
colors1 = ['red', 'blue']
colors2 = colors1

# adding to colors2 changes colors1
colors2 << 'green'

p colors1
# => ["red", "blue", "green"]

p colors2
# => ["red", "blue", "green"]
```

To get a shallow copy of the data within a variable, you need to assign the variable while calling the dup method.

PHP php_to_ruby_language/php/references/assign_by_value.php

```php
$colors1 = array('red', 'blue');
$colors2 = $colors1;

// adding to $colors2 doesn't change $colors1
$colors2[] = 'green';

var_export($colors1);
// => array(0 => 'red', 1 => 'blue')

var_export($colors2);
// => array(0 => 'red', 1 => 'blue', 2 => 'green')
```

Ruby php_to_ruby_language/ruby/references/assign_by_value.rb

```ruby
colors1 = ['red', 'blue']
colors2 = colors1.dup

# adding to colors2 doesn't change colors1
colors2 << 'green'

p colors1
# => ["red", "blue"]
p colors2
# => ["red", "blue", "green"]
```

A step-by-step introduction of variable assignment and references can be found in Section 2.5, *Assigning to Variables*, on page 36.

12.6 External Libraries and Packages

RubyGems is a package distribution system not unlike PEAR in PHP. RubyGems makes it easy to find, install, and update Ruby libraries on your computer. Instead of a PEAR package, we have a gem that includes the source code for the Ruby library, along with metadata about package dependencies. All RubyGem actions are performed using the gem command.

Finding Packages

We can find gem packages by using the gem search command. A great package for parsing HTML in Ruby is the Hpricot library. To find the specific package we want, we can search the remote gem server for this package. This is similar to performing a pear search command.

```
work> gem search -r hpricot
*** REMOTE GEMS ***

hpricot (0.6, 0.5, 0.4)
    a swift, liberal HTML parser with a fantastic library

hpricot-scrub (0.2.0)
    Scrub HTML with Hpricot
...
```

Packages will displayed with the available versions and a short description of what the package does.

Installing Packages

Once we find a package we want to install, we can install using the gem install command, equivalent to performing a pear install. All gem install/uninstall commands need to be run as the root user on *nix-based systems.

```
work> gem install hpricot
Successfully installed hpricot-0.6
1 gem installed
Installing ri documentation for hpricot-0.6...
Installing RDoc documentation for hpricot-0.6...
```

Just like with PEAR, this command installs the package in a system-wide shared directory so that we can include it in all our applications.

Installing gems will not incur any additional overhead in your Rails applications unless they are used within the application. We can view the location in which gems are installed with another gem command.

```
work> gem environment gemdir
/usr/local/lib/ruby/gems/1.8
```

Generating Package Documentation

To use a library, we need to have to figure out how it works. When we install a gem, it automatically generates the docs for us. We can view documentation for all of our installed gems by starting the gem server using the gem server command.

```
work> gem server
[2007-08-07 11:34:32] INFO  WEBrick 1.3.1
[2007-08-07 11:34:32] INFO  ruby 1.8.6 (2007-03-13) [i686-darwin8.9.1]
[2007-08-07 11:34:32] INFO  WEBrick::HTTPServer#start: pid=13 port=8808
```

This started an instance of the WEBrick server to view our docs on port 8808. When we go to http://localhost:8808, we can see a page like that displayed in Figure 12.1, on the following page. From here we can click the syntax library's rdoc link to view the API for the library.

Including Packages

Like in PHP, we need to require a library before we can use it in our code. When we install packages as gems, we'll first need to require the RubyGems library. We'll fire up IRB to perform a quick example of the Hpricot library in use.

```
work> irb
>> require 'rubygems'
=> true
>> require 'hpricot'
=> true
```

Now that we've required the library, we can browse through the docs to view some example code. Here we've found how to pass an HTML-formatted string to Hpricot and be able to parse through the elements.

```
>> doc = Hpricot("<p>Simple <b>test</b></p>")
=> #<Hpricot::Doc {elem <p> "Simple " {elem <b> "test" </b>} </p>}>
>> doc.search("b").inner_html
=> "test"
```

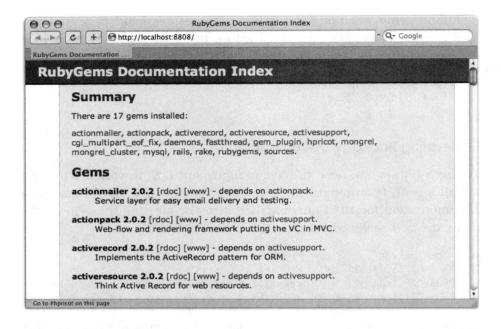

Figure 12.1: GEM SERVER PAGE

When browsing around for additional gems, the source for many gem packages can be found on the RubyForge website.[1] RubyForge is an application repository of open source Ruby projects. This is the most popular location for developers looking to host their code.

12.7 Documenting Code

Ruby takes a more minimal approach to documenting code than PHP, relying heavily on the code itself being self-documenting. This is important to note since it puts a responsibility on the developer to write readable code. Don't be afraid to make long variable or method names. You will regularly see Rubyists use unambiguous method names such as replace_named_bind_variables in order to diminish the need for additional documentation.

---

1. http://rubyforge.org

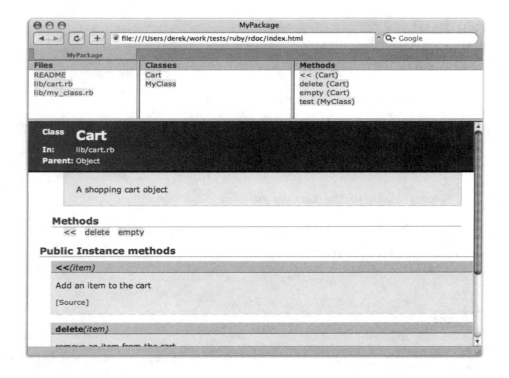

Figure 12.2: Generated RDoc documentation

Comparing PHPDoc and RDoc

Documentation in Ruby is done using an embedded documentation style similar to PHP's PHPDoc-style comments. Ruby's RDoc takes a different approach to code documentation and often has a much smaller footprint when compared to PHPDoc comments. There is no extra step needed to install RDoc, because it is part of the Ruby standard library.

PHPDoc comments are usually composed of a short description, a longer description, and a series of tags. RDoc has no concept of tags and instead favors simple inline formatting for much of the documentation. An example of RDoc's HTML-generated output for a Ruby class is shown in Figure 12.2.

Ruby inline documentation is written using Ruby comments above the class or method signature just as in PHP. Ruby has no special sequence of characters to denote documentation, and all comments are considered documentation unless specified otherwise.

PHP `php_to_ruby_language/php/docs/basics.php`

```php
class Cart {
    protected $items;

    /**
     * Create new cart
     */
    public function __construct() {
        $this->items = array();
    }

    /**
     * Add an item to the cart by id
     *
     * @param    string  $item
     */
    function addItem($item) {
        $this->items[] = $item;
    }
}
```

Ruby `php_to_ruby_language/ruby/docs/basics.rb`

```ruby
class Cart
  # Create new cart
  def initialize
    @items = []
  end

  # Add an item to the cart by id
  def add_item(item)
    @items << item
  end
end
```

Let's take a look at how can use RDoc to document the other various aspects of our code.

Identifying Code Author, Version, and License

The @author, @version, @copyright, and @license tag equivalents of Ruby code are not included in the source files like they are in PHPDoc.

This information for your Rails application is typically stored in a text file named doc/README_FOR_APP, which is used by RDoc as the top-level page for the generated documentation.

`PHP` php_to_ruby_language/php/docs/author.php

```php
/**
 * Movie Sharing Application
 *
 * LICENSE
 *
 * This source file is subject to the proprietary
 * Maintainable license available at:
 * http://maintainable.com/license.txt
 *
 * @author     Joe <joe@example.com>
 * @copyright  Copyright (c) 2007 Maintainable Software
 * @license    http://maintainable.com/license.txt
 */

/**
 * This object represents an application User
 */
class User {
}
```

php_to_rails/ruby/demo_1/doc/README_FOR_APP

```
Movie Sharing Application
=====================

written by Joe <joe@example.com>

License
=====================
Copyright (c) 2007 Maintainable Software

This application is subject to the proprietary
Maintainable license available at:
http://maintainable.com/license.txt
```

This file will used as the top-level page of our generated documentation for the Rails application.

Denoting Packages

RDoc organizes packages automatically based on modules' name-spaces. Because of this, we don't need to worry about specifying the @package or @subpackage tags for a class as we would in PHPDoc.

`PHP` php_to_ruby_language/php/docs/package.php

```php
/**
 * @package Amazon
 */
class Amazon_Category extends ActiveRecord_Base {
}
```

Ruby   php_to_rails/ruby/demo_1/app/models/amazon/category.rb

```ruby
class Amazon::Category < ActiveRecord::Base
end
```

Namespaces are discussed in further detail in Section 3.6, *Organizing Code with Namespaces*, on page 75.

Specifying Parameter and Return Values

Much of the time writing PHPDoc documentation involves identifying the @param and @return values of methods. Ruby documentation does not have an equivalent for specifying this type of information and does not really concern itself with object types in method signatures.

PHP   php_to_ruby_language/php/docs/param.php

```php
class MyClass {
    /**
     * Log a message at a priority
     *
     * @param  string   $message   Message to log
     * @param  integer  $priority  Priority of message
     * @return void
     */
    function log($message, $priority) {
        // ...
    }
}
```

Ruby   php_to_ruby_language/ruby/docs/param.rb

```ruby
class MyClass
  # Log a +message+ at a given +priority+
  def log(message, priority)
    # ...
  end
end
```

RDoc uses inline text to explain the purpose of various parameters. References to the parameter names are usually enclosed in plus signs to (+) to style them using a monospace font.

Formatting Headings and Text

Ruby allows for headings in our documentation to help organize different sections. Different level headings are denoted by the number of equal signs preceding the heading text.

Figure 12.3: Generated headings

Ruby · php_to_ruby_language/ruby/docs/headers.rb

```ruby
# ==This is an H2 style heading
#
# An additional paragraph of text
#
# ===This is an H3 style heading
def my_method
end
```

The resulting headings generated are displayed in Figure 12.3.

RDoc allows for simple formatting of documentation text similar to PHP-Doc but uses a slightly different syntax for doing so. A single word can be enclosed in underscores (_) to italicize, stars (*) to embolden, and plus signs (+) to make monospace styled text. There are tag equivalents of these types of formatting as well for situations where you need to format a series of words or text.

PHP · php_to_ruby_language/php/docs/formatting.php

```php
class MyClass {
    /**
     * This is some <b>bold</b> text, some <i>italic</i>
     * text, and some <kbd>monospaced font</kbd> text
     */
    function myMethod() {}
}
```

Ruby · php_to_ruby_language/ruby/docs/formatting.rb

```ruby
class MyClass
    # This is some <b>bold</b> text, some <em>emphasized</em>
    # text, and some <tt>monospaced font</tt> text
    #
    # This is some *bold* text, some _emphasized_
    # text, and some +monospaced+ text
    def my_method
    end
end
```

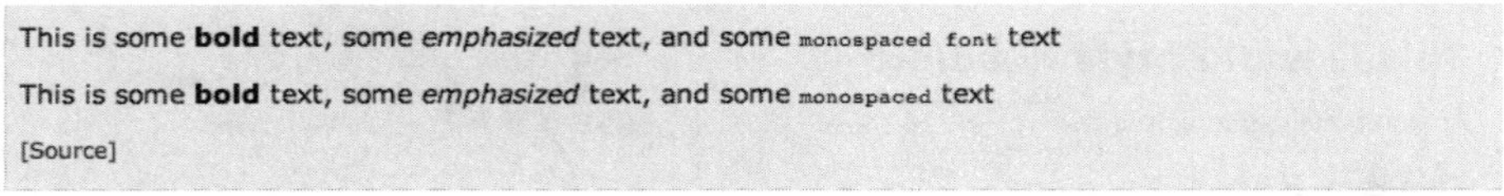

This is some **bold** text, some *emphasized* text, and some `monospaced font` text

This is some **bold** text, some *emphasized* text, and some `monospaced` text

[Source]

Figure 12.4: FORMATTED TEXT

The formatted text can be seen in Figure 12.4.

Creating Lists

Ordered and unordered lists are created pretty similarly in RDoc as they are in PHPDoc syntax. RDoc uses stars (*) to denote unordered list items as opposed to the hyphen (-) used in PHPDoc. RDoc does not have support for ol and ul tags as seen in PHPDoc-style comments.

PHP `php_to_ruby_language/php/docs/lists.php`

```php
class MyClass {
    /**
     * Sample list
     * - item a
     * - item b
     *
     * Ordered list
     * 1. item 1
     * 2. item 2
     */
    function myMethod() {}
}
```

Ruby `php_to_ruby_language/ruby/docs/lists.rb`

```ruby
class MyClass
  # Sample list
  # * item a
  # * item b
  #
  # Ordered list
  # 1. item 1
  # 2. item 2
  def my_method
  end
end
```

The resulting lists are shown in Figure 12.5, on the next page.

Sample list

- item a
- item b

Ordered list

1. item 1
2. item 2

[Source]

Figure 12.5: GENERATED LISTS

Adding Inline Links

Inline links in the documentation text will automatically be converted to hyperlinks. We can add a label for the hyperlink by appending a word with the URL in square brackets. There is no need for anything such as PHPDoc's @link tag.

PHP `php_to_ruby_language/php/docs/links.php`

```php
class MyClass {
    /**
     * see more at {@link http://example.com}
     *
     * see more at {@link http://example.com Example}
     *
     * see more at {@link http://example.com Example Page}
     */
    function myMethod() {}
}
```

Ruby `php_to_ruby_language/ruby/docs/links.rb`

```ruby
class MyClass
  # see more at http://example.com
  #
  # see more at Example[http://example.com]
  #
  # see more at {Example Page}[http://example.com]
  def my_method
  end
end
```

Any references to a class, module, or method will be automatically converted to a link to the documentation for that resource. The hash character (#) is used in Ruby to reference a method as opposed to the double colon (::) in PHP.

see the remove method

see AnotherClass

see the AnotherClass#delete method

[Source]

Figure 12.6: LINKS TO RESOURCES

PHP `php_to_ruby_language/php/docs/see.php`

```php
class MyClass {
    /**
     * @see remove()
     * @see AnotherClass
     * @see AnotherClass::delete()
     */
    function add() {}

    function remove() {}
}

class AnotherClass {
    function delete() {}
}
```

Ruby `php_to_ruby_language/ruby/docs/see.rb`

```ruby
class MyClass
  # see the #remove method
  #
  # see AnotherClass
  #
  # see the AnotherClass#delete method
  def add
  end

  def remove
  end
end

class AnotherClass
  def delete
  end
end
```

The resulting generated resource links can be seen in Figure 12.6.

```
Example:

  if a == 1
    foo = 'bar'
  end

[Source]
```

Figure 12.7: FORMATTED CODE

Displaying Code Examples

Code examples can be displayed in RDoc by indenting text. Any text that is indented will be displayed verbatim in a monospaced text. Unfortunately, RDoc does not do any syntax highlighting or numbering for this type of text as PHPDoc does.

PHP php_to_ruby_language/php/docs/code.php

```php
class MyClass {
    /**
     * Example:
     * <code>
     *   if ($a == 1) {
     *       $foo = 'bar';
     *   }
     * </code>
     */
    function myMethod() {}
}
```

Ruby php_to_ruby_language/ruby/docs/code.rb

```ruby
class MyClass
  # Example:
  #   if a == 1
  #     foo = 'bar'
  #   end
  def my_method
  end
end
```

This example produces the generated documentation shown in Figure 12.7.

Ignoring Documentation

While PHP uses the @ignore tag to notify PHPDoc to ignore certain docs, this is done in RDoc-style comments using the :nodoc: documentation modifier. We can alternately use the :doc: modifier to instruct RDoc to document private methods.

PHP   php_to_ruby_language/php/docs/ignore.php

```php
class MyClass {
    /**
     * @ignore
     */
    public function myMethod() {}
}
```

Ruby   php_to_ruby_language/ruby/docs/ignore.rb

```ruby
class MyClass
  def my_method # :nodoc:
  end

  private
  def private_method # :doc:
  end
end
```

You might want to use the :nodoc: option when you have a method that is not necessary in the public API but is required to be public for object interoperability.

Generating Documentation

Generating HTML-formatted documentation for Ruby projects is generally done using a Rake task, and Rails includes quite a few ways to build documentation for your application. The most common is to generate the docs for all your application-specific files. This is done with the doc:app task and will place the generated documentation in the doc/app directory of your Rails application.

```
work> cd rails_app/
rails_app> rake doc:app
(in /Users/derek/work/rails_app)
          README_FOR_APP:
          application.rb: c
...
Elapsed: 0.134s
```

To see options for generating documentation on other areas of your Rails code, you can view the list of available Rake tasks using rake -T doc.

```
work> cd rails_app
rails_app> rake -T doc
(in /Users/derek/work/rails_app)
rake doc:app       # Build the app HTML Files
...
rake doc:rerails # Force a rebuild of the RDOC files
```

Like PHP's phpdoc command, you can also generate documentation from the command-line prompt using the rdoc command.

```
work> cd php_app
php_app> phpdoc -s on -d lib/ -t docs/

Parsing configuration file phpDocumentor.ini...
...
Total Documentation Time: 0 seconds
work> cd ruby_app
ruby_app> rdoc -S -i lib/ -o docs/
                         cart.rb: c.....
                     my_class.rb: c.
Generating HTML...
...
Elapsed: 0.286s
```

## Chapter 13

PHP to Rails Reference

PHP was primarily written to be used for web development and tightly integrates web programming concepts and practices into the core language. Most web-specific functionality used in Ruby is not in the core Ruby library but added by Rails. Instead of using superglobals and functions of the language, Rails adds features such as sessions and cookies as methods available in the Rails controllers and views.

13.1 Templates

PHP has a variety of template systems used to separate domain and presentation logic in applications. The most popular solutions tend to use a library such as Smarty, Flexy, Savant, or the PHP language. The view system that Rails implements can be fitted with various template solutions but comes packaged with a popular system that uses ERB. ERB works in a similar way to how PHP natively embeds in HTML.

`PHP` `php_to_rails/php/templates/templates.php`

```php
<h1>Meetings</h1>

<? if (!empty($flash['notice'])): ?>
  <div id="flash_notice"><?= htmlentities($flash['notice']) ?></div>
<? endif ?>

<div class="meeting_list">
  <h2>Meetings</h2>
  <ul>
    <? foreach ($meetings as $meeting): ?>
    <li>
      <a href="/meetings/show/<?= htmlentities($meeting->id) ?>">
        <?= htmlentities($meeting->name) ?>
      </a>
    </li>
```

```
    <? endforeach ?>
  </ul>
  <p class="add"><a href="/meetings/new">add meeting</a></p>
</div>
```

`Ruby` `php_to_rails/ruby/demo_1/app/views/meetings/index.html.erb`

```erb
<h1>Meetings</h1>

<% if flash[:notice] %>
  <div id="flash_notice"><%=h flash[:notice] %></div>
<% end %>

<div class="meeting_list">
  <h2>Meetings</h2>
  <ul>
    <% @meetings.each do |meeting| %>
    <li>
      <%= link_to h(meeting.name), :action => "show",
                                   :id     => meeting.id %>
    </li>
    <% end %>
  </ul>
  <p class="add">
    <%= link_to "add meeting", :action    => "new" %>
  </p>
</div>
```

ERB uses the <% and %> start and end tags to invoke and end the Ruby interpreter within our template. We can alternately start the Ruby code with <%= to output the result of the expression in the same way that PHP uses <?= when short tags are enabled.

13.2 $_GET/$_POST

Rails takes a quite different approach to HTTP GET and POST variables than PHP. While PHP makes this data available via the $_GET and $_POST superglobals, Rails provides a single access to this data using the params hash. The params hash can be accessed from both controller methods and view templates.

`PHP` `php_to_rails/php/params/get_post.php`

```php
$name  = $_POST['name'];
$title = $_POST['title'];
```

`Ruby` `php_to_rails/ruby/demo_1/app/controllers/examples_controller.rb`

```ruby
def my_action
  name  = params[:name]
  title = params[:title]
end
```

Instead of differentiating between HTTP GET and POST methods using the superglobal array name, Rails controllers reference an object that represents the current request. The request method will return an object that contains all the properties of the current HTTP request. Two of the methods that are helpful for determining the type of request we're processing are get? and post?.

This is similar to using the $_SERVER['REQUEST_METHOD'] value in PHP to determine the request method.

PHP

php_to_rails/php/params/request_method.php

```php
if ($_SERVER['REQUEST_METHOD'] == 'GET') {
    header("Location: /meetings/show");

} elseif ($_SERVER['REQUEST_METHOD'] == 'POST') {
    $meeting = new Meeting($_POST['meeting']);
}
```

Ruby

php_to_rails/ruby/demo_1/app/controllers/examples_controller.rb

```ruby
def my_action
  if request.get?
    redirect_to :show

  elsif request.post?
    meeting = Meeting.new(params[:meeting])
  end
end
```

13.3 $_FILES

When performing file uploads in Rails, we typically have a model that corresponds to the files being uploaded. For this example, we'll use a Document model that has three attributes: filename, filesize, and content_type. When we upload a file, we'll create an associated record in the database for that file. The database migration used to create this table would look like this.

Ruby

php_to_rails/ruby/demo_1/db/migrate/002_create_documents.rb

```ruby
def self.up
  create_table :documents do |t|
    t.string  :filename
    t.integer :filesize
    t.string  :content_type
    t.timestamps
  end
end
```

```
  def self.down
    drop_table :documents
  end
end
```

We'll create a controller named DocumentsController to handle all actions associated with creating and displaying the uploaded document. Our upload form will be the new action in this controller. This action will instantiate a new Document object that we'll use to build our form using the form_for helper.

Ruby   php_to_rails/ruby/demo_1/app/controllers/documents_controller.rb

```ruby
def new
  @document = Document.new
end
```

The HTML form itself in Rails will work similarly to the form we would make in PHP. The biggest difference is that we'll use some form helpers in our Rails view. Our Rails form will submit to the create action to upload/create the document. Forms that submit a file upload require the :multipart => true value to be included in the :html option of form_for. This will add the appropriate enctype attribute for the form.

PHP   php_to_rails/php/files/file_upload_form.php

```php
<!-- PHP upload form -->
<h1>Upload Document</h1>
<form action="file_upload.php" method="post"
      enctype="multipart/form-data">
  <label for="uploaded_file">File:</label>
  <input type="file" name="uploaded_file" id="uploaded_file" />

  <input type="submit" name="submit" value="Upload" />
</form>
```

Ruby   php_to_rails/ruby/demo_1/app/views/documents/new.html.erb

```erb
<h1>Upload Document</h1>
<% form_for :document, :url  => { :action => "create" },
                       :html => { :multipart => true } do |form| -%>
  <label for="document_uploaded_file">File:</label>
  <%= form.file_field :uploaded_file %>

  <input type="submit" name="submit" value="Upload" />
<% end -%>
```

While we use the $_FILES superglobal in PHP to access the uploaded file information, Rails packages this data into an object that is sent along with the posted parameters from the form. This object contains all the information we need about the file just like the $_FILES array.

php_to_rails/ruby/files.rb

```ruby
# params hash submitted
{ "submit"   => "Upload",
  "document" => { "uploaded_file" => #<File:/tmp/CGI.5112.0> } }
```

The create action for the documents controller will look like that for any other controller. Most of the code that we use to upload the file will end up in our documents controller. We set the attributes for the Document object directly from the data in params[:document].

php_to_rails/ruby/demo_1/app/controllers/documents_controller.rb

```ruby
def create
  @document = Document.new(params[:document])
  if @document.save
    flash[:success] = "File uploaded successfully."
  end
  redirect_to :action => "index"
end
```

This assigns the value of uploaded_file to the document object. This means we need to create an assignment method to handle this data. The uploaded_file= method uses the uploaded file object sent with the request. We'll first get the content of the file using the read method and store it in an instance variable. We'll then use the file object to get the attributes of the file, similarly to how we'd extract this data from the $_FILES array.

php_to_rails/php/files/upload_attributes.php

```php
$filename    = $_FILES['uploaded_file']['name'];
$filesize    = $_FILES['uploaded_file']['size'];
$contentType = $_FILES['uploaded_file']['type'];
```

php_to_rails/ruby/demo_1/app/models/document.rb

```ruby
def uploaded_file=(file)
  # contents of uploaded file
  @contents = file.read

  self.filename     = file.original_filename
  self.filesize     = file.length
  self.content_type = file.content_type
end
```

At this point in our PHP, we'd use the move_uploaded_file function to write our file to disk. In Rails, we need to create a before_save callback for our model so that it writes our file to disk before the document record is saved. We'll add a new method named write_file_upload to use with this callback that will write the file content to disk. In this case, we've created an uploads directory to hold all the file uploads in our application.

`PHP` `php_to_rails/php/files/file_upload.php`

```php
// destination for file
$destDir = dirname(__FILE__)."/uploads/";
$dest    = $destDir.basename($_FILES['uploaded_file']['name']);

if (move_uploaded_file($_FILES['uploaded_file']['tmp_name'], $dest)) {
    echo "File uploaded successfully.";
}
```

`Ruby` `php_to_rails/ruby/demo_1/app/models/document.rb`

```ruby
before_save :write_file_upload

def write_file_upload
  dest = "#{RAILS_ROOT}/uploads/#{self.filename}"
  File.open(dest, 'w') {|f| f << @contents }
end
```

You'll obviously want to perform some validation and error checking for your file uploads just as you would in PHP. You would typically check that the file size isn't zero and that the uploaded file doesn't already exist on disk. Rick Olson has written a useful Rails plug-in that deals with a lot of the issues you may run into while dealing with file uploads. This plug-in is named attachment_fu and can be found in Rick's SVN Repository.[1]

13.4 $_SERVER

Most of the common environment variables you would get through the $_SERVER superglobal array or getenv() function in PHP are set as methods on the request object in Rails. As shown in Figure 13.1, on the facing page, we can access these by referencing these methods from within a controller action.

13.5 Cookies

Setting cookies in Rails is done by assigning a value to the cookies hash within a controller action. We can also assign a hash of parameters to the cookie if we need to specify the expiration date or path constraint.

---

1. http://svn.techno-weenie.net/projects/plugins/attachment_fu/

PHP	Rails
`<?php`	`def my_action`
`$_SERVER['REQUEST_METHOD'];`	`request.method`
`$_SERVER['REQUEST_METHOD'] == 'GET';`	`request.get?`
`$_SERVER['REQUEST_METHOD'] == 'POST';`	`request.post?`
`$_SERVER['REQUEST_METHOD'] == 'PUT';`	`request.put?`
`$_SERVER['REQUEST_METHOD'] == 'DELETE';`	`request.delete?`
`$_SERVER['HTTP_ACCEPT'];`	`request.accepts`
`$_SERVER['HTTP_X_REQUESTED_WITH'] == 'XMLHttpRequest';`	`request.xhr?`
`$_SERVER['REMOTE_ADDR'];`	`request.remote_ip`
`$_SERVER['SERVER_SOFTWARE'];`	`request.server_software`
`!empty($_SERVER['HTTPS']);`	`request.ssl?`
`$_SERVER["HTTP_HOST"];`	`request.host`
`$_SERVER['SERVER_PORT'];`	`request.port`
`$_SERVER['REQUEST_URI'];`	`request.request_uri`
	`end`

Figure 13.1: SERVER VARIABLES

PHP

php_to_rails/php/cookies/set_cookies.php

```php
// expire at the finish of the current session
setcookie('tabState', 'open');

// set additional info for the cookie
setcookie("tabState", 'open', time()+3600*24*14, "/~foo/");
```

Ruby

php_to_rails/ruby/demo_1/app/controllers/examples_controller.rb

```ruby
def my_action
  # expire at the finish of the current session
  cookies[:tab_state] = 'open'

  # set additional info for the cookie
  cookies[:tab_state] = { :value   => 'open',
                          :expires => 14.days.from_now,
                          :path    => "/~foo/" }
end
```

We can retrieve cookies within a Rails controller by simply accessing the value for the cookie from the cookies hash. Remember that this method is not a superglobal such as the $_COOKIE array in PHP and is available only when working in an action or view.

PHP `php_to_rails/php/cookies/get_cookies.php`

```php
$state = isset($_COOKIE['tabState']) ? $_COOKIE['tabState'] : null;
```

Ruby `php_to_rails/ruby/demo_1/app/controllers/examples_controller.rb`

```ruby
def my_action
  state = cookies[:tab_state]
end
```

We delete cookies in PHP by setting an expiration date that has already passed. In Rails, we delete a cookie using the delete method to our cookies proxy object. Simply call this method with the name of the cookie you want to wipe out.

PHP `php_to_rails/php/cookies/delete_cookies.php`

```php
// one hour ago
setcookie("tabState", "", time() - 3600);
```

Ruby `php_to_rails/ruby/demo_1/app/controllers/examples_controller.rb`

```ruby
def my_action
  cookies.delete(:tab_state)
end
```

13.6 Sessions

Session data is set within controller methods by assigning values to the session hash. There is no need for any equivalent of PHP's session_start function.

PHP `php_to_rails/php/sessions/set_session.php`

```php
session_start();

$_SESSION['user'] = $user->id;
```

Ruby `php_to_rails/ruby/demo_1/app/controllers/examples_controller.rb`

```ruby
def my_action
  session[:user] = @user.id
end
```

We retrieve session data in Rails by accessing values of the session hash by key name. This method is not a superglobal such as the $_SESSION array in PHP and is available only when working in an action or view.

PHP `php_to_rails/php/sessions/get_session.php`

```php
session_start();

$userId = isset($_SESSION['user']) ? $_SESSION['user'] : null;
```

`Ruby` | php_to_rails/ruby/demo_1/app/controllers/examples_controller.rb

```ruby
def my_action
  user_id = session[:user]
end
```

We can clear all existing session data using the reset_session method, which works similarly to PHP's session_destroy function.

`PHP` | php_to_rails/php/sessions/reset_session.php

```php
session_destroy();
```

`Ruby` | php_to_rails/ruby/demo_1/app/controllers/examples_controller.rb

```ruby
def my_action
  reset_session
end
```

There are various session storage options in Rails that can be changed to suit your needs. The default session storage mechanism uses cookies and is suitable for most needs. However, in some cases, you may need to store more session data than allowed in a cookie (4KB). You might also at times want to store sensitive information that you would rather not have stored in a cookie. In these scenarios, you may want to use ActiveRecord to store your sessions in the database. Turning on :active_record_store can be done by uncommenting the session_store assignment in the initializer block in config/environment.rb.

`Ruby` | php_to_rails/ruby/demo_1/config/environment.rb

```ruby
config.action_controller.session_store = :active_record_store
```

If we want to use Rails' built-in cross-site request forgery protection, we need to perform an additional step when switching the session store. Any session store other than the default cookies storage requires us to provide a :secret token to the protect_from_forgery method in app/controllers/application.rb. This token is already generated in your source code and just needs to be commented out to work with our active record session storage.

`Ruby` | php_to_rails/ruby/demo_1/app/controllers/application.rb

```ruby
protect_from_forgery :secret => 'ef992b27ee422f2e5b5e44bab9e6f7e0'
```

Once we've done this, we need to create the sessions migration to create the database table needed to store our data. We can do this using a Rake task bundled with Rails.

From your application's root directory, run the following:

```
demo> rake db:sessions:create
(in /Users/derek/work/demo)
exists  db/migrate
create  db/migrate/003_create_sessions.rb
```

Now we can use the new session migration to add this table to our database:

```
demo> rake db:migrate
(in /Users/derek/work/demo)

== 3 CreateSessions: migrating ==========================================
-- create_table(:sessions)
   -> 0.0503s
-- add_index(:sessions, :session_id)
   -> 0.0086s
-- add_index(:sessions, :updated_at)
   -> 0.0559s
== 3 CreateSessions: migrated (0.1157s) ================================
```

Once we've restarted the server, sessions will now be stored in the sessions table instead of the default cookie storage. If we ever want to clear our active record session data, there is another Rake task to handle this.

```
demo> rake db:sessions:clear
```

13.7 Headers and Redirection

We can send arbitrary headers in a controller method by assigning header values on the response object. This works similarly to PHP's header function.

`PHP` php_to_rails/php/headers/headers.php

```php
header('Cache-Control: no-cache, must-revalidate');
header('Content-Type: application/pdf');
```

`Ruby` php_to_rails/ruby/demo_1/app/controllers/examples_controller.rb

```ruby
def my_action
  response.headers['Cache-Control'] = 'no-cache, must-revalidate'
  response.headers['Content-Type']  = 'application/pdf'
end
```

Rails provides a method in our controllers to set proper redirect headers in our application. The redirect_to method uses a hash of parameters that compose the redirection URL.

PHP `php_to_rails/php/headers/redirection.php`

```php
header("Location: /documents/new");
```

Ruby `php_to_rails/ruby/demo_1/app/controllers/examples_controller.rb`

```ruby
def my_action
  redirect_to(:controller => "documents", :action => "new")
end
```

This redirect_to method can also be given a string if the redirection URL is outside the domain of the current application.

PHP `php_to_rails/php/headers/redirection_external.php`

```php
header("Location: http://maintainable.com");
```

Ruby `php_to_rails/ruby/demo_1/app/controllers/examples_controller.rb`

```ruby
def my_action
  redirect_to('http://maintainable.com');
end
```

13.8 Security

There are various security concerns when developing Rails applications. Many of these you'll be familiar with from encountering the same issues in PHP. Others are unique to the conventions used in Rails.

Escape Output

You should always escape variables for output. This eliminates bugs because of improperly escaped entities but more importantly alleviates security concerns such as cross-site scripting attacks. The equivalent of PHP's htmlentities function in Rails is the h helper method. We can use this method just like any other helper method, and a common usage pattern is to leave off the parentheses when outputting a single variable within the Ruby interpreter. In this case, the h method is placed at the beginning of the tags used to open the Ruby interpreter such as <%=h.

PHP `php_to_rails/php/security/escape_output.php`

```php
<div>
  <a href="/documents/show/<?= $document->id ?>">
    <?= htmlentities($document->filename, ENT_QUOTES) ?>
  </a>
</div>

<div>
  <?= htmlentities($document->contentType, ENT_QUOTES) ?>
</div>
```

Ruby `php_to_rails/ruby/demo_1/app/views/examples/escape_output.html.erb`

```
<div>
  <%= link_to h(@document.filename), :controller => "documents",
                                     :action     => "show",
                                     :id         => @document.id %>
</div>

<div><%=h @document.content_type %></div>
```

Filter Input

To avoid SQL Injection attacks in PHP, we always use a function such as mysql_real_escape_string to escape quotes and other potentially dangerous characters within a SQL statement. Rails accomplishes the same thing using replacement variables.

Any SQL fragment in our find statements can be stated as an array instead of a string. The first element is a SQL string with question marks as value placeholders. The rest of the array elements are values to be substituted into the string.

PHP `php_to_rails/php/security/replacement_variables.php`

```php
mysql_connect('localhost', 'root', '');

$id   = isset($_POST['id'])   ? $_POST['id']   : null;
$name = isset($_POST['name']) ? $_POST['name'] : null;
$type = isset($_POST['type']) ? $_POST['type'] : null;

$query = sprintf("SELECT * FROM documents WHERE id='%s' LIMIT 1",
                 mysql_real_escape_string($id));

$query = sprintf("SELECT *
                    FROM documents
                   WHERE filename LIKE '%s'
                     AND content_type = '%s'",
                 mysql_real_escape_string("%$name%"),
                 mysql_real_escape_string($type));
```

Ruby `php_to_rails/ruby/demo_1/app/controllers/examples_controller.rb`

```ruby
def my_action
  id, name, type = params[:id], params[:name], params[:type]

  # condition fragment
  doc = Document.find(:first,
                      :conditions => ["id = ?", id])
```

```
    # sql query
    docs = Document.find_by_sql(["SELECT *
                                    FROM documents
                                    WHERE filename LIKE ?
                                      AND content_type = ?",
                                "%#{name}%", type])
  end

  def my_action
    begin
      @document = Document.find(params[:id])
    rescue ActiveRecord::RecordNotFound
      flash[:notice] = "Invalid document"
      redirect_to :action => :index
    end
  end

  def my_action
    @document = Document.find_by_id(params[:id])
  end

  def my_action
    # deliver the message
    NotificationMailer.deliver_confirm(@user)
  end

  def my_action
    # create, and deliver later
    email = NotificationMailer.create_confirm(@user)
    NotificationMailer.deliver(email)
  end

  def my_action
    render
  end

  protected
    def my_protected
      # this cannot be executed as an action
    end

end
```

Protect Attributes from Bulk Assignment

A common pattern used in Rails during form submission is to group together data for a particular object so that we can perform a bulk assignment in our controller. For example, we might have a Comment model such as the code on the next page.

`Ruby` php_to_rails/ruby/demo_1/db/migrate/004_create_comments.rb

```ruby
class CreateComments < ActiveRecord::Migration
  def self.up
    create_table :comments do |t|
      t.string  :email
      t.text    :content
      t.boolean :verified
      t.timestamps
    end
  end

  def self.down
    drop_table :comments
  end
end
```

Then the interface for a public form to create a comment might include only the email and content attributes, while displaying only the verified attribute for site administrators.

`Ruby` php_to_rails/ruby/demo_1/app/views/comments/new.html.erb

```erb
<form method="post" action="/comments/create">
  <input type="text" name="comment[email]" />
  <input type="text" name="comment[content]" />
  <% if @user.admin? %>
  <input type="text" name="comment[verified]" value="1" />
  <% end %>
</form>
```

When the data for this is submitted, it will combine the data into a single hash that we can assign in the controller when creating our object.

`Ruby` php_to_rails/ruby/demo_1/app/controllers/comments_controller.rb

```ruby
def create
  @comment = Comment.new(params[:comment])
  if @comment.save
    flash[:notice] = 'Created successfully.'
    redirect_to :action => "index"
  else
    render :action => "new"
  end
end
```

The problem is that the verified attribute isn't actually secured for the model and is merely hidden from the view. There is nothing stopping a user from submitting this attribute through some other means such as curl, in which it would mark the comment as verified regardless of whether the user is an administrator.

> php_to_rails/ruby/attr_protected.sh

```
curl -d "comment[verified]=1" http://localhost:3000/comments/create
```

The solution for this is to mark this attribute as protected from bulk assignment using the attr_protected method in our model.

Ruby

> php_to_rails/ruby/demo_1/app/models/comment.rb

```ruby
class Comment < ActiveRecord::Base
  attr_protected :verified
end
```

We can also use a white-list approach, instead using attr_accessible to define the only attributes that are allowed during bulk assignment.

Ruby

> php_to_rails/ruby/demo_1/app/models/comment.rb

```ruby
class Comment < ActiveRecord::Base
  attr_accessible :email, :content
end
```

Once we've secured our models this way, we need to remember that we now need to explicitly assign these attributes in our controller when they are applicable.

Ruby

> php_to_rails/ruby/demo_1/app/controllers/comments_controller.rb

```ruby
@comment = Comment.new(params[:comment])
@comment.verified = params[:comment][:verified] if @user.admin?
```

Handle Missing Records

When we use the find method to load a record by primary key, it expects that the ID given is valid. When the ID given cannot be found, an ActiveRecord::RecordNotFound exception is raised. It is important to not trust that IDs given in the application are valid. Many times it is as easy as changing a number in a URL to throw an invalid ID into your action.

There are two ways of handling missing IDs. The first is to put your find within a begin/rescue block. How you deal with an invalid ID depends on the situation. Most of the time it is sufficient to simply redirect back to the index view with a polite message.

Ruby

> php_to_rails/ruby/demo_1/app/controllers/examples_controller.rb

```ruby
def my_action
  begin
    @document = Document.find(params[:id])
  rescue ActiveRecord::RecordNotFound
    flash[:notice] = "Invalid document"
    redirect_to :action => :index
  end
end
```

If you'd rather the object simply be Nil when the record is not found, you can use find_by_id instead of find. This usage is appropriate when you expect that the ID could not exist, and the code can continue to execute properly when the record is Nil.

Ruby | php_to_rails/ruby/demo_1/app/controllers/examples_controller.rb

```ruby
def my_action
  @document = Document.find_by_id(params[:id])
end
```

Nonaction Controller Methods

All methods in a controller are assumed to be public actions unless stated otherwise. This means methods that were not intended to be accessed can be typed in the URL and cause errors in your application. The simplest way to prevent this is to give a protected visibility to any methods not intended to be actions within the controller.

Ruby | php_to_rails/ruby/demo_1/app/controllers/examples_controller.rb

```ruby
def my_action
  render
end

protected
  def my_protected
    # this cannot be executed as an action
  end
```

13.9 Debugging

The most popular debugging strategy in PHP is done using strategically placed print statements. Although there are certainly more sophisticated debugging solution for PHP, simply printing variables to the screen is usually pretty quick and efficient.

If you've tried to place print statements within your Rails controllers or models, you've probably noticed that they don't have any effect on the output sent to the browser. This is because any output generated in your Rails code has nothing to do with the data that Rails eventually renders to the browser. We do, however, have a few alternate strategies for debugging in Rails.

Logging Data

We'll usually use the logger in Rails to do simple debugging. Log files are written to the log/ directory in our application and are named based on the current environment we are using. We discuss environments in more detail in Section 6.2, *Using Rails Environments*, on page 154. When you are working in the development environment, a lot of useful information is sent to the log automatically. This includes all the SQL executed and the list of parameters sent with each request. Simply viewing the log might give you enough information without further debugging.

Often you'll need to send further data to the log to inspect the contents of a variable. We can send data to the log using the logger.info method. This will work in models, controllers, and views. When you are logging objects, you'll probably want to use their inspect method to get a more useful output of their contents.

`Ruby` `php_to_rails/ruby/demo_1/app/controllers/meetings_controller.rb`

```ruby
def create
  @meeting = Meeting.new(params[:meeting])
  logger.info(@meeting.inspect)
  # ...
end
```

When we run this code, something similar to the following will be sent to our log.

```
#<Meeting id: nil, meets_on: "2007-11-30", location: "The Library",
  description: "Using OpenID", created_at: nil, updated_at: nil>
```

Interactive Debugging

Rails also has a sophisticated debugger based on the ruby-debug gem. To use this debugger, first install ruby-debug using gem install:

```
my_app> gem install ruby-debug
Building native extensions.  This could take a while...
Successfully installed ruby-debug-base-0.9.3
Successfully installed ruby-debug-0.9.3
2 gems installed
...
```

Once we've installed this required gem, we need to restart the server for our application using the --debugger option:

```
my_app> ruby script/server --debugger
=> Booting Mongrel (use 'script/server webrick' to force WEBrick)
=> Rails application starting on http://0.0.0.0:3000
=> Debugger enabled
...
```

Now in our application, we can initialize the debugger by placing debugger somewhere in our application.

Ruby | php_to_rails/ruby/demo_1/app/models/meeting.rb

```ruby
# formatted name based on date
def name
  debugger
  meets_on.to_s(:long)
end
```

When the application reaches this point, it will invoke the interactive debugger.

```
/user_group/app/models/meeting.rb:23 meets_on.to_s(:long)
(rdb:5)
```

From here we can walk through the call stack and inspect our environment using various commands. To see a list of available commands, type help.

```
(rdb:5) help
ruby-debug help v0.9.3
Type 'help "command-name"' for help on a specific command

Available commands:
backtrace break catch cont delete display down eval exit finish frame
help irb list method next p pp quit reload restart save script set
step thread tmate trace undisplay up var where
```

Follow the guidelines here for using the help command to get additional information on the various commands. More detailed usage instructions can also be found on the Ruby-Debug website.[2]

13.10 Accessing the Database

We are quite familiar with writing SQL in PHP. While you are learning Rails, you may wonder how to query the database directly without using ActiveRecord objects. The short answer is that it's possible but not a good idea. ActiveRecord uses callbacks hooks and validations to ensure that the data entering the database adheres to the rules assigned in our model classes. Accessing and querying the database directly will circumvent all the logic we've added to the model layer of our application.

---

2. http://www.datanoise.com/ruby-debug/

With this in mind, there are sometimes performance reasons to bypass validations and callbacks. To perform mass updates, we can use the update_all method. The first argument is a SQL fragment with the updates to apply, and the second argument is the conditions.

```
def update_admin_for_nyc
  self.update_all("admin = 1", "location = 'NYC'")
end
```

We can perform a similar operation for mass deletions using the delete_all method. This method takes a single argument with the conditions on which to delete records.

```
def delete_from_tulsa
  self.delete_all("location = 'Tulsa'")
end
```

Most SELECT-based query operations can (and should) be done using the versatile find method. This method supports options such as :select, :from, :group, :limit, :offset, and :conditions.

```
def find_archives
  self.find(:all, :select     => "id, name",
                  :from       => "user_archives",
                  :conditions => "admin = 1",
                  :limit      => 10,
                  :offset     => 10)
end
```

If the find method is not capable of performing the query you need, you can drop down to using the find_by_sql method to query. This method works just like find(:all) but uses a complete SQL string.

```
def find_including_archives
  sql = "SELECT * FROM users UNION SELECT * FROM user_archives"
  self.find_by_sql(sql)
end
```

If you absolutely need to drop down to execute straight SQL, you can do this within your models using the connection.execute method.

```
def swap_to_archive
  connection.execute("INSERT INTO user_archives SELECT * from users")
end
```

Remember that using execute is usually a last resort. Do some research first to find whether there is a better way to accomplish what you are trying to do.

13.11 Email

We can send email in Rails through a component called ActionMailer. This component of Rails enables us to send email from our application using a mailer model and views.

Instead of the usual ActiveRecord model, we'll use a special mailer model to send email messages in our application. We can generate a mailer model using the generate script. This generator optionally takes the name of the mailer actions we want to create such as confirm in this case.

```
demo> ruby script/generate mailer NotificationMailer confirm
exists  app/models/
create  app/views/notification_mailer
exists  test/unit/
create  test/fixtures/notification_mailer
create  app/models/notification_mailer.rb
create  test/unit/notification_mailer_test.rb
create  app/views/notification_mailer/confirm.html.erb
create  test/fixtures/notification_mailer/confirm
```

Each method in our mailer model contains the data for a message that we'll create and send. The method can take an arbitrary number of arguments to be used when composing the message. In this case, we've passed a user object into the confirm method to help fill out the recipient details.

`Ruby`   php_to_rails/ruby/demo_1/app/models/notification_mailer.rb

```ruby
class NotificationMailer < ActionMailer::Base
  def confirm(user)
    @subject    = 'Membership Confirmation'
    @body       = { "user" => user }
    @recipients = user.email
    @from       = 'confirm@example.com'
    @sent_on    = Time.now
    @headers    = {}
  end
end
```

We've set a series of instance variables that are used to compose the email headers. Data assigned to the @body hash will become instance variables in the view template used to compose the body of this message. In this example, we've assigned the user object to the "user" key of the hash to obtain the @user variable in the view. Our view template is stored in a view directory based on the name of the mailer model, and the template is named after the method we've defined.

Ruby php_to_rails/ruby/demo_1/app/views/notification_mailer/confirm.html.erb

```
Dear <%= @user.username %>,

Thank you for signing up for our newsletter at example.com.
You can change your subscription settings at any time by visiting:

http://example.com/newsletter/<%= @user.unsubscribe_code %>

Thanks,
The Example Team
```

This completes the code needed to set up our confirm email message. To actually send this message, we need to invoke the deliver method on the message. This is a class method on NotificationMailer, with a name starting with deliver_ followed by the name of the mailer method we just created. In this example it will be named deliver_confirm.

Ruby php_to_rails/ruby/demo_1/app/controllers/examples_controller.rb

```ruby
def my_action
  # deliver the message
  NotificationMailer.deliver_confirm(@user)
end
```

Alternately, we can use a similar approach to create the method for later delivery. This time the method name is prefixed with create_ and becomes create_confirm. This method will return the email where it can then be delivered using the NotificationMailer.deliver method.

Ruby php_to_rails/ruby/demo_1/app/controllers/examples_controller.rb

```ruby
def my_action
  # create, and deliver later
  email = NotificationMailer.create_confirm(@user)
  NotificationMailer.deliver(email)
end
```

13.12 Testing Rails Code

Testing is given much more focus in the Ruby community than in PHP. Nearly all Rubyists regularly write extensive unit tests, and this influence is evident in Rails. Tests stubs are created in parallel with all code stubs generated in Rails, and you'll find that most open source libraries and packages you find will have a solid suite of tests.

Comparing PHPUnit and Test::Unit

The most popular unit testing framework in Ruby, and the one that is included in Rails, is the Test::Unit library. This library is based on the popular xUnit-style testing library and is similar to the PHPUnit library written by Sebastian Bergmann.

Just as when we write tests with PHPUnit, test classes generally are stored in their own separate test directory. Test class names are suffixed with Test just as in PHP, so the unit tests for the User class are written in the UserTest class. Instead of inheriting from PHPUnit_Framework_TestCase, Ruby test classes inherit from Test::Unit::TestCase.

PHP
php_to_rails/php/tests/test/UserTest.php

```php
require_once 'PHPUnit/Framework.php';
require_once dirname(dirname(__FILE__)).'/lib/User.php';

class UserTest extends PHPUnit_Framework_TestCase {
    function setUp() {
        // set up test state
    }

    function tearDown() {
        // tear down test state
    }

    function testGetFullNameConcatenatesFirstAndLastName() {
        $user = new User('Derek', 'DeVries');
        $this->assertEquals('Derek DeVries', $user->getFullName());
    }

    function testIsAdminFlagDefaultsToFalse() {
        $user = new User('Derek', 'DeVries');
        $this->assertFalse($user->getIsAdmin());

        $user = new User('Derek', 'DeVries', true);
        $this->assertTrue($user->getIsAdmin());
    }
}
```

Ruby
php_to_rails/ruby/tests/test/user_test.rb

```ruby
require 'test/unit'
require File.dirname(__FILE__) + '/../lib/user'

class UserTest < Test::Unit::TestCase
  def setup
    # set up test state
  end
```

```
  def teardown
    # tear down test state
  end

  def test_full_name_concatenates_first_and_last_name
    user = User.new('Derek', 'DeVries')
    assert_equal 'Derek DeVries', user.full_name
  end

  def test_admin_flag_defaults_to_false
    user = User.new('Derek', 'DeVries')
    assert !user.admin?

    user = User.new('Derek', 'DeVries', true)
    assert user.admin?
  end
end
```

There is no extra step needed to install the Test::Unit library, because it is part of the Ruby standard library. In these examples, both PHPUnit and Test::Unit perform a require on the testing library files along with the class we are testing (User). Test::Unit uses setup and teardown methods to include code to execute before and after each test. These work identically to PHPUnit's setUp and tearDown methods.

There are fairly equivalent assertion methods for many of those found in PHPUnit. The most common are the assert_equal and assert methods. We can execute these tests from the command line using the ruby command just like we use the phpunit command-line runner.

```
work> cd php_app
php_app> phpunit UserTest test/UserTest.php
PHPUnit 3.1.2 by Sebastian Bergmann.
..
Time: 0 seconds

OK (2 tests)
```

The previous PHP command can be done in Ruby as follows.

```
work> cd ruby_app
ruby_app> ruby test/user_test.rb
Loaded suite test/user_test
Started
..
Finished in 0.000601 seconds.

2 tests, 3 assertions, 0 failures, 0 errors
```

Testing in Rails

Rails makes testing convenient by generating your test class stubs whenever you create new classes. Rails includes three different types of testing.

Unit Tests

Unit tests are written in parallel with our model classes. These tests should extensively cover the functionality of the domain logic in your application.

`Ruby` `php_to_rails/ruby/demo_1/test/unit/presentation_test.rb`

```ruby
require File.dirname(__FILE__) + '/../test_helper'

class PresentationTest < Test::Unit::TestCase
  fixtures :meetings, :presentations, :users

  def test_should_belongs_to_meeting
    rjs = presentations(:rjs_templates)
    assert_kind_of Meeting, rjs.meeting
  end

  def test_should_require_title
    attrs = { :title       => nil,
              :description => "Render Javascript Snippets",
              :user        => users(:admin_user) }
    p = Presentation.create(attrs)
    assert p.errors.invalid?(:title)
  end
end
```

We discuss more details of unit testing within the context of our application in Section 6.3, *Testing Our Models*, on page 155.

Functional Tests

Functional tests are paired with Rails controller classes and verify that individual controllers and the logic they employ is working correctly.

They provide a simple way of simulating HTTP requests to our application. We can then perform assertions on the results of the request to make sure the correct response and HTML markup is rendered.

Ruby

php_to_rails/ruby/demo_1/test/functional/homepage_controller_test.rb

```ruby
require File.dirname(__FILE__) + '/../test_helper'

class HomepageControllerTest < ActionController::TestCase
  fixtures :meetings

  # make sure that homepage displays login link
  def test_should_show_login_link_when_logged_out
    get :index, {}, :user => nil
    assert_select '#nav a', 'login'
  end
end
```

The get method simulates a GET request for us, with the first argument (:index) being the requested action. The second argument is a list of parameters we'd like to send to the action, which in this case is empty. In the third argument we've specified that the :user session variable is empty by assigning it to nil.

When this method executes, it performs a request cycle and stores the response text in memory. We can then perform assertions on the response that we're expecting. In this case we've used the assert_select method. This method accepts a CSS-style selector syntax to assert that HTML content was returned correctly. We assert that an HTML tag with an id of nav has a nested anchor (a) tag. The second argument specifies the text we expect to be within the anchor tag, which in this case is "login."

Integration Tests

Integration tests are done at a broader level and allow us to test application interaction across many different controllers. These tests are often a series of use cases for the application that are done in the test to ensure that a series of actions behaves correctly in succession.

Ruby

php_to_rails/ruby/demo_1/test/integration/user_stories_test.rb

```ruby
require "#{File.dirname(__FILE__)}/../test_helper"

class UserStoriesTest < ActionController::IntegrationTest
  fixtures :users, :presentations, :meetings

  def test_should_create_new_user
    # home page
    get "/"
    assert_template "homepage/index"
```

```
      # new user page
      get "/signup"
      assert_template "users/new"

      # post new user creation attempt
      user_params = { :name    => "Bob",
                      :email   => "bob@example.com",
                      :password => "chunkybacon",
                      :password_confirmation => "chunkybacon" }
      post "/users/create", :user => user_params
      assert_response :redirect
  end
end
```

We can use integration tests to build stories for our application. In this test, we've simulated a path that a user might follow in the application:

- The user starts at the home page.

- He then visits the sign-up page.

- He submits the form to register an account.

The test reenacts this by performing a series of GET and POST requests. We then assert that the application reacts as expected.

13.13   Rails Plug-Ins

Rails plug-ins are a way of adding additional functionality to Rails in a format that can be easily shared. You will find that some features have been deliberately left out of Rails to keep the framework as lightweight as possible. In many cases, developers create a plug-in to add this functionality to share between their own projects and the with the community.

Finding Plug-Ins

There are quite a few places to find Rails plug-ins. To view a rather long list of plug-in repositories, we can use the script/plugin discover command from within the root directory of our Rails application. This will find and list locations that have been added as source repositories. The -l option will tell Rails to simply list the plug-in sources.

```
demo> cd rails_app
rails_app> ruby script/plugin discover -l
```

```
http://svn.techno-weenie.net/projects/plugins/
http://topfunky.net/svn/plugins/
svn://errtheblog.com/svn/plugins
...
```

We can choose to add these plug-in sources by using the same command without the -l option. It will ask you whether you'd like to ask each source and will add each accepted location to a file in your home directory named .rails-plugin-sources.

Each source is a Subversion repository of plug-ins. To list the plug-ins within a specific repository, we can use the list --source options along with the repository we are searching. In this case, we'll take a further look into the plug-ins found in the Err repository.

```
rails_app> ruby script/plugin \
        list --source=svn://errtheblog.com/svn/plugins
acts_as_cached svn://errtheblog.com/svn/plugins/acts_as_cached/
cache_fu       svn://errtheblog.com/svn/plugins/cache_fu/
will_paginate  svn://errtheblog.com/svn/plugins/will_paginate/
...
```

This will list quite a few plug-ins that are available in this repository along with the direct location to the plug-in.

Installing Plug-Ins

The Will Paginate plug-in has quickly become one the most popular approaches to pagination in Rails applications. We can install this plug-in using the install option of our script. This will copy and install this plug-in into the vendor/plugins directory of our application. Unlike Ruby-Gems, which are available systemwide, plug-ins are installed and available only within a specific application.

```
rails_app> ruby script/plugin \
        install svn://errtheblog.com/svn/plugins/will_paginate/
A  /Users/derek/work/rails_app/vendor/plugins/will_paginate
A  /Users/derek/work/rails_app/vendor/plugins/will_paginate/test
...
A  /Users/derek/work/rails_app/vendor/plugins/will_paginate/README
Exported revision 321.
```

Once we've installed the plug-in, we'll have to restart our web server for it to become active.

We can generate RDoc documentation for it using a Rake task:

```
rails_app> rake doc:plugins
(in /Users/derek/work/rails_app)
...
Generating HTML...

Files:   5
Classes: 2
Modules: 6
Methods: 19
Elapsed: 0.380s
```

The documentation for all plug-ins will be generated and stored within the doc/plugins directory for your Rails application.

Bibliography

[ZT08]   Ezra Zygmuntowicz and Bruce Tate. *Deploying Rails Applications: A Step-by-Step Guide*. The Pragmatic Programmers, LLC, Raleigh, NC, and Dallas, TX, 2008.

Index

The Pragmatic Web

Welcome to the Pragmatic Community. We hope you've enjoyed this title.

If you want to make Javascript painless, start with *Prototype and script.aculo.us.* And to make your whole website work for *all* audiences—from cell phone browsers to those with physical handicaps—take a look at *Design Accessible Web Sites.*

Prototype and script.aculo.us

Tired of getting swamped in the nitty-gritty of cross-browser, Web 2.0–grade JavaScript? Get back in the game with Prototype and script.aculo.us, two extremely popular JavaScript libraries that make it a walk in the park. Be it Ajax, drag and drop, autocompletion, advanced visual effects, or many other great features, all you need is write one or two lines of script that look so good they could almost pass for Ruby code!

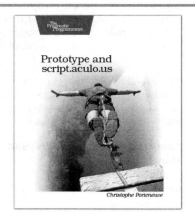

Prototype and script.aculo.us: You never knew JavaScript could do this!
Christophe Porteneuve
(330 pages) ISBN: 1-934356-01-8. $34.95
http://pragprog.com/titles/cppsu

The Accessible Web

The 2000 U.S. Census revealed that 12% of the population is severely disabled. Sometime in the next two decades, one in five Americans will be older than 65. Section 508 of the Americans with Disabilities Act requires your website to provide *equivalent access* to all potential users. But beyond the law, it is both good manners and good business to make your site accessible to everyone. This book shows you how to design sites that excel for all audiences.

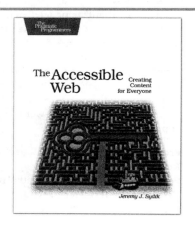

The Accessible Web
Jeremy Sydik
(304 pages) ISBN: 1-934356-02-6. $34.95
http://pragprog.com/titles/jsaccess

Pragmatic Methodology

Every developer can benefit from the award-winning *Practices of an Agile Developer*. And you and your manager can see what it really takes to manage a software project in the critically-acclaimed *Manage It!*.

Manage It!

Manage It! is a risk-based guide to making good decisions about how to plan and guide your projects. Author Johanna Rothman shows you how to beg, borrow, and steal from the best methodologies to fit your particular project. You'll find what works best for *you*.

• Learn all about different project lifecycles • See how to organize a project • Compare sample project dashboards • See how to staff a project • Know when you're done—and what that means.

Your Guide to Modern, Pragmatic Project Management
Johanna Rothman
(360 pages) ISBN: 0-9787392-4-8. $34.95
http://pragprog.com/titles/jrpm

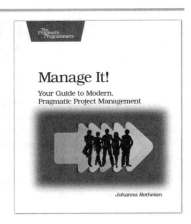

Practices of an Agile Developer

Agility is all about using feedback to respond to change. Learn how to apply the principles of agility throughout the software development process
• establish and maintain an agile working environment • deliver what users really want
• use personal agile techniques for better coding and debugging • use effective collaborative techniques for better teamwork • move to an agile approach

Practices of an Agile Developer: Working in the Real World
Venkat Subramaniam and Andy Hunt
(189 pages) ISBN: 0-9745140-8-X. $29.95
http://pragprog.com/titles/pad

Facets of Ruby Series

See how to integrate Ruby with all varieties of today's technology in *Enterprise Integration with Ruby*. And speaking of today's finest, you'll need a good text editor, too. On the Mac, we recommend TextMate.

Enterprise Integration with Ruby

See how to use the power of Ruby to integrate all the applications in your environment. Learn how to
• use relational databases directly and via mapping layers such as ActiveRecord • harness the power of directory services • create, validate, and read XML documents for easy information interchange
• use both high- and low-level protocols to knit applications together

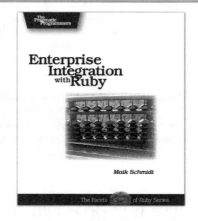

Enterprise Integration with Ruby
Maik Schmidt
(360 pages) ISBN: 0-9766940-6-9. $32.95
http://pragprog.com/titles/fr_eir

TextMate

If you're coding Ruby or Rails on a Mac, then you owe it to yourself to get the TextMate editor. And, once you're using TextMate, you owe it to yourself to pick up this book. It's packed with information that will help you automate all your editing tasks, saving you time to concentrate on the important stuff. Use snippets to insert boilerplate code and refactorings to move stuff around. Learn how to write your own extensions to customize it to the way you work.

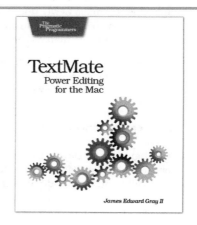

TextMate: Power Editing for the Mac
James Edward Gray II
(200 pages) ISBN: 0-9787392-3-X. $29.95
http://pragprog.com/titles/textmate

Facets of Ruby Series

If you're serious about Ruby, you need the definitive reference to the language. The Pickaxe: *Programming Ruby: The Pragmatic Programmer's Guide, Third Edition*. This is *the* definitive guide for all Ruby programmers. For Rails, we have the definitive reference guide as well: the award-winning and best-selling *Agile Web Development with Rails*.

Programming Ruby (The Pickaxe)

The Pickaxe book, named for the tool on the cover, is the definitive reference to this highly-regarded language. • Up-to-date and expanded for Ruby version 1.9 • Complete documentation of all the built-in classes, modules, and methods • Complete descriptions of all standard libraries • Learn more about Ruby's web tools, unit testing, and programming philosophy

Programming Ruby: The Pragmatic Programmer's Guide, 3rd Edition
Dave Thomas with Chad Fowler and Andy Hunt
(900 pages) ISBN: 978-1-9343560-8-1. $49.95
http://pragprog.com/titles/ruby3

Agile Web Development with Rails

Rails is a full-stack, open-source web framework, with integrated support for unit, functional, and integration testing. It enforces good design principles, consistency of code across your team (and across your organization), and proper release management. This is newly updated Second Edition, which goes beyond the Jolt-award winning first edition with new material on:

• Migrations • RJS templates • Respond_to
• Integration Tests • Additional ActiveRecord features • Another year's worth of Rails best practices

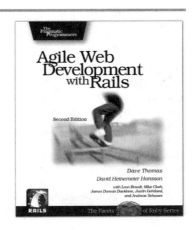

Agile Web Development with Rails: Second Edition
Dave Thomas, and David Heinemeier Hansson with Leon Breedt, Mike Clark, James Duncan Davidson, Justin Gehtland, and Andreas Schwarz
(750 pages) ISBN: 0-9776166-3-0. $39.95
http://pragprog.com/titles/rails2